SCHOLASTIC

LITERATURE ANTHOLOGIES

NOVELS

Edited by

Lauren Weidenman

CURRICULUM CONSULTANTS

Dr. Joan Curry
Professor of Reading
San Diego State University
San Diego, California

Mrs. Fredie Carter
Assistant Principal
Hampton Middle School
Detroit, Michigan

Mary C. Glover
English/Language Arts Consultant
Juvenile Court and Community Schools
Spring Valley, California

STAFF

Editorial Director: Edward C. Haggerty
Art Director: Marijka Kostiw

Design of Scholastic Literature Anthologies based on concept by Joe Borzetta.

COVER ART: "Dickens's Dream," by R.W. Buss, courtesy of the Dickens House, London, England. This unfinished painting depicts Dickens in his study, surrounded by characters from his many novels.

ISBN 0-590-35443-4

12 11 10 9 8 7 6 5 4 3 2 1 9 9/8 0 1 2 3/9
23

ACKNOWLEDGMENT

Grateful acknowledgment is made to the following author and publisher for the use of copyrighted material.
Harper & Row, Publishers, Inc. for SOUNDER by William H. Armstrong. Text copyright © 1969 by William H. Armstrong. Reprinted by permission of Harper & Row, Publishers, Inc.

PHOTOGRAPHY CREDITS

Pages 8-9, 23, 30, 35, 41, 43, 51, 60, 67: SOUNDER (1972), a Radnitz/Mattel Production, courtesy of Twentieth Century Fox.

Pages 72-73, 81, 86, 90, 104, 117, 127, 134, 137, 143, 145, 150, 152: A CHRISTMAS CAROL (1951), a Renown Pictures Presentation, courtesy of United Artists.

Pages 154-155, 158, 167, 205, 209: DR. JEKYLL AND MR. HYDE (1932), courtesy of Paramount.

CONTENTS

DR. JEKYLL AND MR. HYDE

Robert Louis Stevenson

INTRODUCTION

When you recommend a novel to someone, that person is likely to ask, "What's it about?" to see whether the book sounds interesting. You might ask the same question about the three short novels in this anthology: *Sounder,* by William H. Armstrong, *A Christmas Carol,* by Charles Dickens, and *Dr. Jekyll and Mr. Hyde,* by Robert Louis Stevenson.

Sounder is about injustice and racial prejudice and the suffering they cause for a family of black sharecroppers in the South. Though the parents work tirelessly, they can barely keep themselves and their children clothed and fed. Although it is too late for them to make a better life, there is hope for their boy—hope that he will break out of the tradition of silent suffering that keeps his parents captive.

A Christmas Carol is about Ebenezer Scrooge, a miser who hasn't done a good deed for the last thirty years. He is immune to the infectious spirit of Christmas, a season when most people open their hearts and take notice of those less fortunate than themselves. Scrooge doesn't care about poor people or Christmas, he just wants to be left alone. But Scrooge is *not* left alone: he is forced to learn about the Christmas spirit—from three spririts of Christmas.

Dr. Jekyll and Mr. Hyde is about the complexity of human character. It is about the fact that human nature is a mixture of good and evil, and that every individual has a responsibility to keep the evil within himself in check. Dr. Jekyll is a person who recognizes the warring elements within himself, and wants to find a way to free each side of his personality from the other. Using his knowledge of science, he devises a dangerous, radical scheme to accomplish this. The resulting story is what Stevenson himself called "a fine bogey tale."

When you tell someone what a novel is about, you often begin by giving a brief summary of the action, or plot. Sometimes a novel has a main plot and a secondary plot called a subplot. In *A Christmas Carol,* for example, the main plot concerns Scrooge—what he does and what happens to him. The subplot is the story of Bob Cratchit and his family. The outcome of the subplot depends upon the main plot: what happens to Bob Cratchit's family depends upon Scrooge's actions.

In order to have a plot, a novel must have a character, and the character must have a conflict. It is the character's attempt to resolve his conflict that gives the story its action. The conflict may be between different characters, between a character and nature, or between a character and society. The conflict may also be between opposing elements within one character, as it is in the case of Dr. Jekyll. Dr. Jekyll's attempt to resolve his inner conflict by scientific experimentation, and the events caused by this attempt, make up the plot of the novel.

Sometimes the conflict a character faces is determined by the place, time, conditions, and social setting in which the character lives. In *Sounder,* the characters are oppressed by the poverty, isolation, and prejudice that are an integral part of their lives. The hardships and conflicts that these characters face are determined by the fact that they are black sharecroppers living in the South at the turn of the century.

Whether the novel is about the plight of downtrodden sharecroppers, the redemption of a misanthropic miser, or the downfall of a reputable doctor, it must hold your interest in order to be successful. It must capture the truth about its particular subject while telling you something about life in general. Though you read a novel for enjoyment, you emerge from the experience with new knowledge, sometimes about other people, times, and places, and sometimes about yourself.

The photographs used to illustrate Sounder *are stills from the 1972 movie, starring Cicely Tyson and Paul Winfield. You will notice that the moviemakers have taken liberties with the story and have changed some details. For example, they have shifted certain scenes from wintertime to summertime, and have depicted a scene that is not dramatized in the book.*

William H. Armstrong

Radnitz / MATTEL Productions
Presents
"SOUNDER"
A Robert B. Radnitz/Martin Ritt Film
ng CICELY TYSON · PAUL WINFIELD · KEVIN HOOKS · co-starring TAJ MAHAL
ET MACLACHLAN · produced by ROBERT B. RADNITZ · directed by MARTIN RITT
LONNE ELDER, III · based on the Newbery Award winning Novel by WILLIAM H. ARMSTRONG
songs and music by TAJ MAHAL · PANAVISION · COLOR BY DE LUXE
TWENTIETH CENTURY-FOX

Author's Note

Fifty years ago I learned to read at a round table in the center of a large, sweet-smelling, steam-softened kitchen. My teacher was a gray-haired black man who taught the one-room Negro school several miles away from where we lived in the Green Hill district of the county. He worked for my father after school and in the summer. There were no radios or television sets, so when our lessons were finished he told us stories. His stories came from Aesop, the Old Testament, Homer, and history.

There was a lasting, magnificent intoxication about the man that has remained after half a century. There was seldom a preacher at the whitewashed, clapboard Baptist church in the Green Hill district, so he came often to our white man's church and sat alone in the balcony. Sometimes the minister would call on this eloquent, humble man to lead the congregation in prayer. He would move quietly to the foot of the balcony steps, pray with the simplicity of the Carpenter of Nazareth, and then return to where he sat alone, for no other black people ever came to join him.

He had come to our community from farther south, already old when he came. He talked little, or not at all, about his past. But one night at the great center table after he had told the story of Argus, the faithful dog of Odysseus, he told the story of Sounder, a coon dog.

It is the black man's story, not mine. It was not from Aesop, the Old Testament, or Homer. It was history — *his* history.

That world of long ago has almost totally changed. The church balcony is gone. The table is gone from the kitchen. But the story remains.

W. H. ARMSTRONG

• In this novel by William H. Armstrong, a young boy's family struggles with the problems of racial prejudice and poverty. As sharecroppers on someone else's land, the boy's parents have nothing to give him but love, and the strength and courage that come from love. Is that enough to keep this boy's hope alive, even after his family is torn apart?

William H. Armstrong

SOUNDER

CHAPTER ONE

THE TALL MAN STOOD AT THE EDGE OF THE porch. The roof sagged from the two rough posts which held it, almost closing the gap between his head and the rafters. The dim light from the cabin window cast long equal shadows from man and posts. A boy stood nearby shivering in the cold October wind. He ran his fingers back and forth over the broad crown of the head of a coon dog named Sounder.

"Where did you first get Sounder?" the boy asked.

"I never got him. He came to me along the road when he wasn't more'n a pup."

The father turned to the cabin door. It was ajar. Three small children, none as high as the level of the latch, were peering out into the dark. "We just want to pet Sounder," the three all said at once.

"It's too cold. Shut the door."

"Sounder and me must be about the same age," the boy said, tugging gently at one of the coon dog's ears, and then the other. He felt the importance of the years — as a child measures age — which separated him from the younger children. He was old enough to stand out in the cold and run his fingers over Sounder's head.

No dim lights from other cabins punctuated the night. The white man who owned the vast endless fields had scattered the cabins of his Negro sharecroppers[1] far apart, like flyspecks on a whitewashed ceiling. Sometimes on Sundays the boy walked with his parents to set awhile at one of the distant cabins. Sometimes they went to the meetin' house. And there was school too. But it was far away at the edge of town. Its term began after harvest and ended before planting time. Two successive Octobers the boy had started, walking the eight miles morning and evening. But after a few weeks when cold winds and winter sickness came, his mother had said, "Give it up, child. It's too long and too cold." And the boy, remembering how he was always laughed at for getting to school so late, had agreed. Besides, he thought, next year he would be bigger and could walk faster and get to school before it started and wouldn't be laughed at. And when he wasn't dead-tired from walking home from school, his father would let him hunt with Sounder. Having both school and Sounder would be mighty good, but if he couldn't have school, he could always have Sounder.

"There ain't no dog like Sounder," the boy said. But his father did not take up the conversation. The boy wished he would. His father stood silent and motionless. He was looking past the rim of the half-light that came from the cabin window and pushed back the darkness in a circle that lost itself around the ends of the cabin. The man seemed to be listening. But no sounds came to the boy.

Sounder was well named. When he treed a coon or possum in a persimmon tree or on a wild grape vine, his voice would roll across the flatlands. It wavered through the foothills, louder than any other dog's in the whole countryside.

What the boy saw in Sounder would have been totally missed by an outsider. The dog was not much to look at — a mixture of Georgia redbone hound and bulldog. His ears, nose, and color were those of a redbone. The great square jaws and head, his muscular neck and broad chest showed his bulldog blood. When a possum or coon was shaken from a tree, like a flash Sounder would clamp and set his jaw-vise just behind the animal's head. Then he would spread his front paws, lock his shoulder joints, and let the bulging neck muscles fly from left to right. And that was all. The limp body, with not a torn spot or a tooth puncture in the skin, would be laid at his master's feet. His master's calloused hand would rub the great neck, and he'd say "Good Sounder, good Sounder." In the winter when there were no crops and no pay, fifty cents for a possum and two dollars for a coonhide bought flour and overall jackets with blanket linings.

But there was no price that could be put on Sounder's voice. It came out of the great chest cavity and broad jaws as though it had bounced off the walls of a cave. It mellowed into half-echo before it touched the air. The mists of the flatlands strained out whatever coarseness was left over from his bulldog heritage, and only flute-like redbone mellowness came to the listener. But it was louder and clearer than any purebred redbone. The trail barks seemed to be spaced with the precision of a juggler. Each bark bounced from slope to slope in the foothills like a rubber ball. But it was not an ordinary bark. It filled up the night and made music as though the branches of all the trees were being pulled across silver strings.

While Sounder trailed the path the hunted had taken in search of food, the high excited voice was quiet. The warmer the trail grew, the longer the silences, for, by nature, the coon dog would try to surprise his quarry[2] and catch him on the ground, if possible. But the great voice box of Sounder would have burst if he had tried to trail too long in silence. After a last, long-sustained stillness which allowed the great dog to close in on his quarry, the voice would burst forth so fast it overflowed itself and became a melody.

A stranger hearing Sounder's treed bark suddenly fill the night might have thought there were six dogs at the foot of one tree. But all over the countryside, neighbors, leaning against slanting porch posts or standing in open cabin doorways and listening, knew that it was Sounder.

"If the wind does not rise, I'll let you go hunting with me tonight." The father spoke quietly as he glanced down at boy and dog. "Animals don't like to move much when it's windy."

"Why?" the boy asked.

"There are too many noises, and they can't hear a killer slipping up on them. So they stay in their dens, especially possums, because they can't smell much."

The father left the porch and went to the woodpile at the edge of the rim of light. The boy followed, and each gathered a chunk-stick for the cabin stove. At the door, the father took down a lantern that hung on the wall beside a possum sack and shook it. "There's plenty of coal oil," he said.

The boy closed the door quickly. He had heard leaves rattling across the frozen ground. He hoped his father didn't hear it. But he knew the door wouldn't shut it out. His father could sense the rising wind, and besides, it would shake the loose windowpanes.

Inside the cabin, the boy's mother was cutting wedge-shaped

pieces of corn mush from an iron pot that stood on the back of the stove. She browned them in a skillet and put them on the tin-topped table in the middle of the room. The boy and the three younger children ate their supper in silence. The father and mother talked a little about ordinary things, talk the boy had heard so many times he no longer listened. "The crop will be better next year. There'll be more day work. The hunting was better last year."

This winter the hunting was getting worse and worse. The wind came stronger and colder than last year. Sometimes Sounder and his master hunted in the wind. But night after night they came home with an empty brown sack. Coons were scarcely seen at all. People said they had moved south to the big water. There were few scraps and bones for Sounder. Inside the cabin, they were hungry for solid food too. Corn mush had to take the place of stewed possum, dumplings, and potatoes.

Not long after supper, Sounder's master went out of the cabin and stood listening, as he always did, to see if he could hear the cold winter wind beginning to rise in the hills. When he came back into the cabin, he took off his blanket-lined overall jacket and sat behind the stove for a long time. Sounder whined at the door as if he were asking if someone had forgotten to light the lantern and start across the fields of dead stalks to the lowlands or past the cottonwoods and jack oaks to the hills. The boy took Sounder some table scraps in a tin pan. As Sounder licked the bottom of the pan it rattled against a loose board in the porch as if somebody were walking across the floor.

Later, when it was time for the smaller children in the cabin to go to bed, Sounder's master got up, put on his overall jacket, and went outside. He did not take the lantern or Sounder or the boy with him. The stern order to the coon hound to go back under the porch came in through the cabin door, and Sounder's whining continued long after the footsteps on the frozen path had died out.

Inside the cabin, the boy's mother sat by the stove, picking kernels of walnuts with a bent hairpin. The woman watched each year for the walnuts to fall after the first hard frost. Each day she went with the children and gathered all that had fallen. The brownish-green husks, oozing their dark purple stain, were beaten off on a flat rock outside the cabin. On the same rock, the nuts were cracked after they had dried for several weeks in a tin box under the stove. When kernel-picking time came, before it was dark each day, the boy or the father took a hammer with a home-made handle, went to the flat rock, and cracked as many as could be kerneled in a night.

The troubled whimper of a child came through the little door that led to the shed-room where the children slept.

"You must go to bed soon," the mother said. "Your little brother gets addled[3] in his sleep when you ain't in bed with him."

The boy reached into his mother's lap, where the golden half-kernels lay in the folds of her apron. She slapped his hand away. "You eat the crumbs from the bottom of the hull basket," she said. "I try to pick two pounds a night. That's thirty cents' worth. Fifteen cents a pound at the store if they're mostly half-kernels and dry. The man won't pay if they're all in crumbs."

Sometimes the woman told the boy stories she had heard at the meetin' house. "The Lord do powerful things" she would say. The boy liked it when she told her stories. They took away night loneliness. Night loneliness was always bad when the younger children had gone to bed, or when the father was not in the cabin. "Night loneliness is part fearing," the boy's mother had once said to him. But the boy was never afraid when his father was near.

Perhaps she too felt the loneliness that came with the wind as it passed the cabin outside, and the closeness of a world whose farthest border in the night was the place where the lamp light ended, at the edge of the cabin walls. So she told the boy a story of a mighty flood which the Lord had sent to wash away all the evil in the world. When the story was over, she sent the boy to bed and continued picking out kernels and adding them to the neat mound in the folds of her apron.

The boy pressed his head deep into his straw pillow. The pillow was cold, but it felt smooth, and it smelled fresh. He had the same feeling he got when he rubbed his face against the sheets that hung on the clothesline every Monday. His mother washed his pillow-case and sheet every week, just like she did for the people who lived in the big house down the road. He buried himself deep in his side of the straw tick;[4] he felt where the wooden slats of the bed crossed under his body. He rolled close to his little brother and tucked the edge of the coverlet under his body to keep out the cold that seeped up through the straw ticking. His little brother's body warmed him.

He heard Sounder whimpering under the porch. But Sounder was warm because the boy's father had put two burlap sacks under the porch for the time when the hard frosts came. The boy thought there must be two pounds of nuts in the pile on his mother's lap. His mother always said "Two pounds is a good night's work if you can start early and there ain't a sick child to rock."

He wondered where his father had gone without Sounder; they always went together at night. He heard the thump, thump, thump of Sounder's paw hitting the underneath side of the porch floor as he scratched at a flea in his short tan hair.

The boy dreamed of the stalk land covered by the Lord's mighty flood. He wondered where the animals would go if the water rose over the foothills. "Cabins built on posts would just float like boats, porch and all," he assured himself in a whisper. If they floated from the far ends of the land and all came together, that would be a town, and he wouldn't be lonely anymore . . .

When the boy awoke in the morning, he went to the window. He remembered his dream of the flood covering the stalk land. He called the younger children. His breath steamed up the windowpane. He wiped the steam away with the bottom of his fist. His dream had not come true. There was no floodwater rising in the bottom-land. Except for frost on the ground, everything looked just the same as it had yesterday. The younger children looked, saw nothing, and asked, "What is it?"

The big blue-enameled possum kettle was boiling on top of the chunk stove. It had two lids and doubled for cooking and heating. The boy felt the brown paper bag of walnut kernels on the shelf behind the stove. "Yes," he said to his mother, "I think there are two pounds."

He stood close to the warm stovepipe, turning one cheek and then the other to its glowing warmth. He circled his arms in a wide embrace around the pipe and rubbed his hands together. The warmth ran up his sleeves and down over his ribs inside his shirt and soaked inward through his whole body. He pulled in deep breaths from above the stove to catch the steam escaping from under the kettle's lid as it bounced up and down, breaking the rhythm of the bubbles that went *lob, lob, lob* on the surface of the fast-boiling pot.

In a skillet on the second stove lid there were pork sausages! He sniffed the thin lines of smoke curling up from under the edges of each of them. Pork sausage was for Christmas. But he knew it wasn't Christmas yet. His mother put a pan of cold biscuits on the lid of the possum kettle to warm. She was humming to herself. The lid stopped jumping up and down, the steam began to whistle softly as it squeezed from under the lid.

The smell that came from under the lid wasn't possum. It was ham bone. The boy had only smelled it twice in his life, once before in his own cabin, and once when he was walking past the big house down the road. The sausage and ham-bone smells filled up the cabin and leaked out through the cracks in the floor and around the door. They excited Sounder, and now he was scratching at the door.

Sounder hadn't had much to eat yesterday. Besides a few scraps, he had had one cold biscuit. When flour was scarce, the boy's mother would wrap the leftover biscuits in a clean flour sack and put them away for the next meal. Then they would be put in a pan, sprinkled with a little water to keep them soft, and warmed over. The boy called to Sounder to stop and go away. His mother stopped her humming and said, "Shush, child, you'll wake your father."

Then she went back to her humming. His mother always hummed when she was worried. When she held a well child on her lap and rocked back and forth, she sang. But when she held a sick child close in her arms and the rocker moved just enough to squeak a little, she would hum. Sometimes she hummed so softly that the child heard the deep concerned breathing of terror above the sound of the humming. The boy always thought her lips looked as though they were glued together when she hummed. They seemed to be rolled inward and drawn long and thin. Once when she kissed him good night when he was sick, they were cold, he remembered. But when she sang or told stories, her lips were rolled out, big and warm and soft.

Outside, the wind still blew, the sun was weak, and the earth was gray. Several times the boy went out to bring wood for his mother. He ate sausage and biscuits at the tin-topped table with the other children.

When his father got up, he chopped some wood and sat by the fire. The top of the possum kettle bounced up and down again because the biscuit pan had been moved. The father lifted the lid now and then. With the big wire fork that had a wooden handle, he pulled the ham half out of the water and turned it over. The boy felt warm and proud inside when he saw his father's great hand take hold of the handle of the hot lid without using a pot rag the way his mother always did. Finally his father took from the shelf a flat oak slab, bigger than any of the pans or dishes, and put it on the table.

The boy liked to smell the oak slab. It smelled like the Mercy Seat meetin'-house picnic held every summer. He also liked to rub his fingers on the edge of the slab, for it was soft and smooth where the grease had soaked it. His father had hollowed it out during long winter evenings as he sat by the stove. The boy had cleaned up the shavings and slipped them under the door of the stove when the draft was open. They burned with a bright flame, and they made a great mystery for the boy: The curled ones straightened out as they burned, but the straight ones curled up.

The boy remembered when the oak slab had had ham on it before. One year his father had won a pig in a shooting match and raised it to a hog. They had eaten one ham and traded one for beans and flour at the store. That year they had spareribs and chitlins[5] and pan scrapple.[6] Sometimes when the boy's father helped butcher hogs down at the big house, he would bring home spareribs and sowbelly[7] — lots of sowbelly, but not much spareribs.

The boy's father took the ham from the kettle and put it on the oak slab. "Save the ham-boilin' for Sounder," he reminded the boy's mother.

"Sounder will eat good now," the boy said.

The father sharpened the butcher knife with the whetstone[8] he used to whet his scythe[9] and his goose-necked brier hook in the summer when he cut brambles and young sumac in the fencerows. He cut big pieces of ham, and they stuck out from under the brown tops of the biscuits. It was like a Christmas bigger than a pork-sausage Christmas. The boy slipped a piece of the fat rind into a biscuit and took it out to Sounder. When the ham-boiling had cooled, he filled Sounder's pan and ran his fingers up and down the great dog's back as he lapped it up.

The windows of the cabin stayed steamed up almost all day, the kettle had boiled so long. The cold wind continued to blow outside. Nothing moved except what the wind moved — dead leaves under the cabin, brown blades and stalks from the fields which were dead and ready to be blown away, bare branches of poplars, and the spires of tall pines. Toward evening the father wiped the steam away from the glass and looked out a couple of times. The dry cottonwood chunks burned like gunpowder in the stove. In one or two spots the side of the stove gave off a red glow.

With the flavor of ham and biscuit still in his mouth, the boy felt good. He watched his mother as she patched his father's overalls with a piece of ticking. The combination of faded blue overall cloth and gray-and-white-striped ticking looked odd. One time at the meetin'-house picnic, boys with patches the same color as their overalls had laughed at him and pointed to the checkered gingham on the knees of his overalls. He had felt mad and hurt. But his mother had said, "Pay no mind, child," and had led him away. He hoped no one would laugh at his father. His father wouldn't be hurt. He didn't get hurt. He would get mad and fight back, and the boy was always afraid when his father got mad.

When the woman had patched the torn place, she got the walnut basket, folded her apron in her lap, and began to pick out golden-brown kernels. The boy thought she would sing, but the rocker only moved enough to squeak. She hummed softly, and her lips looked glued together. "Look down, look down that lonesome road." The boy wished she would stop humming and tell a story about the Lord or King David, but she kept humming "That Lonesome Road."

The boy decided it was lonesomer in bed in the dark than it was staying up. He was glad he could set a long time after the young children had gone to bed. Once he had been gathering weeds which his father had cut at the edge of a lawn. On the lawn a lady sat under a tree reading a story aloud to some children. He wished his mother or father could read. And if they had a book, he would hold a lamp by the chair so they could see the words and never get tired. "One day I will learn to read," he said to himself. He would have a book with stories in it, then he wouldn't be lonesome even if his mother didn't sing.

1 **sharecroppers:** persons who farm land owned by another in return for part of the crop
2 **quarry:** an animal that is being hunted down
3 **addled:** confused, mixed up
4 **tick:** a cloth case filled with straw to form a mattress
5 **chitlins:** a food made from the small intestines of pigs
6 **scrapple:** cornmeal boiled with scraps of pork, then sliced and fried
7 **sowbelly:** pork preserved in salt
8 **whetstone:** a stone with a rough surface for sharpening knives
9 **scythe:** a tool with a long, single-edged blade on a long, curved handle, used in cutting tall grass or grain

CHAPTER TWO

The road which passed the cabin lay like a thread dropped on a patchwork quilt. Stalk land, fallow[1] fields, and brushland, all appeared to be sewn together by wide fencerow stitches of trees. Their bare branches spread out to join together the separate patches of land. Weeds grew on either side of the road in summer, and a thin strip of green clung to life between the dusty tracks. In summer a horse and wagon made almost no noise in the soft earth. In winter when the ground was frozen, the rattle of wheels and each distinct hoofbeat punctuated the winter quiet. When the wind blew, little clouds of dust would rise in the road and follow the wind tracks across the fields.

The boy was allowed to go as far as he wanted to on the road. But the younger children couldn't go past the pine clump toward the big house and the town, or the bramble patch where they picked blackberries in summer in the other direction. Almost no one passed on the road in winter except to buy flour at the store far down the road or to go to the town of a Saturday. Even in summer a speck on the horizon was a curiosity. People sitting on cabin porches would wonder whether the speck would take the form of a man, woman, or child.

The third day after the boy had awakened to the smell of ham bone and pork sausage, it was still cold and the wind still blew. But the cabin still smelled good, and there was plenty to eat. Just as dark was gathering, the boy started to go to the woodpile to bring in wood for the night. The dim light of the lamp ran past the boy as he stood motionless in the open cabin door.

"Shut the door," the boy's father called from where he sat near the stove. But the boy did not move.

Just past the edge of the porch three white men stood in the dim light. Their heavy boots rattled the porch floor, and the boy backed quickly into the cabin as they pushed their way in.

"There are two things I can smell a mile," the first man said in a loud voice. "One's a ham cookin' and the other's a thievin' nigger."

"Get up," the second man ordered. The warm, but frozen circle of man, woman and three small children around the stove jumped to their feet. A stool on which a child had been sitting fell backward and made a loud noise. One of the men kicked it across the room. The boy did not move from his place just inside the door.

"Here's the evidence," said the first man. He jerked at the grease-spotted cloth on the tin-topped table. The oak slab and the half-eaten ham fell to the floor with a great thud and slid against the wall.

"You know who I am," said the first man as he unbuttoned his heavy brown coat and pulled it back to show a shiny metal star pinned to his vest. "These are my deputies." The stranger nearest the door kicked it shut and swore about the cold.

"Stick out your hands, boy," ordered the second man. The boy started to raise his hands, but the man was already reaching over the stove, snapping handcuffs on the outstretched wrists of his father.

The click of the handcuffs was like the click of a gate latch at the big house where the boy had once gone with his father to work. He had swung on the gate and played with the latch until someone had called out from the house, "If you want to swing on a gate, boy, swing on the one behind the house. Get away from the front."

The third stranger, who had not spoken, turned toward the door. "I'll bring up the wagon." But he did not open the door.

Suddenly the voice of the great dog shattered the heavy, seemingly endless silence that came between the gruff words of the sheriff and those of his men. Sounder was racing toward the cabin from the fields. He had grown restless from waiting to go hunting with his master and had wandered away to hunt alone. That's why he hadn't warned them. He always barked and sometimes, even in daytime, he would start from under the porch, the hair on his back straightening before anyone had sighted a moving speck at the far end of the road. "Somebody's comin' or a creature's movin' " the boy's mother would say.

Now he was growling and scratching at the door. The noise seemed to undo the fearful shock that had held the smaller children ashen and motionless. The youngest child began to cry and hid behind his mother. He tugged at her apron, but the woman did not move.

The men were speaking roughly to Sounder's master. "That tear in your overalls where the striped ticking is — that's where you tore them on the door hook of the smokehouse. We found threads of torn cloth in the hook. You gonna wear nothing but stripes pretty soon. Big, wide black and white stripes. Easy to hit with a shotgun."

The deputy who had started out to bring up the wagon kicked

the closed door and swore at the dog on the other side.

"Go out and hold that mongrel if you don't want him shot." He held the door ajar the width of the boy's body and thrust him out. The boy fell on the back of the dog, whose snarling jaws had pushed into the light between the boy's legs. A heavy boot half pushed, half kicked the entangled feet of the sprawled boy and the nose of the dog and slammed the door. "Get that dog out of the way and hold him if you don't want him dead."

The boy, regaining his balance, dragged Sounder off the porch and to the corner of the cabin. Then the deputy, hearing the barking move back from the door, opened it and came out. He walked out of the circle of light but returned soon leading a horse hitched to a spring wagon. A saddled horse followed behind the wagon.

The appearance of the horses and the added confusion of people coming from the cabin roused Sounder to new fury. The boy felt his knees give. His arms ached, and his grip on the dog's collar was beginning to feel clammy and wet. But he held on.

"Chain him up," said the sheriff.

The boy thought they were telling him to chain up Sounder, but then he saw that one of the men had snapped a long chain on the handcuffs on his father's wrists. As the men pushed his father into the back of the wagon his overalls caught on the end of the tail-gate bolt, and he tore a long hole in his overalls. The bolt took one side of the ticking patch with it. The man holding the chain jerked it, and the boy's father fell backward into the wagon. The man swung the loose end of the chain, and it struck the boy's father across the face. One of the deputies pulled the chain tight and tied it to the wagon seat. The two deputies climbed on the wagon seat; the sheriff mounted the saddled horse. The cabin door was open; the boy's mother was standing in the doorway. He did not see his brother and sisters.

Sounder was making an awful noise, a half-strangled mixture of growl and bark. The boy spoke to him, but the great paws only dug harder to grip the frozen earth. Inch by inch the boy was losing his footing. Numbness was beginning to creep up his arms and legs, and he was being dragged away from the corner of the house.

The wagon started, and the sheriff rode behind it on his horse. Sounder made a great lunge forward, and the boy fell against the corner of the porch. Sounder raced after the wagon. No one yelled after him. The mother stood still in the doorway. The deputy who

wasn't holding the reins turned on the seat, aimed his shotgun at the dog jumping at the side of the wagon, and fired. Sounder fell in the road, and the sheriff rode around him. Sounder's master was still on his back in the wagon, but he did not raise his head to look back.

The boy struggled to his feet. His head hurt where he had hit it against the corner of the porch. Now his mother spoke for the first time since he had opened the door to bring in wood. "Come in, child, and bring in some wood."

Sounder lay still in the road. The boy wanted to cry; he wanted to run to Sounder. His stomach felt sick; he didn't want to see Sounder. He sank to his knees at the woodpile. His foot hurt where the door had been slammed on it. He thought he would carry in two chunk-sticks. Maybe his mother would drag Sounder out of the road. Maybe she would drag him across the fields and bury him. Maybe if she laid him on the porch and put some soft rags under him tonight, he might rise from the dead, like Lazarus[2] did in a meetin'-house story. Maybe his father didn't know Sounder was dead. Maybe his father was dead in the back of the sheriff's wagon now. Maybe his father had said it hurt to bounce over the rough road on his back, and the deputy had turned around on the seat and shot him.

The second chunk-stick was too big. It slipped out of the boy's arms. Two of his fingers were bruised under the falling wood.

Suddenly a sharp yelp came from the road. Just like when a bee stung Sounder under the porch or a brier caught his ear in the bramble, the boy thought. In an instant the boy was on his feet. Bruised foot and fingers, throbbing head were forgotten. He raced into the dark. Sounder tried to rise but fell again. There was another yelp, this one constrained and plaintive. The boy, trained in night-sight when the lantern was dimmed so as not to alert the wood's creatures, picked out a blurred shape in the dark.

Sounder was running, falling, floundering, rising. The hind part of his body stayed up and moved from side to side, trying to lift the front part from the earth. He twisted, fell, and heaved his great shoulders. His hind paws dug into the earth. He pushed himself up. He staggered forward, sideways, then fell again. One front leg did not touch the ground. A trail of blood, smeared and blotted, followed him. There was a large spot of mingled blood, hair, and naked flesh on one shoulder. His head swung from side to side. He fell again and pushed his body along with his hind legs. One side of his head was a mass of blood. The blast had torn off the whole side of his head and shoulder.

The boy was crying and calling Sounder's name. He ran backward in front of Sounder. He held out his hand. Sounder did not make a sign to stop. The boy followed the coon dog under the porch, but he went far back under the cabin. The boy was on his knees, crying and calling, "Sounder, Sounder, Sound . . ." His voice trailed off into a pleading whisper.

The cabin door opened, and the boy's mother stood in the door. The pale light of the lamp inside ran past the woman, over the edge of the porch, and picked out the figure of the boy on his hands and knees. "Come in, child," the woman said. "He is only dying."

Inside the cabin the younger children sat huddled together near the stove. The boy rubbed his hands together near the stovepipe to warm them. His bruised fingers began to throb again. His foot and his head hurt, and he felt a lump rising on the side of his head. If Sounder would whimper or yelp, I would know, the boy thought. But there was no sound, no thump, thump, thump of a paw scratching fleas and hitting the floor underneath.

"Creatures like to die alone," the mother said after a long time. "They like to crawl away where nobody can find them dead, especially dogs. He didn't want to be shot down like a dog in the road. Some creatures are like people."

The road, the boy thought. What would it be like? Did the shotgun blast a hole in the road?

"I ain't got the wood," the boy said at last. "I'll light the lantern and get it."

"You know where the wood is. You won't need a lantern," the woman said.

The boy paused in the doorway. Then he took the lantern from the nail where it hung beside the possum sack. He took the lantern to the stove, lit a splinter of kindling through the open door-draft, and held it to the lantern wick the way his father always did. His mother said nothing to him. She spoke to the younger children instead. "I ain't fed you yet."

When he got outside, the boy did not go to the woodpile. He followed the trail of blood in its zigzag path along the road. At the end of it there was a great wide spot, dark on the frozen ground. Little clumps of Sounder's hair lay in the blood. There was no hole where the shotgun had blasted. At the edge of the dark stain, the boy touched his finger to something. It was more than half of

Sounder's long thin ear. The boy shivered and moved his finger away. He had seen dead lizards and possums and raccoons, but he'd never seen a human animal, like Sounder, dead.

It wouldn't work, he thought. But people always said to put things under your pillow when you go to bed, and if you make a wish, it will come true. He touched Sounder's ear again. It was cold. He picked it up. One edge of it was bloody, and jagged like the edge of a broken windowpane. He followed the zigzag trail back along the road, but he could scarcely see it now. He was crying again. At the corner of the porch he took the possum sack from the nail where it hung and wiped the ear. It gave him the shivers. He jumped down quickly, and holding the lantern near the ground, tried to see under the porch. He called Sounder. There was no sound. He went back to wiping the ear. His throat hurt. He put the ear in the pocket of his overall jacket. He was going to put it under his pillow and wish that Sounder wasn't dead.

The wind had stopped blowing. This would have been a good hunting night, he thought. Far away, a single lantern was moving into the foothills. The boy was still crying. He had not forgotten the wood. Now he put out the lantern and hung it against the wall. He went to the woodpile, picked up two chunk-sticks, and went into the cabin.

The loneliness that was always in the cabin, except when his mother was singing or telling a story about the Lord, was heavier than ever now. It made the boy's tongue heavy. It pressed against his eyes, and they burned. It rolled against his ears. His head seemed to be squeezed inward, and it hurt. He noticed grease spots on the floor where the oak slab and the ham had fallen. He knew his mother had picked them up. His father would be cold, he thought, with that great rip in his overalls.

His mother sat by the stove. "You must eat," the woman said. The boy had been outside a long time. His mother had fed the other children, and they were already in bed. She did not take down her walnut basket to begin the slow filling of her apron with fat kernels. She did not sing or even hum. "Child . . . child" she would say with long spaces between. Sometimes she would murmur to herself with her eyes closed. His little brother would murmur and be addled in his sleep tonight, the boy thought. He would set as long as his mother would let him. Maybe his mother would let him set and listen all night.

The boy listened for a yelp, a whine, a thump, thump, thump

under the floor. There was no sound. His mother's rocker did not even move enough to squeak. One chunk-stick burning atop another in the stove rolled against the stove door with a slight thump. The boy started toward the cabin door.

"You know it was the stove," the mother said as she reached for the poker to push the wood back from the door.

"It sounded outside," the boy said as he pulled the door closed after him.

Soon he returned carrying the lantern. "I want to look more," he said. "I keep hearin' things." He lit the lantern from the stove as he had done before. His mother said nothing. He had thought she might say "Hang it back, child" as she often did when he wanted to go along the fencerows and hunt with Sounder after dark.

Outside, he murmured to himself, "That was the stove, I reckon." He put the lantern on the ground and tried to see under the cabin. Nothing moved in the dim light. He wished the light would shine in Sounder's eyes and he would see them in the dark, but it didn't. Backing from under the porch on his hands and knees, he touched the lantern and tipped it over. He grabbed it by the wire rim that held the top of the globe and burned his hand. "Don't let it fall over; it'll explode" his father had said to him so many times when they hunted together. He sucked his burned fingers to draw out the fire. Sounder's pan was on the ground, and someone had stepped on it. The mean man who had kicked him with his big boot, the boy thought. He straightened it as best he could with his hurt fingers and put it on the porch.

He blew out the lantern and hung it by the possum sack. He stood on the porch and listened to the faraway. The lantern he had seen going into the foothills had disappeared. There were gravestones behind the meetin' house. Some were almost hidden in the brambles. If the deputy sheriff had turned around on the seat of the wagon and shot his father, the visiting preacher and somebody would bring him back and bury him behind the meetin' house, the boy thought. And if Sounder dies, I won't drag him over the hard earth. I'll carry him. I know I can carry him if I try hard enough, and I will bury him across the field, near the fencerow, under the big jack oak tree.

The boy picked up Sounder's bent tin pan and carried it into the cabin. The woman pushed back in her chair for a brief second in surprise and half opened her mouth. But, seeing the boy's face in the lamplight, she closed her mouth, and the rocker came slowly back to its standing position — her head tilted forward again, her eyes fixed on the boy's uneaten supper, still warming on the back of the stove.

In the corner of the room next to the dish cupboard, the boy filled Sounder's tin with cold ham-boiling from the possum kettle. "What's that for, child?" asked the mother slowly, as though she were sorry she had asked and would like to take it back.

"For if he comes out."

"You're hungry, child. Feed yourself."

The boy put Sounder's tin under the porch, closed the door, pushed the night latch, sat down behind the stove, and began to eat his supper.

[1] **fallow:** plowed but left unplanted
[2] **Lazarus:** In the Bible, Lazarus was raised from the dead by Jesus.

A CLOSER LOOK

1. Explain why "Sounder" is a good name for the dog.

2. Why is it important to the boy to learn how to read?

3. On the morning when the boy wakes up to the smell of ham bone and sausage, he hears his mother humming. What is the significance of her humming on this particular morning?

4. Why does the boy start to raise his hands when the sheriff tells the father to stick out his hands? What is inappropriate about the way the sheriff addresses the boy's father?

5. To whom is the sheriff referring when he says, "Chain him up"? Why does the boy think the sheriff must be referring to Sounder?

6. How does the boy react to Sounder's being shot? How is his reaction different from his mother's?

CHAPTER THREE

In the morning the boy's mother did not cook any pork sausage for breakfast. The ham was on the tin-topped table, but she did not uncover it. Everybody had biscuits and milk gravy. There was still a faint smell of ham, but the boy missed the scent of sausage coming up to him as he stood warming himself. He had hurried out and called Sounder and looked under the house before he had finished buttoning his shirt, but his mother had made him come in. She knew he would be crawling under the cabin, so she made him put on last year's worn-out overalls and a ragged jacket of his father's that came down to his knees. It wouldn't keep out much cold because it was full of holes.

The boy's mother put what was left of the pork sausage and the ham in a meal sack. When she had wrapped her walnut kernels in brown paper and tied them with string, she tied a scarf around her head and put on a heavy brown sweater that had pink flannel-outing patches on the elbows. She put the brown package in the basket she always carried when she went to the store. She put the meal sack over her shoulder.

"I'm taking the kernels to the store to sell them," she said to the boy. She did not say where she was going with the meal sack she had swung over her shoulder.

"Watch the fire, child," she said. "Don't go out of hollerin' distance and leave the young ones. Don't let them out in the cold.

"Warm some mush in the skillet for you all to eat at dinnertime. I'll be home before suppertime.

"Whatever you do, child, don't leave the children with a roaring fire and go lookin' for Sounder. You ain't gonna find him this day. If a stranger comes, don't say nothin'."

The boy had nodded each time she spoke. He thought he would say "Yes" or "Don't worry, I will," but he didn't. He pushed the younger children back out of the cold and closed the door.

As his mother stepped off the porch and started for the road she began to hum softly to herself. It was a song the boy had heard her sing many nights in the cabin:

You gotta walk that lonesome valley,
You gotta walk it by yourself,
Ain't nobody else gonna walk it for you.

The boy wanted to run after her. He watched as she became smaller and smaller, until the meal sack over her shoulder was just a white speck. The rest of her became a part of the brown road and the gray earth. When the white speck had faded into the earth, the boy looked up at the sky.

"No sun to thaw things out today," he said aloud to himself. His father always spoke aloud to the wind and the sky, and sometimes to the sun when he stood on the porch in the morning, especially when it rose out of the far lowland cottonwoods and pines like a great ball of fire. "Warmin' the cold bones" his father would say. And preparing for a hunt, his father would caution a full moon, hanging over the foothills, "Don't shine too bright, you'll make the creatures skittish." And Sounder too, settin' on his haunches, would speak to the moon in ghost-stirrin' tones of lonesome dog-talk.

People would be very mean to his mother today, the boy thought. He wondered if she would tell them that the ham had slid across the floor. If she told them, they might just throw it out and

feed it to their dogs. They might let his mother keep it and bring it home again. They wouldn't let her keep the pork sausage, for it was wrapped in clean white paper and not cooked. They might push and pull his mother and put her in the back of a spring wagon and take her away too. She would spill the walnut kernels, and then she wouldn't be able to sell them to buy sowbelly and potatoes.

The boy had hoped the sun would shine. It would soften the frozen crust of earth and make it easier for him to dig a grave for Sounder — if he found Sounder. If Sounder was dead, he hoped no one would come along and see him carrying the grub hoe and shovel across the field to the big jack oak. They would ask what he was doing. If anybody passed while he was digging the grave, he would hide in the fencerow. If they saw him, they might run him off the land.

He felt like crying, but he didn't. Crying would only bother him. He would have his hands full of tools or be carrying Sounder's body. His nose would start dripping and be powerful troublesome because he wouldn't have a free hand to wipe it.

He took in an armload of wood and punched up the fire. "Don't open the stove door," he cautioned the younger children. "I have to go out some more." He went to his bed and took Sounder's ear from under the pillow. He would bury it with Sounder. He smelled his pillow. It still smelled clean and fresh. He put the ear in his pocket so the children wouldn't ask questions as he passed them on the way out. He smoothed his pillow. He was glad his mother washed his sheet and pillowcase every week, just like she did for the people who lived in the big houses with curtains on the windows. About twice a year his mother washed a lot of curtains. The clothesline was filled with them, and they were thin and light and ruffled and fluffy. It was more fun to rub your face against the curtains than on the clean sheets every Monday. The curtains, moving in the breeze, were like the sea's foam. The boy had never seen sea foam, but his mother had told him that when the Lord calmed the mighty Jordan for people to cross over, the water moved in little ripples like curtains in a breeze, and soft white foam made ruffles on top of the water.

The boy had never looked out of a window that had curtains on it. Whenever he passed houses with curtains on the windows, he remembered that if he put his face close against the curtains on the washline he could see through them. He thought there were always eyes, close against the curtains, looking out at him. He watched the windows out of the corner of his eye; he always felt scared until he had passed. Passing a cabin was different. In a cabin window there were just faces with real eyes looking out.

He could go out now, he thought. The wood in the stove had burned down some, and it would be safe. Besides, he would be close by for a while. Getting the body of Sounder from under the cabin wouldn't be easy. The younger children would bother him; they would ask a lot of questions like "Why is Sounder dead?" and "Will he stay dead?" and many more that he would not want to answer.

"When I'm out, don't be yellin' for me. I'll be through in a while," he said to the smallest child, who was looking out of the window, his chin barely high enough to rest on the sill.

There's no hurry, the boy thought. I have all day, and it's still early. And he looked out of the window too. "If you're inside you look out, and if you're outside you look in, but what looks both ways? That's a riddle; what's the answer?" He directed it to no child in particular. And no one answered. "What's the answer?" the boy repeated, and then he answered his own riddle. "The window is the answer; it looks both ways." None of the children paid any attention.

"I must go now," said the boy to his brother and sisters, "before it gets colder. The wind is starting up, so keep the door shut."

Sounder had not died in his favorite spot right behind the porch steps where he had a hole dug out and where the boy's father had put two coffee sacks for a pallet.[1] His mother had said, "Sounder will crawl to the darkest, farthest part of the cabin." That's why she had made the boy put on his ragged clothes.

The boy could not see all the way under the cabin. At one time rats had lived there, and they had pushed up the earth in some places so that it almost touched the beams. They did this so they could gnaw through the floor from below.

He hurt his head and shoulders on nails sticking down from above as he crawled. He hurt his knees and elbows on broken glass, rusty sardine cans, and broken pieces of crockery and dishes. The dry dust got in his mouth and tasted like lime and grease. Under the cabin it smelled stale and dead, like old carcasses and snakes. The boy was glad it was winter because in summer there might have been dry-land moccasins[2] and copperheads under the cabin. He crawled from front to back, looking along the spaces between the beams.

Sounder was not to be seen. The boy would have to go back and forth. Maybe Sounder had pushed with his hind feet and dug a hole into which he had settled. The threadbare knees of last year's overalls opened up, and his bare knees scraped the soil. His father's long jacket caught under his knees as he crawled and jerked his face down into the dust. Cobwebs dropped over his face and mouth. His mouth was so dry with dust that he could not spit them out.

He crawled over every spot under the cabin, but Sounder's body was not there. The boy felt in his pocket. He had lost Sounder's ear under the cabin. It made no difference. It could be buried there.

But where was Sounder's body? he wondered. Perhaps the injuries in the side of his head and shoulder were only skin wounds. They looked so terrible, but maybe they were not bad after all. Perhaps Sounder had limped down the road, the way the wagon had taken his master, and died. Perhaps he had only been knocked senseless and that was why he zigzagged so crazily, running for the cabin.

No wild creature could have carried the dead body away. Foxes could carry off dead squirrels and possums. But no animal was big enough to drag Sounder's body away. Maybe the boy, looking under the cabin with the lantern, had caused Sounder to crawl out the other side and die in the brown stalk land.

The boy was crying now. Not that there was any new or sudden sorrow. There just seemed to be nothing else to fill up the vast lostness of the moment. His nose began to run and itch. The tears ran down through the cobwebs and dust that covered his face, making little rivulets.[3] The boy rubbed his eyes with his dirty hands and mixed dust with tears. His eyes began to smart.

He followed the road the way the wagon had taken his father as far as he dared leave the fire and the children in the cabin, still in hollering distance. There was no sign of Sounder's body. He spiraled the brown stalk land in ever-widening circles, searching the fencerows as he went. Under the jack oaks and the cottonwoods there was nothing. In the matted Scotch-broom tangle he visualized the great tan body as he carefully picked each step. But the dog was not there.

[1] **pallet:** a small, crude bed or straw-filled mattress
[2] **dry-land moccasins:** poisonous snakes found in the southeastern U.S.
[3] **rivulets:** little streams

CHAPTER FOUR

After the boy had fed the children and eaten something himself, he sat down by the warm stove and looked out of the window. There was nothing else to do. Now and then a cloud would cross the sun that had finally burned its way out of the gray. The boy watched the cloud shadows roll over the fields and pass over the cabin. They darkened the windows as they passed.

He carried in wood for the night before the sun began to weaken. Then he looked out of the window again to where his mother would appear. Finally he saw a speck moving on the road. He watched it grow.

"She's coming," he said to the younger children, and they crowded around him and pushed their faces against the window. "She's been gone long enough to walk to town and more," he added.

"What will she bring?" one of the children asked.

"She'll bring nothin', but maybe things to eat. She won't bring no stick candy. Don't ask her for none. Don't ask her nothin'."

Several times during the day the boy had said to himself, "Maybe they'll let him come home if she takes back the stuff. Some people might, but some won't." But his father was not with her.

"I gave the stuff back," she said when she got to the cabin.

The boy's throat hurt with a great lump, and when he swallowed, it would hurt more. If his father had come, it would have been easy. Together they could have found Sounder's body and buried him.

When the boy's mother heard that he had not found Sounder under the cabin, she stood in the doorway and thought for a long time. If one of the children had stood in the door that long, she would have said "Go in or out, child."

"Creatures like to die under somethin'," she said at last, "and there ain't nothin' else close to crawl under. He wasn't hit in his vitals, I reckon. He's got a flesh wound. He's gone into the woods to draw out the poison with oak-leaf acid."

Now she shut the door and put her basket on the tin-topped table. "Poke up the fire," she said to the boy. "Oak leaves has strong acid that toughens the skin, just like the oak bark that they use to tan leather in the tannery. The creature beds down with the wound against a heap of oak leaves. The leaves make a poultice[1] that draws out the poison and heals the wound with a hard brown scab. That's why creatures head for the swampland around the big water when the mange hits. Wet leaves heals better."

"Sounder's blood would wettin the leaves," the boy said after he had stood a long time with the poker in his hand. His eyes were fixed on the open stove door, watching the yellow flame change shape and turn to blue and red.

"Sounder was jumping at the wagon and hard to hit," the boy's mother said. "I think maybe he was hit a glancing shot that tore off the hide on his head and shoulder. If he was, he's gone to the jack-oak woods to heal himself. The Lord shows His creatures how to do. If he ain't dead now, he'll come limpin' home, powerful hungry, in time."

"Tomorrow or the day after?" the boy asked.

"Longer, maybe four days, or more like seven. But don't be all hope, child. If he had deep head wounds, he might be addled crazy and not know where he wandered off to die."

The boy's mother had brought home the empty meal sack. In her basket she had some fat meat, potatoes, and a small bottle of

vanilla flavoring, which she had bought with the money she got for her walnut kernels. From the bottom of the basket she took the folded brown paper bag into which she poured each night's pickin's and put it on the shelf. She also brought home an empty cardboard box which the storekeeper had given her. She didn't say where she had been, besides the store, or what had happened. The boy could see that her eyes were filled with hurt and said nothing. The younger children remembered not to ask anything except, looking in the empty box, one said, "Nothin' in here?"

"I'm gonna use it to put a cake in," the mother said.

"Better go out and crack nuts for the night's pickin' before dark," she said to the boy.

The boy scooped up a tin pail of nuts from the big box under the stove and went out to the flat cracking stone. With his knees still sore from crawling under the cabin, he hesitated a long time before he knelt on the frozen earth. Standing, he looked one way and then another, tracing the fencerows that had more oaks than other trees, the far lowland woods and the foothills. "I'll go there first tomorrow," he said to himself as he faced the foothills. "There's big patches of oak trees there. And whenever Sounder was given his head, he picked the hills for huntin'."

When night came, his mother hummed and picked kernels. She did not tell a story. The boy wanted to ask who carried in wood to keep the people in jail warm. He knew they had big stoves in big jails. Once his mother had told him a story about three people named Shadrach, Meshach, and Abed-nego who were in jail. Some mean governor or sheriff got mad and had them thrown right into the jail stove, big as a furnace, but the Lord blew out the fire and cooled the big stove in a second. And when the jail keeper opened the stove door, there stood Shadrach, Meshach, and Abed-nego singing:

Cool water, cool water;
The Lord's got green pastures and cool water.

"Tell me about Joseph[2] in the jail and the stone quarry in Egypt and chiselin' out rocks to make ole Pharaoh's gravestone," the boy asked. But his mother went on humming, and the boy went back to his thinking.

No stove could be that big, he thought. He watched the red coals through the open draft in the stove door brighten each time the wind blew loud enough to make a low whistling noise in the stovepipe. A burning chunk-stick fell against the inside of the stove, but the boy did not try to convince himself that it might be the thump of Sounder scratching fleas underneath the floor. He was thinking of tomorrow.

Tomorrow he would go into the woods and look for Sounder. "The wind whistlin' in the pipe is bothersome," he said. He hated the cold wind. It blew through his clothes and chilled his body inside and made him shiver. He hoped the wind would not be blowing in the woods tomorrow. The wind made the woods noisy. The boy liked the woods when they were quiet. He understood quiet. He could hear things in the quiet. But quiet was better in the woods than it was in the cabin. He didn't hear things in cabin quiet. Cabin quiet was long and sad.

"Turn the pipe-damper a little and the whistlin' will stop," his mother said at last.

The next day he walked the great woodlands, calling Sounder's name. The wind blew through his clothes and chilled him inside. When he got home after dark, his clothes were torn. His throat hurt with a great lump choking him. His mother fed him and said, "Child, child, you must not go into the woods again. Sounder might come home again. But you must learn to lose, child. The Lord teaches the old to lose. The young don't know how to learn it. Some people is born to keep. Some is born to lose. We was born to lose, I reckon. But Sounder might come back."

But weeks went by, and Sounder did not come back.

One night the boy learned why his mother had brought home the bottle of vanilla flavoring. Now it was Christmas and she was making a cake. When the four layers were spread out on the tin-topped table and she began to ice them, the boy noticed that she put three together in a large cake and made a small one of the leftover layer.

"Why we having two cakes?" the boy asked. But she was humming to herself and did not answer him. When she had finished, she put the small cake on the top shelf of the dish cupboard. The big one she put in the cardboard box she had brought from the store.

The sweet smell of baking and vanilla had drawn the smaller

children from the stove to the edge of the table. The woman reached over or walked around them as she worked. "I'm done," she finally said. "You can lick the pans."

The boy had not moved from his chair by the stove. Today he had searched the oak clumps along the far fencerows for Sounder. He never got the sweet pan till last, anyway. It always went from youngest to oldest, and there was never much left when his turn came.

"You're tired and worried poorly," his mother said. And she handed him the icing pan.

In the morning the woman told the boy that she wanted him to walk to town, to the jail behind the courthouse, and take the cake to his father. "It's a troublesome trip," she said. "But they won't let women in the jail. So you must go." She tied a string around the cardboard box and said, "Carry it flat if your hands don't get too cold. Then it'll look mighty pretty when you fetch it to him." She stood at the edge of the porch until he was far enough away not to be able to look back and see her crying, then called to him, "Whatever you do, child, act perkish and don't grieve your father."

On the road, the boy felt afraid. He had been to the town at Christmastime before. Not on Christmas Day, but a few days before, to help his father carry mistletoe and bunches of bitter-sweet berries that his father sold by the wall in front of the court-house or on the corner by the bank. And sometimes, when it was getting late and they still had trimmings to sell, his father would go to the back door of houses along the street and say "Ma'am, would you need some trimmin's?" and hold up the biggest sprig of mistletoe left in his grain sack. They usually sold most of the mistletoe, the boy remembered, but bunches of bittersweet that the boy had carried all day were always left over to be thrown in a fence corner on the way home. "Ain't no good for nothin' now" his father would say.

From early fall until gathering time, the father and boy kept their eyes peeled for the golden-green clumps with white berries that grew high up in the forks of water elm and sycamore trees. Bittersweet was easy. "Pull down one vine and trim it, and you've got as much as a man can carry" his father always said. "But it takes a heap of fearful climbin' for mistletoe." They had already started gathering, and half a grain sack of mistletoe was still hanging against the side of the cabin. "If she hadn't had such a big load, she might have taken it," the boy said to himself.

The boy's fearful feeling increased as he got nearer town. There were big houses and behind the curtained windows there were eyes looking out at him. There would be more people now, and somebody might say "What you got in that box, boy?" or "Where you goin', boy?"

Church bells were ringing in the town. It was Christmas, and some people went to church on Christmas. In town the people he saw were laughing and talking. No one noticed him and he was glad. He looked at the store windows out of the corner of his eye. They were silvery and gold and green and red and sparkling. They were filled with toys and beautiful things. With the Christmas money from peddling,[3] his father had bought what toys he could for the boy and his little brother and sisters. They had worn-out toys too. People in the big houses where his mother worked had given them to her to bring home.

He always wished they would give his mother an old book. He was sure he could learn to read if he had a book. He could read some of the town signs and the store signs. He could read price figures. He wanted to stop and stand and look straight at the windows, but he was afraid. A policeman would come after him. Perhaps the people had offered his mother old books, but she had said "No use, nobody can read in our cabin." Perhaps the people knew she couldn't read and thought her feelings would be hurt if they offered her the books their children had used up and worn out. The boy had heard once that some people had so many books they only read each book once. But the boy was sure there were not that many books in the world.

It was cold, but there were a few people standing or sitting along the wall in front of the courthouse. Winter or summer, there were always people there. The boy wondered if they knew it was Christmas. They didn't look happy like some of the people he had seen. He knew they were looking at him, so he hurried quickly past and around the corner to the back of the courthouse. The front of the courthouse was red brick with great white marble steps going up to a wide door. But the back was gray cement and three floors high, with iron bars over all the windows.

The only door that led into the jail had a small square of glass at about the height of a man, and there were iron bars over the glass. The boy was not tall enough to see through the glass. He clutched the box close to him. He felt that something was about to burst through the door. In the middle of the door there was a great iron knocker. The boy knew he had to knock at the door; he wished he could be back in the great woods. He could hear voices inside the windows with the iron bars. Somewhere a voice was singing "God's gonna trouble the water." From one of the windows there came the sound of laughter. Now and then a door slammed with the deep clash of iron on iron. There was a rattle of tin pans. The boy felt very lonely. The town was as lonely as the cabin, he thought.

A large red-faced man opened the door and said, "You'll have to wait. It ain't visitin' hours yet. Who do you want to see? You'll have to wait." And he slammed the door before the boy could speak.

It was cold on the gray side of the building, so the boy went to the corner near the wall where the people and visitors stood or sat. The sun was shining there. The boy had forgotten it was still Christmas, the waiting seemed so long. A drunk man staggered along the street in front of the courthouse wall, saying "Merry Christmas" to everyone. He said "Merry Christmas" to the boy, and he smiled at the boy too.

Finally the great clock on the roof of the courthouse struck twelve. It frightened the boy because it seemed to shake the town. Now the red-faced man opened the door and let several people in. Inside, the man lined everybody up and felt their clothes and pockets. He jerked the cardboard box from the boy and tore off the top. The boy could hear iron doors opening and closing. Long hallways, with iron bars from floor to ceiling, ran from the door into the dim center of the building. The man with the red face squeezed the cake in his hands and broke it into four pieces. "This could have a steel file or hacksaw blade in it," he said. Then he swore and threw the pieces back in the box. The boy had been very hungry. Now he was not hungry. He was afraid. The man shoved the box into the boy's hands and swore again. Part of the cake fell to the floor; it was only a box of crumbs now. The man swore again and made the boy pick up the crumbs from the floor.

The boy hated the man with the red face with the same total but helpless hatred he had felt when he saw his father chained, when he saw Sounder shot. He had thought how he would like to chain the deputy sheriff behind his own wagon and then scare the horse so that it would run faster than the cruel man could. The deputy would fall and bounce and drag on the frozen road. His fine leather

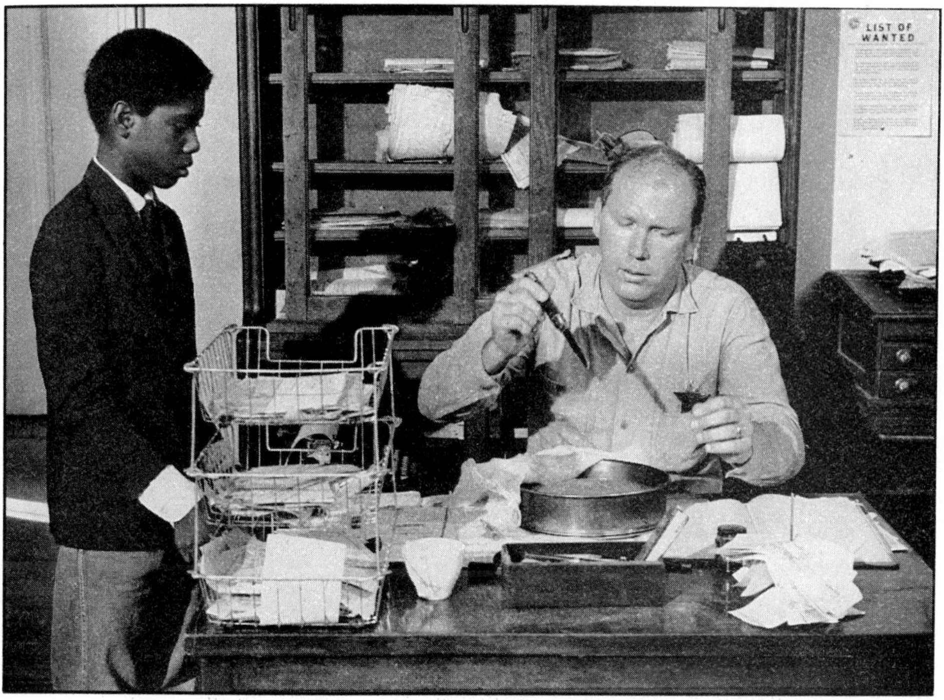

jacket would be torn more than he had torn his father's overalls. He would yell and curse, and that would make the horse go faster. And the boy would just watch, not trying to stop the wagon. . . .

The boy would like to see the big red-faced man crumpled on the floor with the crumbs. Besides the red face, the boy had noticed the fat, bulging neck that folded down over the man's collar and pushed up in wrinkled circles under his chin. The bull neck of the man reminded the boy of the bull he had seen die in the cattle chute at the big house where his father worked. The horse doctor had been trying to vaccinate the bull in the neck, but the rope through the ring in the bull's nose didn't keep the bull from tossing his head from side to side, knocking the horse doctor against the side of the chute. Then the horse doctor had gotten mad and said, "Get a chain. I'll make him stand still."

When the chain was snapped around the bull's neck, the farm hands pulled it over the crossbar of the chute posts and hooked it. But when the horse doctor stuck the bull in the neck, he lunged backward, set his front feet with his whole weight against the chain, and choked himself to death before one of the farm hands could jab him with a pitchfork and make him slacken the chain.

The legs of the bull folded under him and the chain buried itself in the fat of his neck. When the farm hands finally got the chain unhooked from the crossbar, the bull's head fell in the dirt, and blood oozed out of its mouth and nostrils. . . .

The bull-necked man would sag to his knees, the boy thought, and crumple into a heap on the floor. Just the way the bull did, the boy thought, and blood would ooze out of his mouth and nose.

"Get up," the red-faced man said, "you wanta take all day?" The boy stood up. He felt weak and his knees shook, but there were no more tears in his eyes.

The red-faced man took a big iron key on a ring as big around as the boy's head and unlocked one of the iron gates. He pushed the boy in and said, "Fourth door down." Passing the three doors, the boy could feel eyes following him. He saw men, some sitting on cots, some standing behind the iron gates with their hands on the bars, looking at him. Each step echoed against the iron ceiling and made him sound like a giant walking. Far down the long iron-grated corridor a sad voice was singing:

Far away on Judah's plains
The shepherds watched their sheep.

The boy's father stood with his hands on the bars. He did not have his hands and feet chained together. Seeing the hands that could handle a pot lid without a pot rag, open the stove door without using a poker, or skin a possum by holding the hind legs of the carcass with one hand and the hide with the other and just pulling, the boy knew his father could have choked the cruel man with the bull neck.

The father looked at the boy and said, "Child." On the way, the boy had thought about what he would say to his father. He had practiced talking about his mother selling kernels at the store and buying the cake makings, his little brother and sisters being all right, no strangers coming past, not finding Sounder's body. And he was going to ask his father where Sounder came to him along the road when he wasn't more'n a pup. He practiced saying them all over and over to get the quiver and the quiet spells out of his voice because his mother had said, "Whatever you do, child, act perkish and don't grieve your father."

But the boy was full of mixed hate and pity now, and it addled him. There was an opening in the bars with a flat, iron shelf

attached on the inside. The boy had left the lid of the box on the floor. Now he pushed the box through the opening and said, "This was a cake, before—" But he couldn't finish. An awful quiet spell destroyed all his practice.

"Sounder might not be dead," the boy said. He knew his father was grieved, for he swallowed hard and the quiet spells came to him too.

"I'll be back 'fore long," said his father.

From somewhere down the corridor there came a loud belly laugh, and a loud voice called out, "Listen to the man talk."

"Tell her not to grieve." His father was almost whispering now.

"Sounder didn't die under the cabin." But the boy couldn't keep the quivering out of his voice.

"Tell her not to send you no more." The quiet spells were getting longer. The man stopped looking through the bars at the boy and looked down at the cake.

"If he wasn't shot in his vitals," the boy said, "he might get healed in the woods." Then there was a long quiet spell that was split in the middle by the loud clank of an iron door banging shut.

"Tell her I'll send word with the visitin' preacher."

The big red-faced man with the bull neck opened the corridor door and yelled, "Visitin' over." The boy felt numb and cold, like he had felt standing outside the jail door. He choked up. He had grieved his father. He hated the red-faced man, so he wouldn't cry until he got outside.

"Come on, boy," the man yelled, swinging the big key ring.

"Go, child," the father said. "Hurry, child."

The boy was the last person through the big iron door. The bull-necked man pushed him and said, "Git, boy, or next time you won't get in."

[1] **poultice:** a soft, wet mixture applied to a sore part of the body
[2] **Joseph:** The story of Joseph is told in the book of Genesis.
[3] **peddling:** traveling about selling wares

A CLOSER LOOK

1. What makes the mother think that the gunshot probably didn't kill Sounder after all? According to the mother, how will Sounder heal his wounds?

2. Why does the mother want her son not to go into the woods anymore to search for Sounder? Explain what she means when she says, ". . . you must learn to lose, child."

3. In the jail, the boy is reminded of a violent daydream of revenge he had about the deputy sheriff when his father was arrested. Describe the daydream. How is the boy's daydream similar to what actually happened to his father?

4. Why does the father tell his son not to visit him in jail anymore?

CHAPTER FIVE

The boy moved quickly around the corner and out of sight of the iron door and the gray cement walls of the jail. At the wall in front of the courthouse he stood for a while and looked back. When he had come, he was afraid, but he felt good in one way because he would see his father. He was bringing him a cake for Christmas. And he wasn't going to let his father know he was grieved. So his father *wouldn't* be grieved.

Now the sun had lost its strength. There were only a few people loafing around the courthouse wall, so the boy sat for a spell. He felt numb and tired. What would he say to his mother? He would tell her that the jailer was mean to visitors but didn't say nothing to the people in jail. He wouldn't tell her about the cake. When he told her his father had said she shouldn't send him again, that he would send word by the visiting preacher, she would say "You grieved him, child. I told you to be perk so you wouldn't grieve him."

Nobody came near where the boy sat or passed on the street in front of the wall. He had forgotten the most important thing, he thought. He hadn't asked his father where Sounder had come to him on the road when he wasn't more'n a pup. That didn't make any difference.

But along the road on the way to the jail, before the bull-necked man had ruined everything, the boy had thought his father would begin to think and say "If a stray ever follard you and it wasn't near a house, likely somebody's dropped it. So you could fetch it home and keep it for a dog."

"Wouldn't do no good now," the boy murmured to himself. Even if he found a stray on the way home, his mother would say "I'm afraid, child. Don't bring it in the cabin. If it's still here when mornin' comes, you take it down the road and scold it and run so it won't foller you no more. If somebody come lookin', you'd be in awful trouble."

A great part of the way home the boy walked in darkness. In the big houses he saw beautiful lights and candles in the windows. Several times dogs rushed to the front gates and barked as he passed. But no stray pup came to him along the lonely, empty stretches of road. In the dark he thought of the bull-necked man crumpled on the floor in the cake crumbs, like the strangled bull in the cattle chute, and he walked faster. At one big house the mailbox by the road had a lighted lantern hanging on it. The boy walked on the far side of the road so he wouldn't show in the light. "People hangs 'em out when company is comin' at night," the boy's father had once told him.

When court was over, they would take his father to a road camp or a quarry[1] or a state farm. Would his father send word with the visiting preacher where he had gone? Would they take his father away to the chain gang for a year or two years before he could tell the visiting preacher? How would the boy find him then? If he lived closer to the town, he could watch each day, and when they took his father away in the wagons where convicts were penned up in huge wooden crates, he could follow.

The younger children were already in bed when the boy got home. He was glad, for they would have asked a lot of questions that might make his mother feel bad, questions like "Is everybody chained up in jail? How long do people stay in jail at one time?"

The boy's mother did not ask hurtful questions. She asked if the boy got in all right and if it was warm in the jail. The boy told her that the jailer was mean to visitors but that he didn't say nothing to the people in jail. He told her he heard some people singing in the jail.

"Sounder ain't come home?" the boy said to his mother after he had talked about the jail. He had looked under the porch and called before he came into the cabin.

Now he went out, calling and looking around the whole cabin. He started to light the lantern to look more, but his mother said, "Hang it back, child. Ain't no use to fret yourself. Eat your supper, you must be famished."

"He said not to come no more," the boy finally said to his mother when he had finished his supper. "He said he'll send word by the visitin' preacher." He poked up the fire and waited for his mother to ask him if he had been perk and didn't grieve his father, but she didn't. He warmed himself and watched a patch of red glow the size of his hand at the bottom of the stove. He could see the red-faced man lying on the jail floor with blood oozing out of the corners of his mouth. After a long quiet spell the rocker began to squeak, and it made the boy jump, but his mother didn't notice. She began to rock as she picked out walnut kernels. She hummed for a while, and then she began to sing like she was almost whispering for no one to hear but herself:

You gotta walk that lonesome valley,
You gotta walk it by yourself,
Ain't nobody else gonna walk it for you . . .

In bed, the pressure of the bed slats through the straw tick felt good against the boy's body. His pillow smelled fresh, and it was smooth and soft. He was tired, but he lay awake for a long time. He thought of the store windows full of so many things. He thought of the beautiful candles in windows. He dreamed his father's hands were chained against the prison bars and he was still standing there with his head down. He dreamed that a wonderful man had come up to him as he was trying to read the store signs aloud and had said, "Child, you want to learn, don't you?"

In the morning the boy lay listening to his mother as she opened and closed the stove door. He heard the damper squeak in the stovepipe as she adjusted it. She was singing softly to herself. Then the boy thought he heard another familiar sound, a faint whine on the cabin porch. He listened. No, it couldn't be. Sounder always scratched before he whined, and the scratching was always louder than the whine. Besides, it was now almost two months later, and the boy's mother had said he might be back in a week. No, he was not dreaming. He heard it again. He had been sleeping in his shirt to keep warm, so he only had to pull on his overalls as he went. His mother had stopped singing and was listening.

There on the cabin porch, on three legs, stood the living skeleton of what had been a mighty coon hound. The tail began to wag, and the hide made little ripples back and forth over the ribs. One side of the head and shoulders was reddish brown and hairless; the acid of the oak leaves had tanned the surface of the wound the color of leather. One front foot dangled above the floor. The stub of an ear stuck out on one side, and there was no eye on that side, only a dark socket with a splinter of bone showing above it. The dog raised his good ear and whined. His one eye looked up at the lantern and the possum sack where they hung against the wall. The eye looked past the boy and his mother. Where was his master? "Poor creature. Poor creature," said the mother and turned away to get him food. The boy felt sick and wanted to cry, but he touched Sounder on the good side of his head. The tail wagged faster, and he licked the boy's hand.

The shattered shoulder never grew together enough to carry weight, so the great hunter with the single eye, his head held to one side so he could see, never hopped much farther from the cabin than the spot in the road where he had tried to jump on the wagon with his master. Whether he lay in the sun on the cabin porch or by the side of the road, the one eye was always turned in the direction his master had gone.

The boy got used to the way the great dog looked. The stub of ear didn't bother him, and the one eye that looked up at him was warm and questioning. But why couldn't he bark? "He wasn't hit in the neck" the boy would say to his mother. "He eats all right, his throat ain't scarred." But day after day when the boy snapped his fingers and said "Sounder, good Sounder," no excited bark burst from the great throat. When something moved at night, the whine was louder, but it was still a whine.

Before Sounder was shot, the boy's mother always said "Get the pan, child" or "Feed your dog, child." Now she sometimes got the pan herself and took food out to Sounder. The boy noticed that sometimes his mother would stop singing when she put the food pan down at the edge of the porch. Sometimes she would stand and look at the hunting lantern and possum sack where they hung, unused, against the cabin wall. . . .

The town and the jail seemed to become more remote and the distance greater as each day passed. If his father hadn't said "Don't come again," it wouldn't seem so far, the boy thought. Uncertainty made the days of waiting longer too.

The boy waited for the visiting preacher to come and bring word of his father. He thought the people for whom his mother washed the soft curtains could certainly write and would write a letter for his mother. But would someone in the jail read it for his father? Perhaps none of the people in jail could read, and the big man with the red face would just tear it up and swear. The visiting preacher might write a letter for the boy's father. But how would it get to the cabin since no mailman passed and there was no mailbox like the boy had seen on the wider road nearer the town?

The boy wanted to go to the town to find out what had happened to his father. His mother always said "Wait, child, wait." When his mother returned laundry to the big houses, she asked people to read her the court news from their newspapers. One night she came home with word of the boy's father; it had been read to her from the court news. When the younger children had gone to bed, she said to the boy, "Court's over." And then there was one of those long quiet spells that always made the boy feel numb and weak.

"You won't have to fret for a while about seein' him in jail. He's gone to hard labor."

"For how long?" the boy asked.

"It won't be as long as it might. Folks has always said he could do two men's work in a day. He'll get time off for hard work and good behavior. The court news had about good behavior in it. The judge said it."

"Where's he gonna be at?" the boy asked after he had swallowed the great lump that filled up his throat and choked him.

"Didn't say. The people that has the paper says it don't ever say wher' they gonna be at. But it's the county or the state. Ain't never outside the state, the people says."

"He'll send word," the boy said.

[1] **quarry:** an open pit from which stone is obtained by digging, cutting, or blasting

CHAPTER SIX

Now the cabin was even quieter than it had been before loneliness put its stamp on everything. Sounder rolled his one eye in lonely dreaming. The boy's mother had longer periods of just humming without drifting into soft singing. The boy helped her stretch longer clotheslines from the cabin to the cottonwood trees at the edge of the fields. In the spring the boy went to the fields to work. He was younger than the other workers. He was afraid and lonely. He heard them talking quietly about his father. He went to do yard work at the big houses where he had gathered weeds behind his father. "How old are you?" a man asked once when he was paying the boy his wages. "You're a hard worker for your age."

The boy did not remember his age. He knew he had lived a long, long time.

And the long days and months and seasons built a powerful restlessness into the boy. "Don't fret" his mother would say when he first began to talk of going to find his father. "Time's passin'. Won't be much longer now."

To the end of the county might be a far journey, and out of the county would be a far, far journey, but I'll go, the boy thought.

"Why are you so feared for me to go?" he would ask, for now he was old enough to argue with his mother. "In Bible stories everybody's always goin' on a long journey. Abraham goes on a long journey. Jacob goes into a strange land where his uncle lives, and he don't know where he lives, but he finds him easy. Joseph goes on the longest journey of all and has more troubles, but the Lord watches over him. And in Bible-story journeys, ain't no journey hopeless. Everybody finds what they suppose to find."

The state had many road camps which moved from place to place. There were also prison farms and stone quarries. Usually the boy would go searching in autumn when work in the fields was finished. One year he heard "Yes, the man you speak of was here, but I heard he was moved to the quarry in Gilmer County." One year it had been "Yes, he was in the quarry, but he was sick in the winter and was moved to the bean farm in Bartow County." More often a guard would chase him away from the gate or from standing near the high fence with the barbed wire along the top of it. And the guard would laugh and say "I don't know no names; I only know numbers. Besides, you can't visit here, you can only visit in

jail." Another would sneer "You wouldn't know your old man if you saw him, he's been gone so long. You sure you know who your pa is, kid?"

The men in striped convict suits, riding in the mule-drawn wagons with big wooden frames resembling large pig crates, yelled as they rode past the watching boy, "Hey, boy, looking for your big brother? What you doing, kid, seeing how you gonna like it when you grow up?" And still the boy would look through the slats of the crate for a familiar face. He would watch men walking in line, dragging chains on their feet, to see if he could recognize his father's step as he had known it along the road, coming from the fields to the cabin. Once he listened outside the gate on a Sunday afternoon and heard a preacher telling about the Lord loosening the chains of Peter when he had been thrown into prison. Once he stood at the guardhouse door of a quarry, and some ladies dressed in warm heavy coats and boots came and sang Christmas songs.

In his wandering the boy learned that the words men use most are "Get!" "Get out!" and "Keep moving!" Sometimes he followed the roads from one town to another, but if he could, he would follow railroad tracks. On the roads there were people, and they frightened the boy. The railroads usually ran through flat silent countryside where the boy could walk alone with his terrifying thoughts. He learned that railroad stations, post offices, courthouses, and churches were places to escape from the cold for a few hours in the late night.

His journeys in search of his father accomplished one wonderful thing. In the towns he found that people threw newspapers and magazines into trash barrels, so he could always find something with which to practice his reading. When he was tired, or when he waited at some high wire gate, hoping his father would pass in the line, he would read the big-lettered words first and then practice the small-lettered words.

In his lonely journeying, the boy had learned to tell himself the stories his mother had told him at night in the cabin. He liked the way they always ended with the right thing happening. And people in stories were never feared of anything. Sometimes he tried to put together things he had read in the newspapers he found and make new stories. But the ends never came out right, and they made him more afraid. The people he tried to put in stories from the papers always seemed like strangers. Some story people he wouldn't be afraid of if he met them on the road. He thought he liked the David[1] and Joseph[2] stories best of all. "Why you want 'em told over'n over?" his mother had asked so many times. Now, alone on a bed of pine needles, he remembered that he could never answer his mother. He would just wait, and if his mother wasn't sad, with her lips stretched thin, she would stop humming and tell about David the boy, or King David. If she felt good and started long enough before bedtime, he would hear about Joseph the slave-boy, Joseph in prison, Joseph the dreamer, and Joseph the Big Man in Egypt. And when she had finished all about Joseph, she would say "Ain't no earthly power can make a story end as pretty as Joseph's; 'twas the Lord."

The boy listened to the wind passing through the tops of the tall pines; he thought they moved like giant brooms sweeping the sky. The moonlight reached down through the broken spaces of swaying trees and sent bright shafts of light along the ground and over him. The voice of the wind in the pines reminded him of one of the stories his mother had told him about King David. The Lord had said to David that when he heard the wind moving in the tops of the cedar trees, he would know that the Lord was fighting on his side and he would win. When David moved his army around into the hills to attack his enemy, he heard the mighty roar of the wind moving in the tops of the trees, and he cried out to his men that the Lord was moving above them into battle.

The boy listened to the wind. He could hear the mighty roaring. He thought he heard the voice of David and the tramping of many feet. He wasn't afraid with David near. He thought he saw a lantern moving far off in the woods, and as he fell asleep he thought he heard the deep, ringing voice of Sounder rising out of his great throat, riding the mist of the lowlands.

[1] **David:** a Biblical figure who in his youth killed the giant warrior Goliath. He later became king of Israel, and won a battle against the Philistines when the Lord intervened on his behalf.

[2] **Joseph:** a Biblical figure who was sold into slavery by his jealous brothers, and imprisoned unjustly in Egypt, but who was later recognized for his wisdom by the Pharaoh and made a great ruler

A CLOSER LOOK

1. When Sounder comes home he is missing an eye and most of an ear, and has lost the use of one front paw. What else has changed about Sounder that means that he won't live up to his name?

2. The father is sentenced to years of hard labor. Do you think this punishment fits the crime he committed? Explain your answer.

3. As the boy travels in search of his father, he learns some practical things about life. What one thing stands out as wonderful to a boy who, above all else, wants to learn how to read?

4. In the story of Joseph, Joseph suffers because the people around him are jealous, spiteful, and cruel. Yet his wisdom and abilities eventually win him a position of great importance. What parallels exist between Joseph's experiences and those of members of the boy's family? Why does the story of Joseph appeal to the boy?

CHAPTER SEVEN

When the boy came home after each long trip in search of his father, the crippled coon hound would hobble far down the road to meet him, wag his tail, stand on his hind legs, and paw the boy with his good front paw. But never a sound beyond a deep whine came from him. The bits of news he might bring home his mother received in silence. Someone had heard that his father was moved. Someone had been in the same work gang with his father for four months last summer on the Walker county road. When she had heard all he had heard, she would say "There's patience, child, and waitin' that's got to be."

Word drifted back that there had been a terrible dynamite blast in one of the quarries that had killed twelve convicts and wounded several others. His mother had had the people read her the story from their newspapers when she carried the laundry. None of the prisoners killed was the boy's father.

The months and seasons of searching dragged into years. The boy helped his mother carry more and more baskets of laundry to and from the big houses; the clotheslines grew longer and longer. The other children, except for the littlest, could fetch and tote too, but they didn't like to go by themselves.

"Time is passing" the woman would say. "I wish you wouldn't go lookin', child." But when one of the field hands had heard something or when somebody said that a road camp was moving, she would wrap a piece of bread and meat for the boy to eat on the way and say nothing. Looking back from far down the road, the boy would see her watching at the edge of the porch. She seemed to understand the compulsion that started him on each long, fruitless journey with new hope.

Once the boy waited outside the tall wire fence of a road camp. Some convicts were whitewashing stones along the edge of a pathway that came toward the gate near where he stood. One might be his father, he thought. He could not tell until they got closer, for they crawled on their hands and knees as they bent over the stones. He leaned against the fence and hooked his fingers through the wire. If none of them was his father, they might know something anyway, he thought. He wished they would stand up and walk from one stone to the next. Then he would know his father easily by his walk. He could still remember the sound of his footsteps approaching the cabin after dark, the easy roll of the never-hurrying step that was the same when he went to work in the morning and when he came home from the long day in the fields. The boy had even been able to tell his father's walk by the swing of the lantern at his side. But none of the men whitewashing the round rocks that lined the path stood up and walked. They crawled the few feet from stone to stone, and crawling, they all looked the same.

Suddenly something crashed against the fence in front of the boy's face. A jagged piece of iron tore open the skin and crushed the fingers of one of his hands against the fence. Lost in thought and watching the convicts, the boy had not seen the guard, who had been sitting under a tree with a shotgun across his knees, get up and come to a toolbox filled with picks and crowbars which stood near the fence.

The piece of iron lay on the inside of the fence at the boy's feet. Drops of blood from his fingers dripped down the fence from wire to wire and fell on the ground. The boy pulled his fingers away from the wire mesh and began to suck on them to stop the throbbing. Tears ran down over his face and mixed with the blood on his hand. Little rivulets of blood and water ran down his arm and dropped off the end of his elbow.

The guard was swaying back and forth with laughter. His gun lay on the lid of the open toolbox. His arms swung in apelike gyrations of glee, and he held another piece of iron in one hand and his cap in the other. A white strip of forehead, where his uniform cap kept off the sun, shone between his brown hair and his sunburned face. His laughter had burst the button from his tieless shirt collar, and a white strip outlined his gaunt neck. For a second he reminded the boy of a garden scarecrow blowing in the wind, body and head of brown burlap stuffed with straw, the head tied on with a white rag just like the white band around the guard's neck, the head tilting from side to side, inviting a well-placed stone to send it bouncing along a bean row.

The men whitewashing the rocks made no sounds. No one among them suddenly raised himself to the height of a man almost as tall as a cabin porch post.

"He ain't there," the boy murmured to himself. If he was, the boy knew, by now he would be holding the scarecrow of a man in the air with one hand clamped all the way around the strip on the skinny neck, the way he had seen Sounder clamp his great jaws on a weasel once, with the head stuck out one side of the jaws and the body the other. And the man would wheeze and squirm like the weasel had. His legs would paw the air in circles like his hands, then he would go limp, and the boy's father would loosen his grip, and the man in the brown uniform would fall in a heap, like when somebody untied the white rag that held the scarecrow to the stake. And the heap would roll down the slope and lodge against the fence, like the scarecrow rolled along a bean row until it caught in the brambles at the edge of the garden.

Feeling defeat in the midst of his glee because the boy had not run but stood still and defiant, sucking the blood from his bruised fingers, the guard stopped laughing and yelled at him, "That'll show you, boy! Git! And git fast!" The boy turned and, without looking back, began to walk slowly away. The guard began to laugh again and threw the scrap of iron over the fence. It landed a few feet from the boy. He looked at the iron and he looked at the man. The white spot between his hair and his eyes was the spot. The iron would split it open with a wide gash, and blood would darken the white spot and make it the color of the man's sunburned face. And the stone that David slung struck Goliath on his forehead; the stone sank into his forehead, and he fell on his face on the ground, the boy thought. But he left the iron on the ground.

Still sucking his fingers, the boy looked once more at the men whitewashing the stones. They were almost at the gate. He didn't need to wait and ask. His father was not crawling among them.

Later that day, passing along a street in a strange and lonely town, he saw a man dump a box of trash into a barrel. He noticed that a large brown-backed book went in with the trash. He waited until the man went back into the building and then took the book from the barrel. It was a book of stories[1] about what people think. There were titles such as Cruelty, Excellent Men, Education, Cripples, Justice, and many others. The boy sat down, leaned back against the barrel, and began to read from the story called Cruelty.

> I have often heard it said that cowardice is the mother of cruelty, and I have found by experience that malicious and inhuman animosity and fierceness are usually accompanied by weakness. Wolves and filthy bears, and all the baser beasts, fall upon the dying.

The boy was trying to read aloud, for he could understand better if he heard the words. But now he stopped. He did not understand what it said; the words were too new and strange. He was sad. He thought books would have words like the ones he had learned to read in the store signs, words like his mother used when she told him stories of the Lord and Joseph and David. All his life he had wanted a book. Now he held one in his hands, and it was only making his bruised fingers hurt more. He would carry it with him anyway.

He passed a large brick schoolhouse with big windows and children climbing on little ladders and swinging on swings. No one jeered at him or noticed him because he had crossed the street and was walking close up against the hedge on the other side. Soon the painted houses ran out, and he was walking past unpainted cabins. He always felt better on his travels when he came to the part of town where the unpainted cabins were. Sometimes people came out on the porch when he passed and talked to him. Sometimes they gave him a piece to eat on the way. Now he thought they might laugh and say "What you carryin', child? A book?" So he held it close up against him.

"That's a school too," the boy said to himself as he stood facing a small unpainted building with its door at the end instead of the side, the way cabin doors were. Besides, he could always tell a school because it had more windows than a cabin.

At the side of the building two children were sloshing water out of a tin pail near a hand pump. One threw a dipper of water on a dog that came from underneath to bark at the boy. The school was built on posts, and a stovepipe came through the wall and stuck up above the rafters. A rusty tin pipe ran from the corner of the roof down to the cistern[2] where the children were playing.

The dog had gone back under the building, so the boy entered the yard and moved toward the children. If one of them would work the pump handle, he could wash the dried blood off his hand. Just when he reached the cistern, a wild commotion of barking burst from under the floor of the school. Half a dozen dogs, which followed children to school and waited patiently for lunchtime scraps and for school to be over, burst from under the building in pursuit of a pig that had wandered onto the lot. In the wild chase around the building the biggest dog struck the tin drainpipe, and it clattered down the wall and bounced on the cement top of the cistern. With a pig under the building and the dogs barking and racing in and out, the school day ended.

Two dozen or more children raced out of the door, few of them touching the three steps that led from the stoop to the ground. Some were calling the names of dogs and looking under the building. The boy found himself surrounded by strange inquiring eyes. Questions came too fast to answer. "You new here?" "Where you moved to?" "That your book?" "You comin' here to school?" "Kin you read that big a book?" The boy had put his bruised hand into his pocket so no one could see it. Some of the children carried books too, but none were as big as the one he held close against his side.

Just when the commotion was quieting down, a man appeared at the schoolhouse door. The children scattered across the lot in four directions. "Tell your pa that he must keep his pig in the pen," he called to one child.

Then it was quiet. The boy looked at the man in the doorway. They were alone now. The dogs had followed the children. And the pig, hearing a familiar call from the corner of the lot, had come grunting from his sanctuary and gone in the direction of the call.

In his many journeyings among strangers the boy had learned to sniff out danger and spot orneriness[3] quickly. Now, for the first time in his life away from home, he wasn't feared. The lean elderly man, with snow-white hair, wearing Sunday clothes, came down the steps. "This pipe is always falling," he said as he picked it up and put it back in place. "I need to wire it up."

"I just wanted to wash my hand. It's got dried blood on it where I hurt my fingers."

"You should have run home."

"I don't live in these parts."

"Here, I'll hold your book, and I'll pump for you." And the mellow eyes of the man began to search the boy for answers, answers that could be found without asking questions.

"We need warm soapy water," the teacher said. "I live right close. Wait 'til I get my papers and lock the door, and I'll take you home and fix it."

The boy wanted to follow the man into the schoolhouse and see what it was like inside, but by the time he got to the steps the man was back again, locking the door. "I usually put the school in order after the children leave," he said, "but I'll do it in the morning before they get here."

At the edge of the school lot the man took the road that led away from the town. They walked without much talk, and the boy began to wish the man would ask him a lot of questions. When they had passed several cabins, each farther from the other as they went, the man turned off the road and said, "We're home. I live here alone. Have lived alone for a long time." Fingering the small wire hook on the neatly whitewashed gate which led into a yard that was green, the teacher stopped talking.

A cabin with a gate and green grass in the yard is almost a big house, the boy thought as he followed the man.

Inside the gate the man went along the fence, studying some plants tied up to stakes. He began to talk again, not to the boy, but to a plant that was smaller than the others. "You'll make it, little one, but it'll take time to get your roots set again."

The boy looked at the white-haired old man leaning over like he was listening for the plant to answer him. "He's conjured,"[4] the boy whispered to himself. "Lots of old folks is conjured or addled." He moved backward to the gate, thinking he'd better run away. "Conjured folks can conjure you," the boy's mother always said, "if you get yourself plain carried off by their soft spell-talk."

But before the boy could trouble his mind anymore, the man straightened up and began talking to him. "Some animal dug under the roots and tore them loose from the earth. It was wilted badly and might have died. But I reset it, and I water it every day. It's hard to reset a plant if it's wilted too much; the life has gone out of it. But this one will be all right. I see new leaves startin'."

"What grows on it?" the boy asked, thinking it must be something good to eat if somebody cared that much about a plant.

"It's only a flower," the man said. "I'll water it when the earth has cooled a little. If you water a plant when the earth is too warm, it shocks the roots."

Inside the cabin the man started a fire in the cookstove and heated water. As he washed the boy's hand with a soft white rag he said, "You musta slammed these fingers in a awful heavy door or gate." Before the boy could answer, the teacher began to talk about the plant he must remember to water.

He don't wanta know nothin' about me, the boy thought.

"When I saw your book, I thought you were coming to enroll for school. But you don't live in these parts, you say."

"I found the book in a trash barrel. It has words like I ain't used to readin'. I can read store-sign words and some newspaper words."

"This is a wonderful book," said the teacher. "It was written by a man named Montaigne, who was a soldier. But he grew tired of being a soldier and spent his time studying and writing. He also liked to walk on country roads."

The teacher lit two lamps. The boy had never seen two lamps burning in the same room. They made the room as bright as daylight.

"People should read his writings," the man continued. "But few do. He is all but forgotten." But the boy did not hear. He was thinking of a cabin that had two lamps, both lit at the same time, and two stoves, one to cook on and one to warm by.

The man sat in a chair between two tables that held the lamps. There were books on the tables too, and there were shelves filled not with pans and dishes, but with books. The mellow eyes of the man followed the boy's puzzled glances as they studied the strange warm world in which he had suddenly found himself.

"I will read you a little story from your book." The boy watched as the fingers of the man turned the pages one way and then the other until he found what he wanted to read.

"This is a very short story about a king named Cyrus, who wanted to buy the prize horse that belonged to one of his soldiers. Cyrus asked him how much he would sell the horse for, or whether he would exchange him for a kingdom. The soldier said he would not sell his prize horse and he would not exchange him for a kingdom, but that he would willingly give up his horse to gain a friend. . . . But now I have told you the whole story so there's no use for me to read it."

"You've been a powerful good friend to take me in like this," the boy said at last. "My fingers don't hurt no more."

"I am your friend," said the man. "So while I heat some water to soak your hand and make your cot for the night, you tell me all about yourself."

"I had a father and a dog named Sounder," the boy began. . . .

[1] **book of stories:** The book is actually a book of essays by Michel de Montaigne (1533–1592), a French writer who is considered the creator of the personal essay.

[2] **cistern:** a tank for storing rainwater

[3] **orneriness:** irritability; meanness

[4] **conjured:** under a spell

CHAPTER EIGHT

"Who's been kindly to your hurts?" the boy's mother asked as she looked down at the clean white rags that bandaged the boy's fingers. Rocking on the porch, she had seen the white dot swinging back and forth in the sun when the boy wasn't much more than a moving spot far down the road. "For a while I wasn't sure it was you," she said. "Why you walkin' fast? You done found him? Is your hand hurt bad? Is that a Bible somebody's done mistreated?" The woman's eyes had come to rest on the book the boy held in his good hand.

"No. It's a book. I found it in a trash can."

"Be careful what you carry off, child," his mother said. "It can cause a heap o' trouble."

"I got somethin' to tell," the boy said as he sat down on the edge of the porch and ran his bandaged fingers over the head of the great coon dog who had stopped his jumping and whining and lay at the boy's feet with his head cocked to the side, looking up with his one eye. The younger children sat in a line beside the boy, waiting to hear.

"Is he poorly?" the woman asked slowly. "Is he far?"

"It's about somethin' else," the boy said after a long spell of quiet. "I ain't found him yet."

The boy told his mother and the children about his night in the teacher's cabin. The teacher wanted him to come back and go to school. He had been asked to live in the teacher's cabin and do his chores. The children's eyes widened when they heard the cabin had two lamps, two stoves, and grass growing in a yard with a fence and a gate. He told how the teacher could read and that there were lots of books on shelves in the cabin. "Maybe he will write letters to the road camps for you," the mother said, "'cause you'll be so busy with schoolin' and cleanin' the schoolhouse for him that you can't go searchin' no more."

"Maybe I'd have time," the boy said. "But he says like you, 'Better not to go. Just be patient and time will pass.'"

"It's all powerful and puzzlin' and aggravatin', but it's the Lord's will." The boy noticed that his mother had stopped rocking; the loose boards did not rattle as the chair moved on them.

"The teacher said he'd walk all the way and reason about it if you didn't want me to come to him. You don't want me to go, but I'll come home often as I can. And sometimes I might bring word."

"It's a sign; I believes in signs." The rocker began to move back and forth, rattling the loose boards in the porch floor. "Go child. The Lord has come to you."

When he returned to the cabin with books on the shelves and the kind man with the white hair and the gentle voice, all the boy carried was his book with one cover missing — the book that he couldn't understand. In the summers he came home to take his father's place in the fields, for cabin rent had to be paid with field work. In the winter he seldom came because it took "more'n a day's walkin' and sleepin' on the ground."

"Ain't worth it" his mother would say.

Each year, after he had been gone for a whole winter and returned, the faithful Sounder would come hobbling on three legs far down the road to meet him. The great dog would wag his tail and whine. He never barked. The boy sang at his work in the fields, and his mother rocked in her chair and sang on the porch of the cabin. Sometimes when Sounder scratched fleas under the porch, she would look at the hunting lantern and the empty possum sack hanging against the wall. Six crops of persimmons and wild grapes had ripened. The possums and raccoons had gathered them unmolested. The lantern and possum sack hung untouched. "No use to nobody no more," the woman said.

The boy read to his brother and sisters when he had finished his day in the fields. He read the story of Joseph over and over and never wearied of it. "In all the books in the teacher's cabin, there's no story as good as Joseph's story" he would say to them.

The woman, listening and rocking, would say "The Lord has come to you, child. The Lord has certainly come to you."

Late one August afternoon the boy and his mother sat on the shaded corner of the porch. The heat and drought of dog days had parched the earth, and the crops had been laid by. The boy had come home early because there was nothing to do in the fields.

"Dog days is a terrible time," the woman said. "It's when the heat is so bad the dogs go mad." The boy would not tell her that the teacher had told him that dog days got their name from the Dog Star because it rose and set with the sun during that period. She had her own feeling for the earth, he thought, and he would not confuse it.

"It sure is hot," he said instead. "Lucky to come from the fields early." He watched the heat waves as they made the earth look like it was moving in little ripples.

Sounder came around the corner of the cabin from somewhere, hobbled back and forth as far as the road several times, and then went to his cool spot under the porch. "That's what I say about dog days," the woman said. "Poor creature's been addled with the heat for three days. Can't find no place to quiet down. Been down the road nearly out o' sight a second time today, and now he musta come from the fencerows. Whines all the time. A mad dog is a fearful sight. Slobberin' at the mouth and runnin' every which way 'cause they're blind. Have to shoot 'em 'fore they bite some child. It's awful hard."

"Sounder won't go mad," the boy said. "He's lookin' for a cooler spot, I reckon."

A lone figure came on the landscape as a speck and slowly grew into a ripply form through the heat waves. "Scorchin' to be walkin' and totin' far today," she said as she pointed to the figure on the road.

A catbird fussed in the wilted lilac at the corner of the cabin. "Why's that bird fussin' when no cat's prowlin'? Old folks has a sayin' that if a catbird fusses 'bout nothin', somethin' bad is comin'. It's a bad sign."

"Sounder, I reckon," the boy said. "He just passed her bush when he came around the cabin."

In the tall locust at the edge of the fence, its top leaves yellowed from lack of water, a mockingbird mimicked the catbird with half a dozen notes, decided it was too hot to sing, and disappeared. The great coon dog, whose rhythmic panting came through the porch floor, came from under the house and began to whine.

As the figure on the road drew near, it took shape and grew indistinct again in the wavering heat. Sometimes it seemed to be a person dragging something, for little puffs of red dust rose in sulfurous clouds at every other step. Once or twice they thought it might be a brown cow or mule, dragging its hooves in the sand and raising and lowering its weary head.

Sounder panted faster, wagged his tail, whined, moved from the dooryard to the porch and back to the dooryard.

The figure came closer. Now it appeared to be a child carrying something on its back and limping.

"The children still at the creek?" she asked.

"Yes, but it's about dry."

Suddenly the voice of the great coon hound broke the sultry[1] August deadness. The dog dashed along the road, leaving three-pointed clouds of red dust to settle back to earth behind him. The mighty voice rolled out upon the valley, each flutelike bark echoing from slope to slope.

"Lord's mercy! Dog days done made him mad." And the rocker was still.

Sounder was a young dog again. His voice was the same mellow sound that had ridden the November breeze from the lowlands to the hills. The boy and his mother looked at each other. The catbird stopped her fussing in the wilted lilac bush. On three legs, the dog moved with the same lightning speed that had carried him to the throat of a grounded raccoon.

Sounder's master had come home. Taking what might have been measured as a halting half step and then pulling a stiff, dead leg forward, dragging a foot turned sideways in the dust, the man limped into the yard. Sounder seemed to understand that to jump up and put his paw against his master's breast would topple him into the dust, so the great dog smelled and whined and wagged his tail and licked the limp hand dangling at his master's side. He hopped wildly around his master in a circle that almost brought head and tail together.

The head of the man was pulled to the side where a limp arm dangled and where the foot pointed outward as it was dragged through the dust. What had been a shoulder was now pushed up and back to make a one-sided hump so high that the leaning head seemed to rest upon it. The mouth was askew too, and the voice came out of the part farthest away from the withered, wrinkled, lifeless side.

The woman in the still rocker said, "Lord, Lord," and sat suffocated in shock.

"Sounder knew it was you just like you was comin' home from work," the boy said in a clear voice.

Half of the voice of the man was gone too, so in slow, measured stuttering he told how he had been caught in a dynamite blast in the prison quarry, how the dead side had been crushed under an avalanche of limestone, and how he had been missed for a whole night in the search for dead and wounded. He told how the pain of the crushing stone had stopped in the night, how doctors had pushed and pulled and encased the numb side of his body in a cast, how they had spoken kindly to him and told him he would die. But he resolved he would not die, even with a half-dead body, because he wanted to come home again.

"For being hurt, they let me have time off my sentence," the man said, "and since I couldn't work, I guess they was glad to."

"The Lord has brought you home," the woman said.

The boy heard faint laughter somewhere behind the cabin. The children were coming home from the creek. He went around the cabin slowly, then hurried to meet them.

"Pa's home," he said and grabbed his sister, who had started to run toward the cabin. "Wait. He's mighty crippled up, so behave like nothin' has happened."

"Can he walk?" the youngest child asked.

"Yes! And don't you ask no questions."

"You been mighty natural and considerate," the mother said to the younger children later when she went to the woodpile and called them to pick dry kindling for a quick fire. When she came back to the porch she said, "We was gonna just have a cold piece 'cause it's so sultry, but now I think I'll cook."

Everything don't change much, the boy thought. There's eatin' and sleepin' and talkin' and settin' that goes on. One day might be different from another, but there ain't much difference when they're put together.

Sometimes there were long quiet spells. Once or twice the boy's mother said to the boy, "He's powerful proud of your learnin'. Read somethin' from the Scriptures." But mostly they just talked about heat and cold, and wind and clouds, and what's gonna be done, and time passing.

As the days of August passed and September brought signs of autumn, the crippled man sat on the porch step and leaned the paralyzed, deformed side of his body against a porch post. This was the only comfortable sitting position he could find. The old coon dog would lie facing his master, with his one eye fixed and his one ear raised. Sometimes he would tap his tail against the earth. Sometimes the ear would droop and the eye would close. Then the great muscles would flex in dreams of the hunt, and the mighty chest would give off the muffled whisper of a bark. Sometimes the two limped together to the edge of the fields, or wandered off into the pine woods. They never went along the road. Perhaps they knew how strange a picture they made

when they walked together.

About the middle of September the boy left to go back to his teacher. "It's the most important thing," his mother said.

And the crippled man said, "We're fine. We won't need nothin'."

"I'll come for a few days before it's cold to help gather wood and walnuts."

The broken body of the old man withered more and more, but when the smell of harvest and the hunt came with October, his spirit seemed to quicken his dragging step. One day he cleaned the dusty lantern globe, and the old dog, remembering, bounced on his three legs and wagged his tail as if to say "I'm ready."

The boy had come home. To gather the felled trees and chop the standing dead ones was part of the field pay too. He had been cutting and dragging timber all day.

Sometimes he had looked longingly at the lantern and possum sack, but something inside him had said "Wait. Wait and go together." But the boy did not want to go hunting anymore. And without his saying anything, his father had said, "You're too tired, child. We ain't goin' far, no way."

In the early darkness the halting, hesitant swing of the lantern marked the slow path from fields to pine woods toward the lowlands. The boy stood on the porch, watching until the light was lost behind pine branches. Then he went and sat by the stove. His mother rocked as the mound of kernels grew in the fold of her apron. "He been mighty peart,"[2] she said. "I hope he don't fall in the dark. Maybe he'll be happy now he can go hunting again." And she took up her singing where she had left off.

Ain't nobody else gonna walk it for you,
You gotta walk it by yourself.

Sounder's scratching at the door awakened the boy. It was still night, but the first red glow of dawn was rising in a faint crescent over the pine woods.

"Sounder just couldn't poke slow enough for your father," the mother said to the boy as they stood in the doorway, straining and sifting the dark for some movement.

"Lantern wouldn't burn out in this time," the boy said. "No

sign of light. He must have fallen or got tired. Sounder will show me."

Sounder was already across the road into the stalk land, whining, moving his head from one side to the other, looking back to be sure that the boy was following.

Across the stalk land, into the pine woods, into the climbing, brightening glow of the dawn, the boy followed the dog, whose anxious pace slowed from age as they went. "By a dog's age, Sounder is past dying time," the boy said half aloud. Fear had always prompted him to talk to himself.

Deep in the pine woods, along a deserted logging road, the boy and dog came to a small open space where there had once been a log ramp. The sun was just beginning to drive its first splinters of light through the pines, bouncing against tree trunks and earth. At the foot of one of the trees the boy's father sat, the lantern still burning by his side.

"So tuckered out he fell asleep," the boy said to himself.

But the figure did not move when Sounder licked his hand. The boy put his hand on his father's good shoulder and shook ever so gently. The chin did not lift itself; no eyes turned up to meet the boy. "Tired, so tired."

When the boy returned to the cabin and told his mother, her lips grew long and thin and pale. But when she finally spoke, they were warm and soft as when she sang. "When life is so tiresome, there ain't no peace like the greatest peace — the peace of the Lord's hand holding you. And he'll have a store-bought box for burial 'cause all these years I paid close attention to his burial insurance."

They buried the boy's father in the unfenced lot behind the meetin' house. The preacher stood amid the sumac and running briars before the mound of fresh red earth and read:

> The Lord is my shepherd; I shall not want, He maketh me to lie down in green pastures.

"There's plenty of wood, and I must go back to school," the boy told his mother several days after they had buried his father. "Sounder ain't got no spirit left for living. He hasn't gone with me to the woods to chop since Pa died. He doesn't even whine anymore. He just lies on his coffee sacks under the cabin steps. I've dug a grave for him under the big jack oak tree in the stalk land by the fencerow. It'll be ready if the ground freezes. You can carry him on his coffee sacks and bury him. He'll be gone before I come home again."

And the boy was right. Two weeks before he came home for Christmas, Sounder crawled under the cabin and died. The boy's mother told him all there was to tell.

"He just crawled up under the house and died," she said.

The boy was glad. He had learned to read his book with the torn cover better now. He had read in it: "Only the unwise think that what has changed is dead." He had asked the teacher what it meant, and the teacher had said that if a flower blooms once, it goes on blooming somewhere forever. It blooms on for whoever has seen it blooming. It was not quite clear to the boy then, but it was now.

Years later, walking the earth as a man, it would all sweep back over him, again and again, like an echo on the wind.

The pine trees would look down forever on a lantern burning out of oil but not going out. A harvest moon would cast shadows forever of a man walking upright, his dog bouncing after him. And the quiet of the night would fill and echo again with the deep voice of Sounder, the great coon dog.

[1] **sultry:** uncomfortably hot and humid
[2] **peart:** lively; in good spirits

A CLOSER LOOK

1. How are the boy's thoughts about the cruel guard at the road camp similar to his daydream about the bull-necked man at the jail? Why does the boy think of the story of David and Goliath when he sees the scrap of iron?

2. How does the boy feel about the book of essays that he found? What does the boy decide to do with the book? What idea is expressed in the excerpt of the essay on cruelty? How does this idea relate to the themes in **Sounder?**

3. What is the boy's reaction to the teacher upon first meeting him? What is significant about the boy's reaction?

4. Explain what the mother means when she says to her son, "The Lord has come to you."

5. What does Sounder do when the father comes home?

6. What parallels exist between the father's experience and Sounder's experience?

7. What reason might the author have for not giving any of the characters names except Sounder?

The photographs used to illustrate **A Christmas Carol** *are stills from the 1951 British film, starring Alastair Sim as Scrooge. You will notice that the moviemakers have changed certain minor details of the story.*

RY THAT HAS BROUGHT
MILLIONS !
A new screen triumph!
a
ristmas
Carol"
Starring the Incomparable
Alastair SIM
as Charles Dickens'
"SCROOGE"
CHARLES DICKENS'
HARRISON
f the J.A.R.O.)
by Noel Langley
ed Artists
B

• This short novel by Charles Dickens tells the story of Ebenezer Scrooge, a man who values money above everything else in life. Increasing his wealth is his one passion, his one concern, every day of the year. Then one Christmas everything changes.

Charles Dickens

A CHRISTMAS CAROL

STAVE ONE

Marley's Ghost

MARLEY WAS DEAD, TO BEGIN WITH. THERE IS no doubt whatever about that. The register of his burial was signed by the clergyman, the clerk, the undertaker, and the chief mourner. Scrooge signed it; and Scrooge's name was good upon 'Change[1] for anything he chose to put his hand to. Old Marley was as dead as a doornail.

Mind! I don't mean to say that I know, of my own knowledge, what there is particularly dead about a doornail. I might have been inclined, myself, to regard a coffin nail as the deadest piece of iron-mongery in the trade. But the wisdom of our ancestors is in the simile; and my unhallowed hands shall not disturb it, or the Country's done for. You will therefore permit me to repeat, emphatically, that Marley was as dead as a doornail.

Scrooge knew he was dead? Of course he did. How could it be otherwise? Scrooge and he were partners for I don't know how many years. Scrooge was his sole executor,[2] his sole administrator,[2] his sole assign,[2] his sole residuary legatee,[2] his sole friend, and sole mourner. And even Scrooge was not so dreadfully cut up by the sad event, but that he was an excellent man of business on the very day of the funeral, and solemnized it with an undoubted bargain.

The mention of Marley's funeral brings me back to the point I started from. There is no doubt that Marley was dead. This must be distinctly understood, or nothing wonderful can come of the story I am going to relate. If we were not perfectly convinced that Hamlet's father[3] died before the play began, there would be nothing more remarkable in his taking a stroll at night, in an easterly wind, upon his own ramparts, than there would be in any other middle-aged gentleman rashly turning out after dark in a breezy spot — say Saint Paul's Churchyard, for instance — literally to astonish his son's weak mind.

Scrooge never painted out old Marley's name. There it stood, years afterwards, above the warehouse door: Scrooge and Marley. The firm was known as Scrooge and Marley. Sometimes people new to the business called Scrooge Scrooge, and sometimes Marley, but he answered to both names. It was all the same to him.

Oh! But he was a tight-fisted hand at the grindstone, Scrooge! a squeezing, wrenching, grasping, scraping, clutching, covetous old sinner! Hard and sharp as flint, from which no steel had ever struck out generous fire; secret, and self-contained, and solitary as an oyster. The cold within him froze his old features, nipped his pointed nose, shriveled his cheek, stiffened his gait, made his eyes red, his thin lips blue, and spoke out shrewdly in his grating voice. A frosty rime was on his head, and on his eyebrows, and his wiry chin. He carried his own low temperature always about with him; he iced his office in the dog days, and didn't thaw it one degree at Christmas.

External heat and cold had little influence on Scrooge. No warmth could warm, no wintry weather chill him. No wind that blew was bitterer than he, no falling snow was more intent upon its purpose, no pelting rain less open to entreaty. Foul weather didn't know where to have him. The heaviest rain, and snow, and hail, and sleet could boast of the advantage over him in only one respect. They often "came down" handsomely, and Scrooge never did.

Nobody ever stopped him in the street to say, with gladsome looks, "My dear Scrooge, how are you? When will you come to see me?" No beggars implored him to bestow a trifle, no children asked him what it was o'clock, no man or woman ever once in all his life inquired the way to such and such a place, of Scrooge. Even the blind men's dogs appeared to know him, and, when they saw him coming on, would tug their owners into doorways and up courts, and then would wag their tails as though they said, "No eye at all is better than an evil eye, dark master!"

But what did Scrooge care! It was the very thing he liked. To edge his way along the crowded paths of life, warning all human sympathy to keep its distance, was what the knowing ones call "nuts"[4] to Scrooge.

Once upon a time — of all the good days in the year, on Christmas Eve — old Scrooge sat busy in his counting-house. It was cold, bleak, biting weather, foggy withal,[5] and he could hear the people in the court outside go wheezing up and down, beating their hands upon their breasts, and stamping their feet upon the pavement stones to warm them. The city clocks had only just gone three, but it was quite dark already — it had not been light all day — and candles were flaring in the windows of the neighboring offices, like ruddy smears upon the palpable brown air. The fog came pouring in at every chink and keyhole, and was so dense without, that, although the court was of the narrowest, the houses opposite were mere phantoms. To see the dingy cloud come drooping down, obscuring everything, one might have thought that Nature lived hard by, and was brewing on a large scale.

The door of Scrooge's counting-house was open that he might keep his eye upon his clerk, who, in a dismal little cell beyond, a sort of tank, was copying letters. Scrooge had a very small fire, but the clerk's fire was so very much smaller that it looked like one coal. But he couldn't replenish it, for Scrooge kept the coal-box in his own room; and so surely as the clerk came in with the shovel, the master predicted that it would be necessary for them to part. Wherefore the clerk put on his white comforter, and tried to warm himself at the candle, in which effort, not being a man of strong imagination, he failed.

"A merry Christmas, uncle! God save you!" cried a cheerful voice. It was the voice of Scrooge's nephew, who came upon him so quickly that this was the first intimation he had of his approach.

"Bah!" said Scrooge, "Humbug!"

He had so heated himself with rapid walking in the fog and frost, this nephew of Scrooge's, that he was all in a glow; his face was ruddy and handsome; his eyes sparkled, and his breath smoked again.

"Christmas a humbug, uncle!" said Scrooge's nephew. "You don't mean that, I am sure."

"I do," said Scrooge. "Merry Christmas! What right have you to be merry? What reason have you to be merry? You're poor enough."

"Come, then," returned the nephew gaily. "What right have you to be dismal? What reason have you to be morose? You're rich enough."

Scrooge, having no better answer ready on the spur of the moment, said, "Bah!" again, and followed it up with "Humbug."

"Don't be cross, uncle," said the nephew.

"What else can I be," returned the uncle, "when I live in such a world of fools as this? Merry Christmas! Out upon Merry Christmas! What's Christmastime to you but a time for paying bills without money; a time for finding yourself a year older, and not an hour richer; a time for balancing your books, and having every item in 'em through a round dozen of months presented dead against you? If I could work my will," said Scrooge indignantly, "every idiot who goes about with 'Merry Christmas' on his lips should be boiled with his own pudding, and buried with a stake of holly through his heart. He should!"

"Uncle!" pleaded the nephew.

"Nephew!" returned the uncle sternly, "keep Christmas in your own way, and let me keep it in mine."

"Keep it!" repeated Scrooge's nephew. "But you don't keep it."

"Let me leave it alone, then," said Scrooge. "Much good may it do you! Much good it has ever done you!"

"There are many things from which I might have derived good, by which I have not profited, I dare say," returned the nephew, "Christmas among the rest. But I am sure I have always thought of Christmastime, when it has come round — apart from the veneration due to its sacred name and origin, if anything belonging to it can be apart from that — as a good time; a kind, forgiving, charitable, pleasant time; the only time I know of, in the long calendar of the year, when men and women seem by one consent to open their shut-up hearts freely, and to think of people below them as if they really were fellow passengers to the grave, and not another race of creatures bound on other journeys. And therefore, uncle, though it has never put a scrap of gold or silver in my pocket, I believe that it *has* done me good, and *will* do me good; and I say, God bless it!"

The clerk in the tank involuntarily applauded: becoming immediately sensible of the impropriety, he poked the fire, and extinguished the last frail spark forever.

"Let me hear another sound from *you,*" said Scrooge, "and you'll keep your Christmas by losing your situation. You're quite a powerful speaker, sir," he added, turning to his nephew. "I wonder you don't go into Parliament."

"Don't be angry, uncle. Come! Dine with us tomorrow."

Scrooge said that he would see him—[6] Yes, indeed he did. He went the whole length of the expression, and said that he would see him in that extremity first.

"But why?" cried Scrooge's nephew. "Why?"

"Why did you get married?" said Scrooge.

"Because I fell in love."

"Because you fell in love!" growled Scrooge, as if that were the only one thing in the world more ridiculous than a merry Christmas. "Good afternoon!"

"Nay, uncle, but you never came to see me before that happened. Why give it as a reason for not coming now?"

"Good afternoon," said Scrooge.

"I want nothing from you; I ask nothing of you; why cannot we be friends?"

"Good afternoon," said Scrooge.

"I am sorry, with all my heart, to find you so resolute. We have never had any quarrel, to which I have been a party. But I have made the trial in homage to Christmas, and I'll keep my Christmas humor to the last. So a merry Christmas, uncle!"

"Good afternoon!" said Scrooge.

"And a happy New Year!"

"Good afternoon!" said Scrooge.

His nephew left the room without an angry word, notwithstanding. He stopped at the outer door to bestow the greetings of the season on the clerk, who, cold as he was, was warmer than Scrooge; for he returned them cordially.

"There's another fellow," muttered Scrooge, who overheard him: "my clerk, with fifteen shillings a week, and a wife and family, talking about a merry Christmas. I'll retire to Bedlam."[7]

This lunatic, in letting Scrooge's nephew out, had let two other people in. They were portly gentlemen, pleasant to behold, and now stood, with their hats off, in Scrooge's office. They had books and papers in their hands, and bowed to him.

"Scrooge and Marley's, I believe," said one of the gentlemen, referring to his list. "Have I the pleasure of addressing Mr. Scrooge, or Mr. Marley?"

"Mr. Marley has been dead these seven years," Scrooge replied. "He died seven years ago, this very night."

"We have no doubt his liberality is well represented by his

surviving partner," said the gentleman, presenting his credentials.

It certainly was; for they had been two kindred spirits. At the ominous word "liberality," Scrooge frowned, and shook his head, and handed the credentials back.

"At this festive season of the year, Mr. Scrooge," said the gentleman, taking up a pen, "it is more than usually desirable that we should make some slight provision for the poor and destitute, who suffer greatly at the present time. Many thousands are in want of common necessaries; hundreds of thousands are in want of common comforts, sir."

"Are there no prisons?" asked Scrooge.

"Plenty of prisons," said the gentleman, laying down the pen again.

"And the Union workhouses?" demanded Scrooge. "Are they still in operation?"

"They are. Still," returned the gentleman, "I wish I could say they were not."

"The Treadmill and the Poor Law are in full vigor, then?" said Scrooge.

"Both very busy, sir."

"Oh! I was afraid, from what you said at first, that something had occurred to stop them in their useful course," said Scrooge. "I'm very glad to hear it."

"Under the impression that they scarcely furnish Christian cheer of mind or body to the multitude," returned the gentleman, "a few of us are endeavoring to raise a fund to buy the poor some meat and drink, and means of warmth. We choose this time, because it is a time, of all others, when Want is keenly felt, and Abundance rejoices. What shall I put you down for?"

"Nothing!" Scrooge replied.

"You wish to be anonymous?"

"I wish to be left alone," said Scrooge. "Since you ask me what I wish, gentlemen, that is my answer. I don't make merry myself at Christmas, and I can't afford to make idle people merry. I help to support the establishments I have mentioned — they cost enough — and those who are badly off must go there."

"Many can't go there; and many would rather die."

"If they would rather die," said Scrooge, "they had better do it, and decrease the surplus population. Besides — excuse me — I don't know that."

"But you might know it," observed the gentleman.

"It's not my business," Scrooge returned. "It's enough for a man to understand his own business, and not to interfere with other people's. Mine occupies me constantly. Good afternoon, gentlemen!"

Seeing clearly that it would be useless to pursue their point, the gentlemen withdrew. Scrooge resumed his labors with an improved opinion of himself, and in a more facetious[8] temper than was usual with him.

Meanwhile the fog and darkness thickened so, that people ran about with flaring links, proffering their services to go before horses in carriages, and conduct them on their way. The ancient tower of a church, whose gruff old bell was always peeping slyly down at Scrooge out of a Gothic window in the wall, became invisible, and struck the hours and quarters in the clouds, with tremulous vibrations afterwards, as if its teeth were chattering in its frozen head up there. The cold became intense. In the main street, at the corner of the court, some laborers were repairing the gas-pipes, and had lighted a great fire in a brazier, round which a party of ragged men and boys were gathered, warming their hands and winking their eyes before the blaze in rapture. The water-plug being left in solitude, its overflowings sullenly congealed, and turned to misanthropic ice. The brightness of the shops, where holly sprigs and berries crackled in the lamp heat of the windows, made pale faces ruddy as they passed. Poulterers' and grocers' trades became a splendid joke: a glorious pageant, with which it was next to impossible to believe that such dull principles as bargain and sale had anything to do. The Lord Mayor, in the stronghold of the mighty Mansion House, gave orders to his fifty cooks and butlers to keep Christmas as a Lord Mayor's household should; and even the little tailor, whom he had fined five shillings on the previous Monday for being drunk and bloodthirsty in the streets, stirred up tomorrow's pudding in his garret, while his lean wife and baby sallied out to buy the beef.

Foggier yet, and colder! Piercing, searching, biting cold. If the good Saint Dunstan had but nipped the Evil Spirit's nose with a touch of such weather as that, instead of using his familiar weapons, then indeed he would have roared to lusty purpose. The owner of one scant young nose, gnawed and mumbled[9] by the hungry cold as bones are gnawed by dogs, stooped down at Scrooge's keyhole to regale him with a Christmas carol; but at the first sound of *God rest you merry, gentleman,/May nothing you dismay*, Scrooge seized the ruler with such energy of action, that the singer fled in terror, leaving the keyhole to the fog and even more congenial frost.

At length the hour of shutting up the counting-house arrived. With an ill will Scrooge dismounted from his stool, and tacitly admitted the fact to the expectant clerk in the tank, who instantly snuffed his candle out, and put on his hat.

"You'll want all day tomorrow, I suppose?" said Scrooge.

"If quite convenient, sir."

"It's not convenient," said Scrooge, "and it's not fair. If I was to stop half-a-crown for it, you'd think yourself ill used, I'll be bound?"

The clerk smiled faintly.

"And yet," said Scrooge, "you don't think *me* ill used when I

pay a day's wages for no work."

The clerk observed that it was only once a year.

"A poor excuse for picking a man's pocket every twenty-fifth of December!" said Scrooge, buttoning his greatcoat to the chin. "But I suppose you must have the whole day. Be here all the earlier next morning!"

The clerk promised that he would; and Scrooge walked out with a growl. The office was closed in a twinkling, and the clerk, with the long ends of his white comforter dangling below his waist (for he boasted no greatcoat), went down a slide on Cornhill, at the end of a lane of boys, twenty times, in honor of its being Christmas Eve, and then ran home to Camden Town, as hard as he could pelt, to play at blindman's buff.

Scrooge took his melancholy dinner in his usual melancholy tavern, and having read all the newspapers, and beguiled the rest of the evening with his banker's book, went home to bed. He lived in chambers which had once belonged to his deceased partner. They were a gloomy suite of rooms, in a lowering pile of building up a yard, where it had so little business to be, that one could scarcely help fancying it must have run there when it was a young house, playing at hide-and-seek with other houses, and have forgotten the way out again. It was old enough now, and dreary enough, for nobody lived in it but Scrooge, the other rooms being all let out as offices. The yard was so dark that even Scrooge, who knew its every stone, was fain[10] to grope with his hands. The fog and frost so hung about the black old gateway of the house, that it seemed as if the Genius of the Weather sat in mournful meditation on the threshold.

Now it is a fact that there was nothing at all particular about the knocker on the door, except that it was very large. It is also a fact that Scrooge had seen it, night and morning, during his whole residence in that place, also that Scrooge had as little of what is called fancy about him as any man in the City of London, even including — which is a bold word — the corporation, aldermen, and livery. Let it also be borne in mind that Scrooge had not bestowed one thought on Marley, since his last mention of his seven-years' dead partner that afternoon. And then let any man explain to me, if he can, how it happened that Scrooge, having his key in the lock of the door, saw in the knocker, without its undergoing any intermediate process of change — not a knocker, but Marley's face.

Marley's face. It was not in impenetrable shadow, as the other objects in the yard were, but had a dismal light about it, like a bad lobster in a dark cellar. It was not angry or ferocious, but looked at Scrooge as Marley used to look: with ghostly spectacles turned up upon its ghostly forehead. The hair was curiously stirred, as if by breath or hot air; and though the eyes were wide open, they were perfectly motionless. That, and its livid[11] color, made it horrible; but its horror seemed to be in spite of the face, and beyond its control, rather than a part of its own expression.

As Scrooge looked fixedly at this phenomenon, it was a knocker again.

To say that he was not startled, or that his blood was not conscious of a terrible sensation to which it had been a stranger from infancy, would be untrue. But he put his hand upon the key he had relinquished, turned it sturdily, walked in, and lighted his candle.

He *did* pause, with a moment's irresolution, before he shut the door; and he *did* look cautiously behind it first, as if he half expected to be terrified with the sight of Marley's pigtail sticking out into the hall. But there was nothing on the back of the door, except the screws and nuts that held the knocker on; so he said, "Pooh, pooh!" and closed it with a bang.

The sound resounded through the house like thunder. Every room above, and every cask in the wine-merchant's cellar below, appeared to have a separate peal of echoes of its own. Scrooge was not a man to be frightened by echoes. He fastened the door, and walked across the hall, and up the stairs, slowly, too, trimming his candle as he went.

You may talk vaguely about driving a coach-and-six up a good old flight of stairs, or through a bad young Act of Parliament; but I mean to say you might have got a hearse up that staircase, and taken it broadwise, with the splinter-bar towards the wall, and the door towards the balustrades, and done it easy. There was plenty of width for that, and room to spare, which is perhaps the reason why Scrooge thought he saw a locomotive hearse going on before him in the gloom. Half a dozen gas-lamps out of the street wouldn't have lighted the entry too well, so you may suppose that it was pretty dark with Scrooge's dip.

Up Scrooge went, not caring a button for that: darkness is cheap, and Scrooge liked it. But before he shut his heavy door, he walked through his rooms to see that all was right. He had just enough recollection of the face to desire to do that.

Sitting room, bedroom, lumber room. All as they should be. Nobody under the table, nobody under the sofa; a small fire in the grate; spoon and basin ready; and the little saucepan of gruel (Scrooge had a cold in his head) upon the hob. Nobody under the bed; nobody in the closet; nobody in his dressing gown, which was hanging up in a suspicious attitude against the wall. Lumber room as usual. Old fireguard, old shoes, two fish-baskets, washing-stand on three legs, and a poker.

Quite satisfied, he closed his door, and locked himself in: double-locked himself in, which was not his custom. Thus secured against surprise, he took off his cravat, put on his dressing gown and slippers, and his nightcap, and sat down before the fire to take his gruel.

It was a very low fire indeed; nothing on such a bitter night. He was obliged to sit close to it, and brood over it, before he could extract the least sensation of warmth from such a handful of fuel. The fireplace was an old one, built by some Dutch merchant long ago, and paved all round with quaint Dutch tiles, designed to illustrate the Scriptures. There were Cains and Abels, Pharaoh's daughters, Queens of Sheba, angelic messengers descending through the air on clouds like featherbeds, Abrahams, Belshazzars, Apostles putting off to sea in butter-boats, hundreds of figures to attract his thoughts; and yet that face of Marley, seven years dead, came like the ancient Prophet's rod, and swallowed up the whole. If each smooth tile had been a blank at first, with power to shape some picture on its surface from the disjointed fragments of his thoughts, there would have been a copy of old Marley's head on every one.

"Humbug!" said Scrooge; and walked across the room.

After several turns, he sat down again. As he threw his head back in the chair, his glance happened to rest upon a bell, a disused bell, that hung in the room and communicated, for some purpose now forgotten, with a chamber in the highest story of the building. It was with great astonishment, and with a strange, inexplicable dread, that, as he looked, he saw this bell begin to swing. It swung so softly in the outset that it scarcely made a sound; but soon it rang out loudly, and so did every bell in the house.

This might have lasted half a minute, or a minute, but it seemed an hour. The bells ceased as they had begun, together. They were succeeded by a clanking noise, deep down below, as if some person were dragging a heavy chain over the casks in the wine-merchant's cellar. Scrooge then remembered to have heard that ghosts in haunted houses were described as dragging chains.

The cellar door flew open with a booming sound, and then he heard the noise much louder, on the floors below; then coming up the stairs; then coming straight towards his door.

"It's humbug still!" said Scrooge. "I won't believe it."

His color changed, though, when, without a pause, it came on through the heavy door, and passed into the room before his eyes. Upon its coming in, the dying flame leaped up, as though it cried, "I know him! Marley's Ghost!" and fell again.

The same face, the very same. Marley in his pigtail, usual waistcoat, tights, and boots; the tassels on the latter bristling, like his pigtail, and his coat-skirts, and the hair upon his head. The chain he drew was clasped about his middle. It was long, and wound about him like a tail; and it was made (for Scrooge observed it closely) of cash-boxes, keys, padlocks, ledgers, deeds, and heavy purses wrought in steel. His body was transparent: so that Scrooge, observing him, and looking through his waistcoat, could see the two buttons on his coat behind.

Scrooge had often heard it said that Marley had no bowels, but he had never believed it until now.

No, nor did he believe it even now. Though he looked the phantom through and through, and saw it standing before him; though he felt the chilling influence of its death-cold eyes; and marked the very texture of the folded kerchief bound about its head and chin, which wrapper he had not observed before; he was still incredulous, and fought against his senses.

"How now!" said Scrooge, caustic and cold as ever. "What do you want with me?"

"Much!" — Marley's voice, no doubt about it.

"Who are you?"

"Ask me who I *was.*"

"Who *were* you, then?" said Scrooge, raising his voice. "You're particular — for a shade." He was going to say, "*to* a shade," but substituted this, as more appropriate.

"In life I was your partner, Jacob Marley."

"Can you — can you sit down?" asked Scrooge, looking doubtfully at him.

"I can."

"Do it, then."

Scrooge asked the question because he didn't know whether a ghost so transparent might find himself in a condition to take a

chair, and felt that in the event of its being impossible, it might involve the necessity of an embarrassing explanation. But the Ghost sat down on the opposite side of the fireplace, as if he were quite used to it.

"You don't believe in me," observed the Ghost.

"I don't," said Scrooge.

"What evidence would you have of my reality, beyond that of your senses?"

"I don't know," said Scrooge.

"Why do you doubt your senses?"

"Because," said Scrooge, "a little thing affects them. A slight disorder of the stomach makes them cheats. You may be an undigested bit of beef, a blot of mustard, a crumb of cheese, a fragment of an underdone potato. There's more of gravy than of grave about you, whatever you are!"

Scrooge was not much in the habit of cracking jokes, nor did he feel, in his heart, by any means waggish then. The truth is, that he tried to be smart, as a means of distracting his own attention, and keeping down his terror; for the specter's voice disturbed the very marrow in his bones.

To sit, staring at those fixed, glazed eyes, in silence for a moment would play, Scrooge felt, the very deuce with him. There was something very awful, too, in the specter's being provided with an infernal atmosphere of its own. Scrooge could not feel it himself, but this was clearly the case; for though the Ghost sat perfectly motionless, its hair, and skirts, and tassels were still agitated as by the hot vapor from an oven.

"You see this toothpick?" said Scrooge, returning quickly to the charge, for the reason just assigned, and wishing, though it were only for a second, to divert the vision's stony gaze from himself.

"I do," replied the Ghost.

"You are not looking at it," said Scrooge.

"But I see it," said the Ghost, "notwithstanding."

"Well!" returned Scrooge. "I have but to swallow this, and be for the rest of my days persecuted by a legion of goblins, all my own creation. Humbug, I tell you; humbug!"

At this, the spirit raised a frightful cry, and shook its chain with such a dismal and appalling noise, that Scrooge held on tight to his chair, to save himself from falling in a swoon. But how much greater was his horror, when the phantom taking off the bandage round its head, as if it were too warm to wear indoors, its lower jaw dropped down upon its breast!

Scrooge fell upon his knees, and clasped his hands before his face.

"Mercy!" he said. "Dreadful apparition, why do you trouble me?"

"Man of the worldly mind!" replied the Ghost, "do you believe in me or not?"

"I do," said Scrooge. "I must. But why do spirits walk the earth, and why do they come to me?"

"It is required of every man," the Ghost returned, "that the spirit within him should walk abroad among his fellowmen, and travel far and wide; and if that spirit goes not forth in life, it is condemned to do so after death. It is doomed to wander through the world — oh, woe is me! — and witness what it cannot share, but might have shared on earth, and turned to happiness!"

Again the specter raised a cry, and shook its chain, and wrung his shadowy hands.

"You are fettered," said Scrooge, trembling. "Tell me why?"

"I wear the chain I forged in life," replied the Ghost. "I made it link by link, and yard by yard; I girded it on of my own free will, and of my own free will I wore it. Is its pattern strange to *you?*"

Scrooge trembled more and more.

"Or would you know," pursued the Ghost, "the weight and length of the strong coil you bear yourself? It was full as heavy and as long as this, seven Christmas Eves ago. You have labored on it, since. It is a ponderous chain!"

Scrooge glanced about him on the floor, in the expectation of finding himself surrounded by some fifty or sixty fathoms of iron cable; but he could see nothing.

"Jacob," he said imploringly. "Old Jacob Marley, tell me more. Speak comfort to me, Jacob."

"I have none to give," the Ghost replied. "It comes from other regions, Ebenezer Scrooge, and is conveyed by other ministers, to other kinds of men. Nor can I tell you what I would. A very little more is all permitted to me. I cannot rest, I cannot stay, I cannot linger anywhere. My spirit never walked beyond our counting-house — mark me! — in life my spirit never roved beyond the narrow limits of our money-changing hole; and weary journeys lie before me!"

It was a habit with Scrooge, whenever he became thoughtful, to put his hands in his breeches pockets. Pondering on what the Ghost had said, he did so now, but without lifting up his eyes, or getting off his knees.

"You must have been very slow about it, Jacob," Scrooge observed in a businesslike manner, though with humility and deference.

"Slow!" the Ghost repeated.

"Seven years dead," mused Scrooge. "And traveling all the time?"

"The whole time," said the Ghost. "No rest, no peace. Incessant torture of remorse."

"You travel fast?" said Scrooge.

"On the wings of the wind," replied the Ghost.

"You might have got over a great quantity of ground in seven years," said Scrooge.

The Ghost, on hearing this, set up another cry, and clanked its chain so hideously in the dead silence of the night, that the Ward would have been justified in indicting it for a nuisance.

"Oh! captive, bound, and double-ironed," cried the phantom, "not to know that ages of incessant labor by immortal creatures, for this earth, must pass into eternity before the good of which it is susceptible is all developed. Not to know that any Christian spirit working kindly in its little sphere, whatever it may be, will find its mortal life too short for its vast means of usefulness. Not to know that no space of regret can make amends for one life's opportunities misused! Yet such was I! Oh! such was I!

"But you were always a good man of business, Jacob," faltered Scrooge, who now began to apply this to himself.

"Business!" cried the Ghost, wringing its hands again. "Mankind was my business. The common welfare was my business; charity, mercy, forbearance, and benevolence were, all, my business. The dealings of my trade were but a drop of water in the comprehensive ocean of my business!"

It held up its chain at arm's length, as if that were the cause of all its unavailing grief, and flung it heavily upon the ground again.

"At this time of the rolling year," the specter said, "I suffer most. Why did I walk through crowds of fellow beings with my eyes turned down, and never raise them to that blessed Star which led the Wise Men to a poor abode? Were there no poor homes to which its light would have conducted *me!*"

Scrooge was very much dismayed to hear the specter going on at this rate, and began to quake exceedingly.

"Hear me!" cried the Ghost. "My time is nearly gone."

"I will," said Scrooge. "But don't be hard upon me! Don't be flowery, Jacob! Pray!"

"How it is that I appear before you in a shape that you can see, I may not tell. I have sat invisible beside you many and many a day."

It was not an agreeable idea. Scrooge shivered, and wiped the perspiration from his brow.

"That is no light part of my penance," pursued the Ghost. "I am here tonight to warn you, that you have yet a chance and hope of escaping my fate. A chance and hope of my procuring, Ebenezer."

"You were always a good friend to me," said Scrooge. "Thank'ee!"

"You will be haunted," resumed the Ghost, "by Three Spirits."

Scrooge's countenance fell almost as low as the Ghost's had done.

"Is that the chance and hope you mentioned, Jacob?" he

demanded, in a faltering voice.

"It is."

"I — I think I'd rather not," said Scrooge.

"Without their visits," said the Ghost, "you cannot hope to shun the path I tread. Expect the first tomorrow, when the bell tolls One."

"Couldn't I take 'em all at once, and have it over, Jacob?" hinted Scrooge.

"Expect the second on the next night at the same hour. The third, upon the next night when the last stroke of Twelve has ceased to vibrate. Look to see me no more; and look that, for your own sake, you remember what has passed between us!"

When it had said these words, the specter took its wrapper from the table, and bound it round its head, as before. Scrooge knew this, by the smart sound its teeth made when the jaws were brought together by the bandage. He ventured to raise his eyes again, and found his supernatural visitor confronting him in an erect attitude, with its chain wound over and about its arm.

The apparition walked backward from him; and at every step it took, the window raised itself a little, so that when the specter reached it, it was wide open. It beckoned Scrooge to approach, which he did. When they were within two paces of each other, Marley's Ghost held up its hand, warning him to come no nearer. Scrooge stopped.

Not so much in obedience, as in surprise and fear; for on the raising of the hand, he became sensible of confused noises in the air: incoherent sounds of lamentation and regret, wailings inexpressibly sorrowful and self-accusatory. The specter, after listening for a moment, joined in the mournful dirge, and floated out upon the bleak, dark night.

Scrooge followed to the window, desperate in his curiosity. He looked out.

The air was filled with phantoms, wandering hither and thither in restless haste, and moaning as they went. Every one of them wore chains like Marley's Ghost; some few (they might be guilty governments) were linked together; none were free. Many had been personally known to Scrooge in their lives. He had been quite familiar with one old ghost, in a white waistcoat, with a monstrous iron safe attached to its ankle, who cried piteously at being unable to assist a wretched woman with an infant, whom it saw below, upon a doorstep. The misery with them all was, clearly, that they sought to interfere, for good, in human matters, and had lost the power forever.

Whether these creatures faded into mist, or mist enshrouded them, he could not tell. But they and their spirit voices faded together; and the night became as it had been when he walked home.

Scrooge closed the window, and examined the door by which the Ghost had entered. It was double-locked, as he had locked it with his own hands, and the bolts were undisturbed. He tried to say "Humbug!" but stopped at the first syllable. And being, from the emotion he had undergone, or the fatigues of the day, or his glimpse of the Invisible World, or the dull conversation of the Ghost, or the lateness of the hour, much in need of repose, went straight to bed, without undressing, and fell asleep upon the instant.

[1] **'Change:** the Royal Exchange, the financial center of London
[2] **executor:** one appointed to carry out the directions in someone's will
administrator: one appointed to settle the estate of someone who has died
assign: a person to whom property is transferred
residuary legatee: one to whom money or property is left in a will
[3] **Hamlet's father:** In Shakespeare's play *Hamlet,* Hamlet's father has been killed before the action of the play begins, and therefore appears as a ghost.
[4] **nuts:** In this old expression, "nuts" means a source of pleasure.
[5] **withal:** besides
[6] **he would see him—:** The rest of the expression is "in hell first."
[7] **Bedlam:** popular name for the Hospital of St. Mary of Bethlehem, an insane asylum in London
[8] **facetious:** joking or humorous, often inappropriately
[9] **mumbled:** chewed
[10] **fain:** forced
[11] **livid:** pale

A CLOSER LOOK

1. In what ways does Scrooge show himself to be a miser?

2. What is Scrooge's attitude toward Christmas and the spirit of generosity that Christmas brings? What does he say to his nephew and to the gentlemen collecting for charity to explain his position?

3. Who was Jacob Marley? Why does his ghost wear a chain? Describe the chain. What does it represent?

4. Why does Marley's ghost visit Scrooge?

STAVE TWO

The First of the Three Spirits

When Scrooge awoke it was so dark, that, looking out of bed, he could scarcely distinguish the transparent window from the opaque walls of his chamber. He was endeavoring to pierce the darkness with his ferret eyes, when the chimes of a neighboring church struck the four quarters. So he listened for the hour.

To his great astonishment the heavy bell went on from six to seven, and from seven to eight, and regularly up to twelve; then stopped. Twelve! It was past two when he went to bed. The clock was wrong. An icicle must have got into the works. Twelve!

He touched the spring of his repeater, to correct this most preposterous clock. Its rapid little pulse beat twelve; and stopped.

"Why, it isn't possible," said Scrooge, "that I can have slept through a whole day and far into another night. It isn't possible that anything has happened to the sun, and this is twelve at noon!"

The idea being an alarming one, he scrambled out of bed, and groped his way to the window. He was obliged to rub the frost off with the sleeve of his dressing gown before he could see anything, and could see very little then. All he could make out was, that it was still very foggy and extremely cold, and that there was no noise of people running to and fro, and making a great stir, as there unquestionably would have been if night had beaten off bright day, and taken possession of the world. This was a great relief, because "three days after sight of this First of Exchange pay to Mr. Ebenezer Scrooge or his order," and so forth, would have become a mere United States' security if there were no days to count by.[1]

Scrooge went to bed again, and thought, and thought, and thought it over and over and over, and could make nothing of it. The more he thought, the more perplexed he was; and the more he endeavored not to think, the more he thought. Marley's Ghost bothered him exceedingly. Every time he resolved within himself, after mature inquiry, that it was all a dream, his mind flew back again, like a strong spring released, to its first position, and presented the same problem to be worked all through, "Was it a dream or not?"

Scrooge lay in this state until the chimes had gone three quarters more, when he remembered, on a sudden, that the Ghost had warned him of a visitation when the bell tolled One. He resolved to lie awake until the hour was past; and, considering that he could no more go to sleep than go to Heaven, this was perhaps the wisest resolution in his power.

The quarter was so long, that he was more than once convinced he must have sunk into a doze unconsciously, and missed the clock. At length it broke upon his listening ear.

"Ding, dong!"

"A quarter past," said Scrooge, counting.

"Ding, dong!"

"Half past!" said Scrooge.

"Ding, dong!"

"A quarter to it," said Scrooge.

"Ding, dong!"

"The hour itself," said Scrooge, triumphantly, "and nothing else!"

He spoke before the hour bell sounded, which it now did with a deep, dull, hollow, melancholy ONE. Light flashed up in the room upon the instant, and the curtains of his bed were drawn.

The curtains of his bed were drawn aside, I tell you, by a hand. Not the curtains at his feet, nor the curtains at his back, but those to which his face was addressed. The curtains of his bed were drawn aside; and Scrooge, starting up into a half-recumbent attitude, found himself face to face with the unearthly visitor who drew them: as close to it as I am now to you, and I am standing in the spirit at your elbow.

It was a strange figure — like a child: yet not so like a child as like an old man, viewed through some supernatural medium, which gave him the appearance of having receded from the view, and being diminished to a child's proportions. Its hair, which hung about its neck and down its back, was white, as if with age; and yet the face had not a wrinkle in it, and the tenderest bloom was on the skin. The arms were very long and muscular, the hands the same, as if its hold were of uncommon strength. Its legs and feet, most delicately formed, were, like those upper members, bare. It wore a tunic of the purest white; and round its waist was bound a lustrous belt, the sheen of which was beautiful. It held a branch of fresh green holly in its hand; and, in singular contradiction of that wintry emblem, had its dress trimmed with summer flowers. But the strangest thing about it was, that from the crown of its head there sprung a bright, clear jet of light, by which all this was visible; and which was doubtless the occasion of its using, in its duller moments, a great extinguisher for a cap, which it now held under its arm.

Even this, though, when Scrooge looked at it with increasing steadiness, was *not* its strangest quality. For as its belt sparkled and glittered now in one part and now in another, and what was light one instant, at another time was dark, so the figure itself fluctuated in its distinctness: being now a thing with one arm, now with one leg, now with twenty legs, now a pair of legs without a head, now a head without a body: of which dissolving parts, no outline would be visible in the dense gloom wherein they melted away. And, in the very wonder of this, it would be itself again, distinct and clear as ever.

"Are you the Spirit, sir, whose coming was foretold to me?" asked Scrooge.

"I am!"

The voice was soft and gentle. Singularly low, as if instead of being so close beside him, it were at a distance.

"Who, and what are you?" Scrooge demanded.

"I am the Ghost of Christmas Past."

"Long Past?" inquired Scrooge, observant of its dwarfish stature.

"No. Your past."

Perhaps, Scrooge could not have told anybody why, if anybody could have asked him, but he had a special desire to see the Spirit in his cap, and begged him to be covered.

"What!" exclaimed the Ghost, "would you so soon put out, with worldly hands, the light I give? Is it not enough that you are one of those whose passions made this cap, and force me through whole trains of years to wear it low upon my brow!"

Scrooge reverently disclaimed all intention to offend, or any knowledge of having wilfully "bonneted" the Spirit at any period of his life. He then made bold to inquire what business brought him there.

"Your welfare!" said the Ghost.

Scrooge expressed himself much obliged, but could not help thinking that a night of unbroken rest would have been more conducive to that end. The Spirit must have heard him thinking, for it said immediately:

"Your reclamation,[2] then. Take heed!"

It put out its strong hand as it spoke, and clasped him gently by the arm.

"Rise! and walk with me!"

It would have been in vain for Scrooge to plead that the weather and the hour were not adapted to pedestrian purposes; that bed was warm, and the thermometer a long way below freezing; that he was clad but lightly in his slippers, dressing gown, and nightcap; and that he had a cold upon him at that time. The grasp, though gentle as a woman's hand, was not to be resisted. He rose; but finding that the Spirit made towards the window, clasped its robe in supplication.

"I am a mortal," Scrooge remonstrated, "and liable to fall."

"Bear but a touch of my hand *there,*" said the Spirit, laying it upon his heart, "and you shall be upheld in more than this!"

As the words were spoken, they passed through the wall, and stood upon an open country road, with fields on either hand. The city had entirely vanished. Not a vestige of it was to be seen. The darkness and the mist had vanished with it, for it was a clear, cold, winter day, with snow upon the ground.

"Good Heaven!" said Scrooge, clasping his hands together, as he looked about him. "I was bred in this place. I was a boy here!"

The Spirit gazed upon him mildly. Its gentle touch, though it had been light and instantaneous, appeared still present to the old man's sense of feeling. He was conscious of a thousand odors floating in the air, each one connected with a thousand thoughts, and hopes, and joys, and cares long, long forgotten!

"Your lip is trembling," said the Ghost. "And what is that upon your cheek?"

Scrooge muttered, with an unusual catching in his voice, that it was a pimple, and begged the Ghost to lead him where he would.

"You recollect the way?" inquired the Spirit.

"Remember it!" cried Scrooge with fervor, "I could walk it blindfold."

"Strange to have forgotten it for so many years!" observed the Ghost. "Let us go on."

They walked along the road, Scrooge recognizing every gate, and post, and tree; until a little market-town appeared in the distance, with its bridge, its church, and winding river. Some shaggy ponies now were seen trotting towards them with boys upon their backs, who called to other boys in country gigs and carts, driven by farmers. All these boys were in great spirits, and shouted to each other, until the broad fields were so full of merry music that the crisp air laughed to hear it.

"These are but shadows of the things that have been," said the Ghost. "They have no consciousness of us."

The jocund travelers came on; and as they came, Scrooge knew and named them every one. Why was he rejoiced beyond all bounds to see them! Why did his cold eye glisten, and his heart leap up as they went past! Why was he filled with gladness when he heard them give each other Merry Christmas, as they parted at crossroads and byways, for their several homes! What was merry Christmas to Scrooge? Out upon Merry Christmas! What good had it ever done to him?

"The school is not quite deserted," said the Ghost. "A solitary child, neglected by his friends, is left there still."

Scrooge said he knew it. And he sobbed.

They left the highroad, by a well-remembered lane, and soon approached a mansion of dull red brick, with a little weathercock-surmounted cupola on the roof, and a bell hanging in it. It was a large house, but one of broken fortunes; for the spacious offices were little used, their walls were damp and mossy, their windows broken, and their gates decayed. Fowls clucked and strutted in the stables; and the coach-houses and sheds were overrun with grass. Nor was it more retentive of its ancient state, within; for entering the dreary hall, and glancing through the open doors of many rooms, they found them poorly furnished, cold, and vast. There was an earthy savor in the air, a chilly bareness in the place, which associated itself somehow with too much getting up by candle-light, and not too much to eat.

They went, the Ghost and Scrooge, across the hall, to a door at the back of the house. It opened before them, and disclosed a long, bare, melancholy room, made barer still by lines of plain deal forms and desks. At one of these a lonely boy was reading near a feeble fire; and Scrooge sat down upon a form, and wept to see his poor forgotten self as he had used to be.

Not a latent echo in the house, not a squeak and scuffle from the mice behind the paneling, not a drip from the half-thawed water-spout in the dull yard behind, not a sigh among the leafless boughs of one despondent poplar, not the idle swinging of an empty store-house door, no, not a clicking in the fire, but fell upon the heart of Scrooge with softening influence, and gave a freer passage to his tears.

The Spirit touched him on the arm, and pointed to his younger self, intent upon his reading. Suddenly a man, in foreign garments, wonderfully real and distinct to look at, stood outside the window, with an ax stuck in his belt, and leading an ass laden with wood by the bridle.

"Why, it's Ali Baba!"[3] Scrooge exclaimed in ecstasy. "It's dear old honest Ali Baba! Yes, yes, I know! One Christmastime, when yonder solitary child was left here all alone, he *did* come, for the first time, just like that. Poor boy! And Valentine," said Scrooge, "and his wild brother, Orson; there they go! And what's his name, who was put down in his drawers, asleep, at the Gate of Damascus; don't you see him! And the Sultan's Groom turned upside down by the Genii; there he is upon his head! Serve him right! I'm glad of it. What business had *he* to be married to the Princess!"

To hear Scrooge expending all the earnestness of his nature on such subjects, in a most extraordinary voice between laughing and crying, and to see his heightened and excited face would have been a surprise to his business friends in the city, indeed.

"There's the Parrot!" cried Scrooge. "Green body and yellow tail, with a thing like a lettuce growing out of the top of his head; there he is! Poor Robin Crusoe, he called him, when he came home again after sailing round the island. 'Poor Robin Crusoe, where have you been, Robin Crusoe?' The man thought he was dreaming, but he wasn't. It was the Parrot, you know. There goes Friday, running for his life to the little creek! Halloa! Hoop! Halloo!"

Then, with a rapidity of transition very foreign to his usual character, he said, in pity for his former self, "Poor boy!" and cried again.

"I wish," Scrooge muttered, putting his hand in his pocket, and looking about him, after drying his eyes with his cuff, "but it's too late now."

"What is the matter?" asked the Spirit.

"Nothing," said Scrooge. "Nothing. There was a boy singing a Christmas carol at my door last night. I should like to have given him something; that's all."

The Ghost smiled thoughtfully, and waved its hand, saying, as it did so, "Let us see another Christmas!"

Scrooge's former self grew larger at the words, and the room became a little darker and more dirty. The panels shrunk, the windows cracked; fragments of plaster fell out of the ceiling, and the naked laths were shown instead; but how all this was brought about, Scrooge knew no more than you do. He only knew that it was quite correct; that everything had happened so; that there he was, alone again, when all the other boys had gone home for the jolly holidays.

He was not reading now, but walking up and down despairingly. Scrooge looked at the Ghost, and, with a mournful shaking of his head, glanced anxiously towards the door.

It opened; and a little girl, much younger than the boy, came darting in, and, putting her arms about his neck, and often kissing him, addressed him as her "dear, dear brother."

"I have come to bring you home, dear brother!" said the child, clapping her tiny hands, and bending down to laugh. "To bring you home, home, home!"

"Home, little Fan?" returned the boy.

"Yes!" said the child, brimful of glee. "Home, for good and all. Home, for ever and ever. Father is so much kinder than he used to be, that home's like Heaven! He spoke so gently to me one dear night when I was going to bed that I was not afraid to ask him once more if you might come home; and he said Yes, you should, and sent me in a coach to bring you. And you're to be a man!" said the child, opening her eyes, "and are never to come back here; but first, we're to be together all the Christmas long, and have the merriest time in all the world."

"You are quite a woman, little Fan!" exclaimed the boy.

She clapped her hands and laughed, and tried to touch his head; but, being too little, laughed again, and stood on tiptoe to embrace him. Then she began to drag him, in her childish eagerness, towards the door; and he, nothing loath to go, accompanied her.

A terrible voice in the hall cried, "Bring down Master Scrooge's box, there!" and in the hall appeared the schoolmaster himself, who glared on Master Scrooge with a ferocious condescension, and threw him into a dreadful state of mind by shaking hands with him. He then conveyed him and his sister into the veriest old well of a shivering best-parlor that ever was seen, where the maps upon the wall, and the celestial and terrestial globes in the windows were waxy with cold. Here he produced a decanter of curiously light wine, and a block of curiously heavy cake, and administered installments of those dainties to the young people, at the same time, sending out a meager servant to offer a glass of "something" to the postboy, who answered that he thanked the gentleman, but if it was the same tap as he had tasted before, he had rather not. Master Scrooge's trunk being by this time tied on to the top of the chaise, the children bade the schoolmaster good-bye right willingly, and, getting into it, drove gaily down the garden sweep, the quick wheels dashing the hoar-frost and snow from off the dark leaves of the evergreens like spray.

"Always a delicate creature, whom a breath might have withered," said the Ghost. "But she had a large heart!"

"So she had," cried Scrooge. "You're right. I will not gainsay[4] it, Spirit. God forbid!"

"She died a woman," said the Ghost, "and had, as I think, children."

"One child," Scrooge returned.

"True," said the Ghost. "Your nephew!"

Scrooge seemed uneasy in his mind, and answered briefly, "Yes."

Although they had but that moment left the school behind them, they were now in the busy thoroughfares of a city, where shadowy passengers passed and repassed, where shadowy carts and coaches battled for the way, and all the strife and tumult of a real city were. It was made plain enough, by the dressing of the shops, that here too it was Christmastime again; but it was evening, and the streets were lighted up.

The Ghost stopped at a certain warehouse door, and asked Scrooge if he knew it.

"Know it!" said Scrooge. "Was I apprenticed here!"

They went in. At sight of an old gentleman in a Welsh wig, sitting behind such a high desk that if he had been two inches taller he must have knocked his head against the ceiling, Scrooge cried in great excitement:

"Why, it's old Fezziwig! Bless his heart; it's Fezziwig alive again!"

Old Fezziwig laid down his pen, and looked up at the clock, which pointed to the hour of seven. He rubbed his hands; adjusted his capacious[5] waistcoat; laughed all over himself, from his shoes to his organ of benevolence;[6] and called out in a comfortable, oily, rich, fat, jovial voice:

"Yo ho, there! Ebenezer! Dick!"

Scrooge's former self, now grown a young man, came briskly in, accompanied by his fellow-'prentice.

"Dick Wilkins, to be sure!" said Scrooge to the Ghost. "Bless me, yes. There he is. He was very much attached to me, was Dick. Poor Dick! Dear, dear!"

"Yo ho, my boys!" said Fezziwig. "No more work tonight. Christmas Eve, Dick. Christmas, Ebenezer! Let's have the shutters up," cried old Fezziwig, with a sharp clap of his hands, "before a man can say Jack Robinson!"

You wouldn't believe how those two fellows went at it! They charged into the street with the shutters — one, two, three — had 'em up in their places — four, five, six — barred 'em and pinned 'em — seven, eight, nine — and came back before you could have got to twelve, panting like racehorses.

"Hilli-ho!" cried old Fezziwig, skipping down from the high desk with wonderful agility. "Clear away, my lads, and let's have lots of room here! Hilli-ho, Dick! Chirrup, Ebenezer!"

Clear away! There was nothing they wouldn't have cleared away, or couldn't have cleared away, with old Fezziwig looking on. It was done in a minute. Every movable was packed off, as if it were dismissed from public life forevermore; the floor was swept and watered, the lamps were trimmed, fuel was heaped upon the fire; and the warehouse was as snug, and warm, and dry, and bright a ballroom as you would desire to see upon a winter's night.

In came a fiddler with a music book, and went up to the lofty desk, and made an orchestra of it, and tuned like fifty stomachaches. In came Mrs. Fezziwig, one vast substantial smile. In came the three Miss Fezziwigs, beaming and lovable. In came the six young followers whose hearts they broke. In came all the young men and women employed in the business. In came the housemaid, with her cousin, the baker. In came the cook, with her brother's particular friend, the milkman. In came the boy from over the way, who was suspected of not having board enough from his master, trying to hide himself behind the girl from next door but one, who was proved to have had her ears pulled by her mistress. In they all came, one after another; some shyly, some boldly, some gracefully, some awkwardly, some pushing, some pulling; in they all came, anyhow and everyhow. Away they all went, twenty couples at once, hands half round and back again the other way; down the middle and up again; round and round in various stages of affectionate grouping; old top couple always turning up in the wrong place; new top couple starting off again, as soon as they got there; all top couples at last, and not a bottom one to help them. When this result was brought about, old Fezziwig, clapping his hands to stop the dance, cried out, "Well done!" and the fiddler plunged his hot face into a pot of porter, especially provided for that purpose. But, scorning rest, upon his reappearance he instantly began again, though there were no dancers yet, as if the other fiddler had been carried home, exhausted, on a shutter, and he were a brand-new man resolved to beat him out of sight, or perish.

There were more dances, and there were forfeits, and more dances, and there was cake, and there was negus,[7] and there was a great piece of cold roast, and there was a great piece of cold boiled, and there were mince pies, and plenty of beer. But the great effect of the evening came after the roast and boiled, when the fiddler (an artful dog, mind! The sort of man who knew his business better than you or I could have told it him!) struck up "Sir Roger de Coverley." Then old Fezziwig stood out to dance with Mrs. Fezziwig. Top couple, too, with a good stiff piece of work cut out for them; three or four and twenty pair of partners; people who were not to be trifled with; people who *would* dance, and had no notion of walking.

But if they had been twice as many — ah, four times — old Fezziwig would have been a match for them, and so would Mrs. Fezziwig. As to *her,* she was worthy to be his partner in every sense of the term. If that's not high praise, tell me higher, and I'll use it. A positive light appeared to issue from Fezziwig's calves. They shone in every part of the dance like moons. You couldn't have predicted, at any given time, what would become of 'em next. And when old Fezziwig and Mrs. Fezziwig had gone all through the dance; advance and retire, hold hands with your partner; bow and curtsy; corkscrew; thread-the-needle, and back again to your place; Fezziwig "cut" — cut so deftly, that he appeared to wink with his legs, and came upon his feet again without a stagger.

When the clock struck eleven, this domestic ball broke up. Mr. and Mrs. Fezziwig took their stations, one on either side of the door, and shaking hands with every person individually as he or she went out, wished him or her a merry Christmas. When everybody had retired but the two 'prentices, they did the same to them; and thus the cheerful voices died away, and the lads were left to their beds, which were under a counter in the back-shop.

During the whole of this time, Scrooge had acted like a man out of his wits. His heart and soul were in the scene, and with his former self. He corroborated[8] everything, remembered everything, enjoyed everything, and underwent the strangest agitation.

It was not until now, when the bright faces of his former self and Dick were turned from them, that he remembered the Ghost, and became conscious that it was looking full upon him, while the light upon its head burned very clear.

"A small matter," said the Ghost, "to make these silly folks so full of gratitude."

"Small!" echoed Scrooge.

The Spirit signed to him to listen to the two apprentices, who were pouring out of their hearts in praise of Fezziwig, and, when he had done so, said:

"Why! Is it not? He has spent but a few pounds of your mortal money: three or four, perhaps. Is that so much that he deserves this praise?"

"It isn't that," said Scrooge, heated by the remark, and speaking unconsciously like his former, not his latter, self. "It isn't that, Spirit. He has the power to render us happy or unhappy, to make our service light or burdensome, a pleasure or a toil. Say that his power lies in words and looks, in things so slight and insignificant that it is impossible to add and count 'em up; what then? The happiness he gives is quite as great as if it cost a fortune."

He felt the Spirit's glance, and stopped.

"What is the matter?" asked the Ghost.

"Nothing particular," said Scrooge.

"Something, I think?" the Ghost insisted.

"No," said Scrooge, "no. I should like to be able to say a word or two to my clerk just now! That's all."

His former self turned down the lamps as he gave utterance to the wish; and Scrooge and the Ghost again stood side by side in the open air.

"My time grows short," observed the Spirit. "Quick!"

This was not addressed to Scrooge, or to anyone whom he could see, but it produced an immediate effect. For again Scrooge saw himself. He was older now, a man in the prime of life. His face had not the harsh and rigid lines of later years; but it had begun to wear the signs of care and avarice. There was an eager, greedy, restless motion in the eye, which showed the passion that had taken root, and where the shadow of the growing tree would fall.

He was not alone, but sat by the side of a fair young girl in a mourning-dress, in whose eyes there were tears, which sparkled in the light that shone out of the Ghost of Christmas Past.

"It matters little," she said softly. "To you, very little. Another idol[9] has displaced me; and if it can cheer and comfort you in time to come, as I would have tried to do, I have no just cause to grieve."

"What idol has displaced you?" he rejoined.

"A golden one."[10]

"This is the even-handed dealing of the world!" he said. "There is nothing on which it is so hard as poverty; and there is nothing it professes to condemn with such severity as the pursuit of wealth!"

"You fear the world too much," she answered gently. "All your other hopes have merged into the hope of being beyond the chance of its sordid reproach. I have seen your nobler aspirations fall off one by one, until the master passion, Gain, engrosses you. Have I not?"

"What then?" he retorted. "Even if I have grown so much wiser, what then? I am not changed towards you."

She shook her head.

"Am I?"

"Our contract is an old one. It was made when we were both poor and content to be so, until, in good season, we could improve our worldly fortune by our patient industry. You *are* changed.

When it was made, you were another man."

"I was a boy," he said impatiently.

"Your own feeling tells you that you were not what you are," she returned. "I am. That which promised happiness when we were one in heart is fraught with misery now that we are two. How often and how keenly I have thought of this, I will not say. It is enough that I *have* thought of it, and can release you."

"Have I ever sought release?"

"In words, no. Never."

"In what, then?"

"In a changed nature, in an altered spirit, in another atmosphere of life, another Hope as its great end. In everything that made my love of any worth or value in your sight. If this had never been between us," said the girl, looking mildly, but with steadiness, upon him, "tell me, would you seek me out and try to win me now? Ah, no!"

He seemed to yield to the justice of this supposition, in spite of himself. But he said, with a struggle, "You think not."

"I would gladly think otherwise if I could," she answered, "Heaven knows! When *I* have learned a Truth like this, I know how strong and irresistible it must be. But if you were free today, tomorrow, yesterday, can even I believe that you would choose a dowerless[11] girl — you who, in your very confidence with her, weigh everything by Gain: or, choosing her, if for a moment you were false enough to your one guiding principle to do so, do I not know that your repentance and regret would surely follow? I do; and I release you. With a full heart, for the love of him you once were."

He was about to speak; but, with her head turned from him, she resumed:

"You may — the memory of what is past half makes me hope you will — have pain in this. A very, very brief time, and you will dismiss the recollection of it, gladly, as an unprofitable dream, from which it happened well that you awoke. May you be happy in the life you have chosen!"

She left him; and they parted.

"Spirit!" said Scrooge, "show me no more! Conduct me home. Why do you delight to torture me?"

"One shadow more!" exclaimed the Ghost.

"No more!" cried Scrooge. "No more. I don't wish to see it. Show me no more!"

But the relentless Ghost pinioned[12] him in both his arms, and forced him to observe what happened next.

They were in another scene and place: a room, not very large or handsome, but full of comfort. Near to the winter fire sat a beautiful young girl, so like that last that Scrooge believed it was the same, until he saw *her,* now a comely matron, sitting opposite her daughter. The noise in this room was perfectly tumultuous, for there were more children there than Scrooge in his agitated state of mind could count; and, unlike the celebrated herd in the poem, they were not forty children conducting themselves like one, but every child was conducting itself like forty. The consequences were uproarious beyond belief; but no one seemed to care; on the contrary, the mother and daughter laughed heartily, and enjoyed it very much; and the latter, soon beginning to mingle in the sports, got pillaged by the young brigands most ruthlessly. What would I not have given to be one of them! Though I never could have been so rude, no, no! I wouldn't for the wealth of all the world have crushed that braided hair, and torn it down; and for the precious little shoe, I wouldn't have plucked it off, God bless my soul! to save my life. As to measuring her waist in sport, as they did, bold young brood, I couldn't have done it; I should have expected my arm to have grown round it for a punishment, and never come straight again. And yet I should have dearly liked, I own, to have touched her lips; to have questioned her, that she might have opened them; to have looked upon the lashes of her downcast eyes, and never raised a blush; to have let loose waves of hair, an inch of which would be a keepsake beyond price: in short, I should have liked, I do confess, to have had the lightest license of a child, and yet been man enough to know its value.

But now a knocking at the door was heard, and such a rush immediately ensued that she, with laughing face and plundered dress, was borne towards it, the center of a flushed and boisterous group, just in time to greet the father, who came home attended by a man laden with Christmas toys and presents. Then the shouting and the struggling, and the onslaught that was made on the defenseless porter! The scaling him, with chairs for ladders, to dive into his pockets, despoil him of brown paper parcels, hold on tight by his cravat, hug him round the neck, pommel his back, and kick his legs in irrepressible affection! The shouts of wonder and delight with which the development of every package was received! The terrible announcement that the baby had been taken in the act of putting a doll's frying pan into his mouth, and was more than suspected of having swallowed a fictitious turkey, glued on a wooden platter! The immense relief of finding this a false alarm! The joy, and gratitude, and ecstacy! They are all indescribable alike. It is enough that, by degrees, the children and their emotions got out of the parlor and, by one stair at a time, up to the top of the house, where they went to bed, and so subsided.

And now Scrooge looked on more attentively than ever, when the master of the house, having his daughter leaning fondly on him, sat down with her and her mother at his own fireside; and when he thought that such another creature, quite as graceful and as full of promise, might have called him father, and been a springtime in the haggard winter of his life, his sight grew very dim indeed.

"Belle," said the husband, turning to his wife with a smile, "I saw an old friend of yours this afternoon."

"Who was it?"

"Guess!"

"How can I? Tut, don't I know," she added in the same breath, laughing as he laughed. "Mr. Scrooge."

"Mr. Scrooge it was. I passed his office window; and as it was not shut up, and he had a candle inside, I could scarcely help seeing him. His partner lies upon the point of death, I hear; and there he sat alone. Quite alone in the world, I do believe."

"Spirit!" said Scrooge in a broken voice, "remove me from this place."

"I told you these were shadows of the things that have been," said the Ghost. "That they are what they are, do not blame me!"

"Remove me!" Scrooge exclaimed. "I cannot bear it!"

He turned upon the Ghost, and, seeing that it looked upon him with a face in which, in some strange way, there were fragments of all the faces it had shown him, wrestled with it.

"Leave me! Take me back. Haunt me no longer!"

In the struggle, if that can be called a struggle in which the Ghost, with no visible resistance on its own part, was undisturbed by any effort of its adversary, Scrooge observed that its light was burning high and bright; and dimly connecting that with its influence over him, he seized the extinguisher-cap, and by a sudden action pressed it down upon its head.

The Spirit dropped beneath it, so that the extinguisher covered its whole form; but though Scrooge pressed it down with all his force, he could not hide the light, which streamed from under it in an unbroken flood upon the ground.

He was conscious of being exhausted, and overcome by an irresistible drowsiness, and, further, of being in his own bedroom. He gave the cap a parting squeeze, in which his hand relaxed, and had barely time to reel to bed before he sank into a heavy sleep.

[1] **This was a great relief . . . no days to count by:** Scrooge's main concern is that, if days cannot be counted, his stock or bond certificates payable after a certain number of days will become worthless.
[2] **reclamation:** rescue from sin
[3] **Ali Baba:** Ali Baba and the other figures mentioned in these paragraphs are characters from books that Scrooge remembers reading as a boy.
[4] **gainsay:** deny
[5] **capacious:** able to hold much
[6] **organ of benevolence:** According to *phrenology,* a pseudoscience (false science) popular in the 19th century, the organ of benevolence (good will) is located at the top of the head. Phrenologists believed that different sections of the brain's surface, called organs, controlled different personality traits or mental abilities.
[7] **negus:** a sweet, spicy beverage of hot water, wine, and lemon juice
[8] **corroborated:** confirmed
[9] **idol:** an object of worship
[10] **"a golden one":** a golden idol; that is, money
[11] **dowerless:** without a dowry, which is money or property brought by a bride to her husband at marriage
[12] **pinioned:** kept from moving by binding the arms

A CLOSER LOOK

1. What does Scrooge remember when he sees himself as a schoolboy? What emotion does he feel? How does this feeling change his attitude toward the young caroler who had come to his door that evening?

2. How does old Fezziwig's treatment of his employees differ from Scrooge's treatment of his clerk? After seeing Fezziwig, Scrooge mentions that he would like to have a word with his clerk. Why? What do you think Scrooge would say to him?

3. What does Belle, Scrooge's fiancée, mean when she says that a "golden idol" has replaced her in his heart? How has Scrooge's younger self changed?

4. What information about Scrooge do we learn from Belle's conversation with her husband? What does this information tell us about the kind of man Scrooge has become?

STAVE THREE

The Second of the Three Spirits

Awaking in the middle of a prodigiously tough snore, and sitting up in bed to get his thoughts together, Scrooge had no occasion to be told that the bell was again upon the stroke of One. He felt that he was restored to consciousness in the right nick of time, for the especial purpose of holding a conference with the second messenger dispatched to him through Jacob Marley's intervention. But, finding that he turned uncomfortably cold when he began to wonder which of his curtains this new specter would draw back, he put them every one aside with his own hands, and, lying down again, established a sharp lookout all round the bed. For he wished to challenge the Spirit on the moment of its appearance, and did not wish to be taken by surprise, and made nervous.

Gentlemen of the free-and-easy sort, who plume themselves on being acquainted with a move or two, and being usually equal to the time of day, express the wide range of their capacity for adventure by observing that they are good for anything from pitch-and-toss to manslaughter; between which opposite extremes, no doubt, there lies a tolerably wide and comprehensive range of subjects. Without venturing for Scrooge quite as hardily as this, I don't mind calling on you to believe that he was ready for a good broad field of strange appearances, and that nothing between a baby and a rhinoceros would have astonished him very much.

Now, being prepared for almost anything, he was not by any means prepared for nothing; and, consequently, when the bell struck One, and no shape appeared, he was taken with a violent fit of trembling. Five minutes, ten minutes, a quarter of an hour went by, yet nothing came. All this time he lay upon his bed, the very core and center of a blaze of ruddy light, which streamed upon it when the clock proclaimed the hour, and which, being only light, was more alarming than a dozen ghosts, as he was powerless to make out what it meant, or would be at, and was sometimes apprehensive that he might be at that very moment an interesting case of spontaneous combustion,[1] without having the consolation of knowing it. At last, however, he began to think — as you or I would have thought at first; for it is always the person not in the predicament who knows what ought to have been done in it, and would unquestionably have done it too — at last, I say, he began to think that the source and secret of this ghostly light might be in the adjoining room, from whence, on further tracing it, it seemed to shine. This idea taking full possession of his mind, he got up softly, and shuffled in his slippers to the door.

The moment Scrooge's hand was on the lock, a strange voice called him by his name, and bade him enter. He obeyed.

It was his own room. There was no doubt about that. But it had undergone a surprising transformation. The walls and ceiling were so hung with living green that it looked a perfect grove, from every part of which bright, gleaming berries glistened. The crisp leaves of holly, mistletoe, and ivy reflected back the light, as if so many little mirrors had been scattered there; and such a mighty blaze went roaring up the chimney, as that dull petrifaction of a hearth had never known in Scrooge's time, or Marley's, or for many and many a winter season gone. Heaped up on the floor, to form a kind of throne, were turkeys, geese, game, poultry, brawn,[2] great joints of meat, sucking-pigs, long wreaths of sausages, mince pies, plum puddings, barrels of oysters, red-hot chestnuts, cherry-cheeked apples, juicy oranges, luscious pears, immense twelfth-cakes, and seething bowls of punch, that made the chamber dim with their delicious steam. In easy state upon this couch, there sat a jolly Giant, glorious to see, who bore a glowing torch, in shape not unlike Plenty's horn, and held it up, high up, to shed its light on Scrooge, as he came peeping round the door.

"Come in!" exclaimed the Ghost. "Come in! and know me better, man!"

Scrooge entered timidly, and hung his head before this Spirit. He was not the dogged Scrooge he had been; and though the Spirit's eyes were clear and kind, he did not like to meet them.

"I am the Ghost of Chrismas Present," said the Spirit. "Look upon me!"

Scrooge reverently did so. It was clothed in one simple, deep-green robe, or mantle, bordered with white fur. This garment hung so loosely on the figure that its capacious breast was bare, as if disdaining to be warded or concealed by any artifice. Its feet, observable beneath the ample folds of the garment, were also bare; and on its head it wore no other covering than a holly wreath, set here and there with shining icicles. Its dark brown curls were long and free, free as its genial face, its sparkling eye, its open hand, its cheery voice, its unconstrained demeanor, and its joyful air. Girded round its middle was an antique scabbard; but no sword was in it, and the ancient sheath was eaten up with rust.

"You have never seen the like of me before!" exclaimed the Spirit.

"Never," Scrooge made answer to it.

"Have never walked forth with the younger members of my family, meaning (for I am very young) my elder brothers born in these later years?" pursued the Phantom.

"I don't think I have," said Scrooge. "I am afraid I have not. Have you had many brothers, Spirit?"

"More than eighteen hundred," said the Ghost.

"A tremendous family to provide for!" muttered Scrooge.

The Ghost of Christmas Present rose.

"Spirit," said Scrooge submissively, "conduct me where you will. I went forth last night on compulsion, and I learned a lesson which is working now. Tonight, if you have aught to teach me, let me profit by it."

"Touch my robe!"

Scrooge did as he was told, and held it fast.

Holly, mistletoe, red berries, ivy, turkeys, geese, game, poultry, brawn, meat, pigs, sausages, oysters, pies, puddings, fruit, and punch, all vanished instantly. So did the room, the fire, the ruddy glow, the hour of the night, and they stood in the city streets on Christmas morning, where (for the weather was severe) the people made a rough, but brisk and not unpleasant kind of music, in scraping the snow from the pavement in front of their dwellings, and from the tops of their houses, whence it was mad delight to the boys to see it come plumping down into the road below, and splitting into artificial little snowstorms.

The house-fronts looked black enough, and the windows blacker, contrasting with the smooth white sheet of snow upon the roofs, and with the dirtier snow upon the ground, which last deposit had been plowed up in deep furrows by the heavy wheels of carts and wagons, furrows that crossed and recrossed each other hundreds of times where the great streets branched off, and made intricate channels, hard to trace, in the thick yellow mud and icy water. The sky was gloomy, and the shortest streets were choked up with a dingy mist, half thawed, half frozen, whose heavier particles descended in a shower of sooty atoms, as if all the chimneys in Great Britain had, by one consent, caught fire, and were blazing away to their dear hearts' content. There was nothing very cheerful in the climate or the town, and yet was there an air of cheerfulness abroad that the clearest summer air and brightest summer sun might have endeavored to diffuse in vain.

For the people who were shoveling away on the housetops were jovial and full of glee, calling out to one another from the parapets, and now and then exchanging a facetious snowball — better-natured missile far than many a wordy jest — laughing heartily if it went right, and not less heartily if it went wrong. The poulterers' shops were still half open, and the fruiterers' were radiant in their glory. There were great, round, pot-bellied baskets of chestnuts, shaped like the waistcoats of jolly old gentlemen, lolling at the doors, and tumbling out into the street in their apoplectic opulence. There were ruddy, brown-faced, broad-girthed Spanish onions, shining in the fatness of their growth like Spanish friars, and winking from their shelves in wanton slyness at the girls as they went by, and glanced demurely at the hung-up mistletoe. There were pears and apples, clustered high in blooming pyramids; there were bunches of grapes, made, in the shopkeepers' benevolence, to dangle from conspicuous hooks, that people's mouths might water gratis as they passed; there were piles of filberts, mossy and brown, recalling, in their fragrance, ancient walks among the woods, and pleasant shufflings ankle-deep through withered leaves; there were Norfolk Biffins, squab and swarthy, setting off the yellow of the oranges and lemons, and, in the great compactness of their juicy persons, urgently entreating and beseeching to be carried home in paper bags and eaten after dinner. The very gold- and silverfish, set forth among these choice fruits in a bowl, though members of a dull and stagnant-blooded race, appeared to know that there was something going on, and, to a fish, went gasping round and round their little world in slow and passionless excitement.

The grocers'! oh, the grocers'! nearly closed, with perhaps two shutters down, or one, but through those gaps such glimpses! It was not alone that the scales descending on the counter made a merry sound, or that the twine and roller parted company so briskly, or that the canisters were rattled up and down like juggling tricks, or even that the blended scents of tea and coffee were so grateful to the nose, or even that the raisins were so plentiful and rare, the almonds so extremely white, the sticks of cinnamon so long and straight, the other spices so delicious, the candied fruits so caked and spotted with molten sugar as to make the coldest lookers-on feel faint and subsequently bilious.[3] Nor was it that the figs were moist and pulpy, or that the French plums blushed in modest tartness from their highly decorated boxes, or that everything was good to eat and in its Christmas dress: but the customers were all so hurried and so eager in the hopeful promise of the day, that they tumbled up against each other at the door, crashing their wicker baskets wildly, and left their purchases upon the counter, and came running back to fetch them, and committed hundreds of the like mistakes in the best humor possible, while the grocer and his people were so frank and fresh that the polished hearts with which they fastened their aprons behind might have been their own, worn outside for general inspection, and for Christmas daws to peck at if they chose.

But soon the steeples called good people all to church and chapel, and away they came, flocking through the streets in their best clothes, and with their gayest faces. And at the same time there emerged from scores of by-streets, lanes, and nameless turnings, innumerable people, carrying their dinners to the bakers' shops.[4] The sight of these poor revelers appeared to interest the Spirit very much, for he stood with Scrooge beside him in a baker's doorway, and, taking off the covers as their bearers passed, sprinkled incense on their dinners from his torch. And it was a very uncommon kind of torch, for once or twice when there were angry words between some dinner-carriers who had jostled each other, he shed a few drops of water on them from it, and their good humor was restored directly. For they said, it was a shame to quarrel upon Christmas Day. And so it was! God love it, so it was!

In time the bells ceased, and the bakers' were shut up, and yet there was a genial shadowing forth of all these dinners and the progress of their cooking, in the thawed blotch of wet above each baker's oven, where the pavement smoked as if its stones were cooking too.

"Is there a peculiar flavor in what you sprinkle from your torch?" asked Scrooge.

"There is. My own."

"Would it apply to any kind of dinner on this day?" asked Scrooge.

"To any kindly given. To a poor one most."

"Why to a poor one most?" asked Scrooge.

"Because it needs it most."

"Spirit," said Scrooge, after a moment's thought, "I wonder you, of all the beings in the many worlds about us, should desire to cramp these people's opportunities of innocent enjoyment."

"I!" cried the Spirit.

"You would deprive them of their means of dining every seventh day, often the only day on which they can be said to dine at all," said Scrooge. "Wouldn't you?"

"I!" cried the Spirit.

"You seek to close these places on the Seventh Day," said Scrooge. "And it comes to the same thing."

"*I* seek!" exclaimed the Spirit.

"Forgive me if I am wrong. It has been done in your name, or at least in that of your family," said Scrooge.

"There are some upon this earth of yours," returned the Spirit, "who lay claim to know us, and who do their deeds of passion, pride, ill will, hatred, envy, bigotry, and selfishness in our name, who are as strange to us, and all our kith and kin, as if they had never lived. Remember that, and charge their doings on themselves, not us."

Scrooge promised that he would; and they went on, invisible, as they had been before, into the suburbs of the town. It was a remarkable quality of the Ghost (which Scrooge had observed at the baker's), that notwithstanding his gigantic size, he could accommodate himself to any place with ease, and that he stood beneath a low roof quite as gracefully, and like a supernatural creature, as it was possible he could have done in any lofty hall.

And perhaps it was the pleasure the good Spirit had in showing off this power of his, or else it was his own kind, generous, hearty nature, and his sympathy with all poor men, that led him straight to Scrooge's clerk's; for there he went, and took Scrooge with him, holding to his robe; and on the threshold of the door the Spirit smiled, and stopped to bless Bob Cratchit's dwelling with the sprinklings of his torch. Think of that! Bob had but fifteen "Bob" a week himself; he pocketed on Saturdays but fifteen copies of his Christian name; and yet the Ghost of Christmas Present blessed his four-roomed house!

Then up rose Mrs. Cratchit, Cratchit's wife, dressed out but poorly in a twice-turned gown, but brave in ribbons, which are cheap and make a goodly show for sixpence; and she laid the cloth, assisted by Belinda Cratchit, second of her daughters, also brave in ribbons; while Master Peter Cratchit plunged a fork into the saucepan of potatoes, and getting the corners of his monstrous shirt-collar (Bob's private property, conferred upon his son and heir in honor of the day) into his mouth, rejoiced to find himself so gallantly attired, and yearned to show his linen in the fashionable Parks. And now two smaller Cratchits, boy and girl, came tearing in, screaming that outside the baker's they had smelled the goose, and known it for their own; and, basking in luxurious thoughts of sage and onion, these young Cratchits danced about the table, and exalted Master Peter Cratchit to the skies, while he (not proud, although his collars nearly choked him) blew the fire, until the slow potatoes, bubbling up, knocked loudly at the saucepan lid to be let out and peeled.

"What has ever got your precious father, then?" said Mrs. Cratchit. "And your brother, Tiny Tim? And Martha warn't as late last Christmas Day by half an hour!"

"Here's Martha, mother," said a girl, appearing as she spoke.

"Here's Martha, mother!" cried the two young Cratchits. "Hurrah! There's *such* a goose, Martha!"

"Why, bless your heart alive, my dear, how late you are!" said Mrs. Cratchit, kissing her a dozen times, and taking off her shawl and bonnet for her with officious zeal.

"We'd a deal of work to finish up last night," replied the girl, "and had to clear away this morning, mother!"

"Well! Never mind so long as you are come," said Mrs. Cratchit. "Sit ye down before the fire, my dear, and have a warm, Lord bless ye!"

"No, no! There's father coming," cried the two young Cratchits, who were everywhere at once. "Hide, Martha, hide!"

So Martha hid herself, and in came little Bob, the father, with at least three feet of comforter, exclusive of the fringe, hanging down before him, and his threadbare clothes darned up and brushed, to look seasonable, and Tiny Tim upon his shoulder. Alas for Tiny Tim, he bore a little crutch, and had his limbs supported by an iron frame!

"Why, where's our Martha?" cried Bob Cratchit, looking around.

"Not coming," said Mrs. Cratchit.

"Not coming!" said Bob, with a sudden declension in his high spirits; for he had been Tim's blood-horse all the way from church, and had come home rampant. "Not coming upon Christmas Day!"

Martha didn't like to see him disappointed, if it were only in joke; so she came out prematurely from behind the closet door, and ran into his arms, while the two young Cratchits hustled Tiny Tim, and bore him off into the washhouse, that he might hear the pudding singing in the copper.[5]

"And how did little Tim behave?" asked Mrs. Cratchit, when she had rallied Bob on his credulity,[6] and Bob had hugged his daughter to his heart's content.

"As good as gold," said Bob, "and better. Somehow he gets thoughtful, sitting by himself so much, and thinks the strangest things you ever heard. He told me, coming home, that he hoped the people saw him in the church, because he was a cripple, and it might be pleasant to them to remember, upon Christmas Day, who made lame beggars walk and blind men see."

Bob's voice was tremulous when he told them this, and trembled more when he said that Tiny Tim was growing strong and hearty.

His active little crutch was heard upon the floor, and back came Tiny Tim before another word was spoken, escorted by his brother and sister to his stool beside the fire; and while Bob, turning up his cuffs — as if, poor fellow, they were capable of being made more shabby — compounded some hot mixture in a jug with gin and lemons, and stirred it round and round and put it on the hob to simmer, Master Peter and the two ubiquitous young Cratchits went to fetch the goose, with which they soon returned in high procession.

Such a bustle ensued that you might have thought a goose the rarest of all birds, a feathered phenomenon, to which a black swan was a matter of course — and in truth it was something very like it in that house. Mrs. Cratchit made the gravy (ready beforehand in a little saucepan) hissing hot; Master Peter mashed the potatoes with incredible vigor; Miss Belinda sweetened up the applesauce; Martha dusted the hot plates; Bob took Tiny Tim beside him in a tiny corner at the table; the two young Cratchits set chairs for everybody, not forgetting themselves, and mounting guard upon their posts, crammed spoons into their mouths, lest they should shriek for goose before their turn came to be helped. At last the dishes were set on, and grace was said. It was succeeded by a breathless pause, as Mrs. Cratchit, looking slowly all along the carving knife, prepared to plunge it in the breast, but when she did, and when the long-expected gush of stuffing issued forth, one murmur of delight arose all round the board, and even Tiny Tim, excited by the two young Cratchits, beat on the table with the handle of his knife, and feebly cried Hurrah!

There never was such a goose. Bob said he didn't believe there

ever was such a goose cooked. Its tenderness and flavor, size and cheapness, were the themes of universal admiration. Eked out by the applesauce and mashed potatoes, it was a sufficient dinner for the whole family; indeed, as Mrs. Cratchit said with great delight (surveying one small atom of a bone upon the dish), they hadn't ate it all at last! Yet everyone had had enough, and the youngest Cratchits in particular were steeped in sage and onion to the eyebrows! But now, the plates being changed by Miss Belinda, Mrs. Cratchit left the room alone — too nervous to bear witnesses — to take the pudding up, and bring it in.

Suppose it should not be done enough! Suppose it should break in turning out! Suppose somebody should have got over the wall of the backyard, and stolen it, while they were merry with the goose — a supposition at which the two young Cratchits became livid! All sorts of horrors were supposed.

Hallo! A great deal of steam! The pudding was out of the copper. A smell like a washing-day! That was the cloth. A smell like an eating-house and a pastry cook's next door to each other, with a laundress's next door to that! That was the pudding! In half a minute Mrs. Cratchit entered — flushed, but smiling proudly —

with the pudding, like a speckled cannonball, so hard and firm, blazing in half of half-a-quartern of ignited brandy, and bedight with Christmas holly stuck into the top.

Oh, a wonderful pudding! Bob Cratchit said, and calmly, too, that he regarded it as the greatest success achieved by Mrs. Cratchit since their marriage. Mrs. Cratchit said that, now the weight was off her mind, she would confess she had had her doubts about the quantity of flour. Everybody had something to say about it, but nobody said or thought it was at all a small pudding for a large family. It would have been flat heresy to do so. Any Cratchit would have blushed to hint at such a thing.

At last the dinner was all done, the cloth was cleared, the hearth swept, and the fire made up. The compound in the jug being tasted and considered perfect, apples and oranges were put upon the table, and a shovelful of chestnuts on the fire. Then all the Cratchit family drew round the hearth in what Bob Cratchit called a circle, meaning half a one, and at Bob Cratchit's elbow stood the family display of glass — two tumblers and a custard-cup without a handle.

These held the hot stuff from the jug, however, as well as golden goblets would have done, and Bob served it out with beaming looks, while the chestnuts on the fire sputtered and crackled noisily. Then Bob proposed:

"A merry Christmas to us all, my dears. God bless us!"

Which all the family re-echoed.

"God bless us, every one!" said Tiny Tim, the last of all.

He sat very close to his father's side, upon his little stool. Bob held his withered little hand in his, as if he loved the child, and wished to keep him by his side, and dreaded that he might be taken from him.

"Spirit," said Scrooge, with an interest he had never felt before, "tell me if Tiny Tim will live."

"I see a vacant seat," replied the Ghost, "in the poor chimney-corner, and a crutch without an owner, carefully preserved. If these shadows remain unaltered by the Future, the child will die."

"No, no," said Scrooge. "Oh, no, kind Spirit! say he will be spared."

"If these shadows remain unaltered by the Future, none other of my race," returned the Ghost, "will find him here. What then? If he be like to die, he had better do it, and decrease the surplus population."

Scrooge hung his head to hear his own words quoted by the Spirit, and was overcome with penitence and grief.

"Man," said the Ghost, "if man you be in heart, not adamant, forbear that wicked cant[7] until you have discovered What the surplus is, and Where it is. Will you decide what men shall live, what men shall die? It may be, that in the sight of Heaven, you are more worthless and less fit to live than millions like this poor man's child. Oh God! to hear the insect on the leaf pronouncing on the too much life among his hungry brothers in the dust!"

Scrooge bent before the Ghost's rebuke, and, trembling, cast his eyes upon the ground. But he raised them speedily, on hearing his own name.

"Mr. Scrooge!" said Bob; "I'll give you Mr. Scrooge, the Founder of the Feast!"

"The Founder of the Feast indeed!" cried Mrs. Cratchit, reddening. "I wish I had him here. I'd give him a piece of my mind to feast upon, and I hope he'd have a good appetite for it."

"My dear," said Bob, "the children! Christmas Day."

"It should be Christmas Day, I am sure," said she, "on which one drinks the health of such an odious, stingy, hard, unfeeling man as Mr. Scrooge. You know he is, Robert! Nobody knows it better than you do, poor fellow!"

"My dear," was Bob's mild answer, "Christmas Day."

"I'll drink his health for your sake, and the Day's," said Mrs. Cratchit, "not for his. Long life to him! A merry Christmas and a happy New Year! He'll be very merry and very happy, I have no doubt!"

The children drank the toast after her. It was the first of their proceedings which had no heartiness in it. Tiny Tim drank it last of all, but he didn't care twopence for it. Scrooge was the Ogre of the family. The mention of his name cast a dark shadow on the party, which was not dispelled for full five minutes.

After it had passed away, they were ten times merrier than before, from the mere relief of Scrooge the Baleful[8] being done with. Bob Cratchit told them how he had a situation in his eye for Master Peter, which would bring in, if obtained, full five-and-sixpence weekly. The two young Cratchits laughed tremendously at the idea of Peter's being a man of business; and Peter himself looked thoughtfully at the fire from between his collars, as if he were deliberating what particular investments he should favor when he came into the receipt of that bewildering income. Martha, who was a poor apprentice at a milliner's, then told them what kind of work she had to do, and how many hours she worked at a stretch, and how she meant to lie abed tomorrow morning for a good long rest, tomorrow being a holiday she passed at home. Also how she had seen a countess and a lord some days before, and how the lord "was much about as tall as Peter"; at which Peter pulled up his collars so high that you couldn't have seen his head if you had been there. All this time the chestnuts and the jug went round and round, and by the by they had a song, about a lost child traveling in the snow, from Tiny Tim, who had a plaintive little voice, and sang it very well indeed.

There was nothing of high mark in this. They were not a handsome family, they were not well dressed, their shoes were far from being waterproof, their clothes were scanty, and Peter might have known, and very likely did, the inside of a pawnbroker's. But they were happy, grateful, pleased with one another, and contented with the time, and when they faded, and looked happier yet in the bright sprinklings of the Spirit's torch at parting, Scrooge had his eye upon them, especially on Tiny Tim, until the last.

By this time it was getting dark, and snowing pretty heavily; and as Scrooge and the Spirit went along the streets, the brightness of the roaring fires in kitchens, parlors, and all sorts of rooms, was wonderful. Here, the flickering of the blaze showed preparations for a cozy dinner, with hot plates baking through and through before the fire, and deep-red curtains, ready to be drawn to shut out cold and darkness. There, all the children of the house were running out into the snow to meet their married sisters, brothers, cousins, uncles, aunts, and be the first to greet them. Here, again, were shadows on the window-blind of guests assembling; and there a group of handsome girls, all hooded and fur-booted, and all chattering at once, tripped lightly off to some near neighbor's house, where woe upon the single man who saw them enter — artful witches! well they knew it — in a glow.

But, if you had judged from the numbers of people on their way to friendly gatherings, you might have thought that no one was at home to give them welcome when they got there, instead of every house expecting company, and piling up its fires half-chimney high. Blessings on it, how the Ghost exulted! How it bared its breadth of breast, and opened its capacious palm, and floated on, outpouring, with a generous hand, its bright and harmless mirth on everything within its reach! The very lamplighter, who ran on before, dotting the dusky street with specks of light, and who was dressed to spend the evening somewhere, laughed out loudly as the Spirit passed, though little kenned[9] the lamplighter that he had any company but Christmas!

And now, without a word of warning from the Ghost, they stood upon a bleak and desert moor, where monstrous masses of rude stone were cast about, as though it were the burial-place of giants, and water spread itself wheresoever it listed,[10] or would have done so but for the frost that held it prisoner, and nothing grew but moss and furze and coarse, rank grass. Down in the west the setting sun had left a streak of fiery red, which glared upon the desolation for an instant, like a sullen eye, and frowning lower, lower, lower yet, was lost in the thick gloom of darkest night.

"What place is this?" asked Scrooge.

"A place where miners live, who labor in the bowels of the earth," returned the Spirit. "But they know me. See!"

A light shone from the window of a hut, and swiftly they advanced towards it. Passing through the wall of mud and stone, they found a cheerful company assembled round a glowing fire. An old, old man and woman, with their children and their children's children, and another generation beyond that, all decked out gaily in their holiday attire. The old man, in a voice that seldom rose above the howling of the wind upon the barren waste, was singing them a Christmas song — it had been a very old song when he was a boy — and from time to time they all joined in the chorus. So surely as they raised their voices, the old man got quite blithe[11] and loud; and so surely as they stopped, his vigor sank again.

The Spirit did not tarry here, but bade Scrooge hold his robe, and, passing on above the moor, sped — whither? Not to sea? To sea. To Scrooge's horror, looking back, he saw the last of the land, a frightful range of rocks, behind them; and his ears were deafened by the thundering of water, as it rolled, and roared, and raged among the dreadful caverns it had worn, and fiercely tried to undermine the earth.

Built upon a dismal reef of sunken rocks, some leagues or so from the shore, on which the waters chafed and dashed, the wild year through, there stood a solitary lighthouse. Great heaps of seaweed clung to its base, and storm-birds — born of the wind one might suppose, as seaweed of the water — rose and fell about it, like the waves they skimmed.

But even here, two men who watched the light had made a fire, that through the loophole in the thick stone wall shed out a ray of brightness on the awful sea. Joining their horny hands over the rough table at which they sat, they wished each other Merry Christmas in their can of grog; and one of them, the elder, too, with his face all damaged and scarred with hard weather, as the figurehead of an old ship might be, struck up a sturdy song that was like a gale in itself.

Again the Ghost sped on, above the black and heaving sea —on, on — until, being far away, as he told Scrooge, from any shore, they lighted on a ship. They stood beside the helmsman at the wheel, the lookout in the bow, the officers who had the watch, dark, ghostly figures in their several stations, but every man among them hummed a Christmas tune, or had a Christmas thought, or spoke below his breath to his companion of some bygone Christmas Day, with homeward hopes belonging to it. And every man on board, waking or sleeping, good or bad, had had a kinder word for another on that day than on any day in the year, and had shared to some extent in its festivities, and had remembered those he cared for at a distance, and had known that they delighted to remember him.

It was a great surprise to Scrooge, while listening to the moaning of the wind, and thinking what a solemn thing it was to move on through the lonely darkness over an unknown abyss, whose depths were secrets as profound as death — it was a great surprise to Scrooge, while thus engaged, to hear a hearty laugh. It was a much greater surprise to Scrooge to recognize it as his own nephew's, and to find himself in a bright, dry, gleaming room, with the Spirit standing smiling by his side, and looking at that same nephew with approving affability!

"Ha, ha!" laughed Scrooge's nephew. "Ha, ha, ha!"

If you should happen, by any unlikely chance, to know a man more blessed in a laugh than Scrooge's nephew, all I can say is, I should like to know him too. Introduce him to me, and I'll cultivate his acquaintance.

It is a fair, even-handed, noble adjustment of things, that, while there is infection in disease and sorrow, there is nothing in the world so irresistibly contagious as laughter and good humor. When Scrooge's nephew laughed in this way — holding his sides, rolling his head, and twisting his face into the most extravagant contortions — Scrooge's niece, by marriage, laughed as heartily as he. And their assembled friends being not a bit behindhand, roared out, lustily.

"Ha, ha! Ha, ha, ha, ha!"

"He said that Christmas was a humbug, as I live!" cried Scrooge's nephew. "He believed it, too!"

"More shame for him, Fred!" said Scrooge's niece, indignantly. Bless those women; they never do anything by halves. They are always in earnest.

She was very pretty, exceedingly pretty. With a dimpled, surprised-looking, capital face; a ripe little mouth, that seemed made to be kissed — as no doubt it was; all kinds of good little dots about her chin, that melted into one another when she laughed; and the sunniest pair of eyes you ever saw in any little creature's head. Altogether she was what you would have called provoking, you know, but satisfactory, too. Oh, perfectly satisfactory!

"He's a comical old fellow," said Scrooge's nephew, "that's the truth; and not so pleasant as he might be. However, his offenses carry their own punishment, and I have nothing to say against him."

"I'm sure he is very rich, Fred," hinted Scrooge's niece. "At least you always tell *me* so."

"What of that, my dear!" said Scrooge's nephew. "His wealth is of no use to him. He doesn't do any good with it. He doesn't make himself comfortable with it. He hasn't the satisfaction of thinking — ha, ha, ha! — that he is ever going to benefit us with it."

"I have no patience with him," observed Scrooge's niece. Scrooge's niece's sisters, and all the other ladies, expressed the same opinion.

"Oh, I have!" said Scrooge's nephew. "I am sorry for him; I couldn't be angry with him if I tried. Who suffers by his ill whims? Himself, always. Here, he takes it into his head to dislike us, and he won't come and dine with us. What's the consequence? He doesn't lose much of a dinner."

"Indeed, I think he loses a very good dinner," interrupted Scrooge's niece. Everybody else said the same, and they must be allowed to have been competent judges, because they had just had dinner, and, with the dessert upon the table, were clustered round the fire, by lamplight.

"Well! I am very glad to hear it," said Scrooge's nephew,

"because I haven't any great faith in these young housekeepers. What do *you* say, Topper?"

Topper had clearly got his eye upon one of Scrooge's niece's sisters, for he answered that a bachelor was a wretched outcast, who had no right to express an opinion on the subject. Whereat Scrooge's niece's sister — the plump one with the lace tucker, not the one with the roses — blushed.

"Do go on, Fred," said Scrooge's niece, clapping her hands. "He never finishes what he begins to say! He is such a ridiculous fellow!"

Scrooge's nephew reveled in another laugh, and as it was impossible to keep the infection off, though the plump sister tried hard to do it with aromatic vinegar, his example was unanimously followed.

"I was only going to say," said Scrooge's nephew, "that the consequence of his taking a dislike to us, and not making merry with us, is, as I think, that he loses some pleasant moments, which could do him no harm. I am sure he loses pleasanter companions than he can find in his own thoughts, either in his moldy old office, or his dusty chambers. I mean to give him the same chance every year, whether he likes it or not, for I pity him. He may rail at Christmas till he dies, but he can't help thinking better of it — I defy him — if he finds me going there, in good temper, year after year, and saying, 'Uncle Scrooge, how are you?' If it only puts him in the vein to leave his poor clerk fifty pounds, *that's* something; and I think I shook him, yesterday."

It was their turn to laugh now, at the notion of his shaking Scrooge. But being thoroughly good-natured, and not much caring what they laughed at, so that they laughed at any rate, he encouraged them in their merriment, and passed the bottle, joyously.

After tea, they had some music. For they were a musical family, and knew what they were about when they sung a glee or catch, I can assure you: especially Topper, who could growl away in the bass like a good one, and never swell the large veins in his forehead, or get red in the face over it. Scrooge's niece played well upon the harp, and played, among other tunes, a simple little air (a mere nothing: you might learn to whistle it in two minutes) which had been familiar to the child who fetched Scrooge from the boarding-school, as he had been reminded by the Ghost of Christmas Past. When this strain of music sounded, all the things that Ghost had shown him came upon his mind; he softened more and more, and thought that if he could have listened to it often, years ago, he might have cultivated the kindnesses of life for his own happiness with his own hands, without resorting to the sexton's spade that buried Jacob Marley.

But they didn't devote the whole evening to music. After a while they played at forfeits; for it is good to be children sometimes, and never better than at Christmas, when its mighty Founder was a child himself. Stop! There was first a game at blindman's buff. Of course there was. And I no more believe Topper was really blind than I believe he had eyes in his boots. My opinion is, that it was a done thing between him and Scrooge's nephew, and that the Ghost of Christmas Present knew it. The way he went after that plump sister in the lace tucker was an outrage on the credulity of human nature. Knocking down the fire-irons, tumbling over the chairs, bumping up against the piano, smothering himself among the curtains, wherever she went, there went he! He always knew where the plump sister was. He wouldn't catch anybody else. If you had fallen up against him, as some of them did, and stood there, he would have made a feint of endeavoring to seize you, which would have been an affront to your understanding, and would instantly have sidled off in the direction of the plump sister. She often cried out that it wasn't fair, and it really was not. But when at last he caught her — when, in spite of all her silken rustlings, and her rapid flutterings past him, he got her into a corner whence there was no escape — then his conduct was the most execrable.[12] For his pretending not to know her, his pretending that it was necessary to touch her head-dress, and further to assure himself of her identity by pressing a certain ring upon her finger, and a certain chain about her neck, was vile, monstrous! No doubt she told him her opinion of it, when, another blind man being in office, they were so very confidential together, behind the curtains.

Scrooge's niece was not of the blindman's buff party, but was made comfortable with a large chair and a footstool, in a snug corner, where the Ghost and Scrooge were close behind her. But she joined in the forfeits, and loved her love to admiration with all the letters of the alphabet. Likewise at the game of How, When, and Where, she was very great, and, to the secret joy of Scrooge's nephew, beat her sisters hollow, though they were sharp girls too, as Topper could have told you. There might have been twenty people there, young and old, but they all played, and so did Scrooge; for, wholly forgetting in the interest he had in what was going on, that his voice made no sound in their ears, he sometimes came out with his guess quite loud, and very often guessed right, too; for the sharpest needle, best Whitechapel, warranted not to cut in the eye, was not sharper than Scrooge, blunt as he took it in his head to be.

The Ghost was greatly pleased to find him in this mood, and looked upon him with such favor that he begged like a boy to be allowed to stay until the guests departed. But this the Spirit said could not be done.

"Here is a new game," said Scrooge. "One half-hour, Spirit, only one!"

It was a game called Yes and No, where Scrooge's nephew had to think of something, and the rest must find out what, he only answering to their questions yes or no as the case was. The brisk fire of questioning to which he was exposed, elicited from him that he was thinking of an animal, a live animal, rather a disagreeable animal, a savage animal, an animal that growled and grunted sometimes, and talked sometimes, and lived in London, and walked about the streets, and wasn't made a show of, and wasn't led by anybody, and didn't live in a menagerie, and was never killed in a market, and was not a horse, or an ass, or a cow, or a bull, or a tiger, or a dog, or a pig, or a cat, or a bear. At every fresh question that was put to him, this nephew burst into a fresh roar of laughter, and was so inexpressibly tickled, that he was obliged to get up off the sofa and stamp. At last the plump sister, falling into a similar state, cried out:

"I have found it out! I know what it is, Fred! I know what it is!"

"What is it?" cried Fred.

"It's your Uncle Scro-o-o-o-oge!"

Which it certainly was. Admiration was the universal sentiment, though some objected that the reply to "Is it a bear?" ought to have been "Yes," inasmuch as an answer in the negative was sufficient to have diverted their thoughts from Mr. Scrooge, supposing they had ever had any tendency that way.

"He has given us plenty of merriment, I am sure," said Fred, "and it would be ungrateful not to drink his health. Here is a glass of mulled wine ready to our hand at the moment, and I say, 'Uncle Scrooge!'"

"Well! Uncle Scrooge!" they cried.

"A merry Christmas and a happy New Year to the old man, whatever he is!" said Scrooge's nephew. "He wouldn't take it from me, but may he have it, nevertheless. Uncle Scrooge!"

Uncle Scrooge had imperceptibly become so gay and light of heart, that he would have pledged the unconscious company in return, and thanked them in an inaudible speech, if the Ghost had given him time. But the whole scene passed off in the breath of the last word spoken by his nephew; and he and the Spirit were again upon their travels.

Much they saw, and far they went, and many homes they visited, but always with a happy end. The Spirit stood beside sick-beds, and they were cheerful; on foreign lands, and they were close at home; by struggling men, and they were patient in their greater hope; by poverty, and it was rich. In alms-house, hospital, and jail, in misery's every refuge, where vain man in his little brief authority had not made fast the door, and barred the Spirit out, he left his blessing, and taught Scrooge his precepts.

It was a long night, if it were only a night; but Scrooge had his doubts of this, because the Christmas holidays appeared to be condensed into the space of time they passed together. It was strange, too, that while Scrooge remained unaltered in his outward form, the Ghost grew older, clearly older. Scrooge had observed this change, but never spoke of it, until they left a children's Twelfth Night party, when, looking at the Spirit as they stood

together in an open place, he noticed that its hair was gray.

"Are spirits' lives so short?" asked Scrooge.

"My life upon this globe is very brief," replied the Ghost. "It ends tonight."

"Tonight!" cried Scrooge.

"Tonight at midnight. Hark! The time is drawing near."

The chimes were ringing the three quarters past eleven at that moment.

"Forgive me if I am not justified in what I ask," said Scrooge, looking intently at the Spirit's robe, "but I see something strange, and not belonging to yourself, protruding from your skirts. Is it a foot or a claw?"

"It might be a claw, for the flesh there is upon it," was the Spirit's sorrowful reply. "Look here."

From the foldings of its robe, it brought two children, wretched, abject, frightful, hideous, miserable. They knelt down at its feet, and clung upon the outside of its garment.

"O Man! look here! Look, look, down here!" exclaimed the Ghost.

They were a boy and a girl. Yellow, meager, ragged, scowling, wolfish; but prostrate,[13] too, in their humility. Where graceful youth should have filled their features out, and touched them with its freshest tints, a stale and shriveled hand, like that of age, had pinched, and twisted them, and pulled them into shreds. Where angels might have sat enthroned, devils lurked, and glared out menacing. No change, no degradation, no perversion of humanity, in any grade, through all the mysteries of wonderful creation, has monsters half so horrible and dread.

Scrooge started back, appalled. Having them shown to him in this way, he tried to say they were fine children, but the words choked themselves, rather than be parties to a lie of such enormous magnitude.

"Spirit! are they yours?" Scrooge could say no more.

"They are Man's," said the Spirit, looking down upon them. "And they cling to me, appealing from their fathers. This boy is Ignorance. This girl is Want.[14] Beware them both, and all of their degree, but most of all beware this boy, for on his brow I see that written which is Doom, unless the writing be erased. Deny it!" cried the Spirit, stretching out its hand toward the city. "Slander those who tell it ye! Admit it for your factious[15] purposes, and make it worse! And bide the end!"

"Have they no refuge or resource?" cried Scrooge.

"Are there no prisons?" said the Spirit, turning on him for the last time with his own words. "Are there no workhouses?"

The bell struck Twelve.

Scrooge looked about him for the Ghost, and saw it not. As the last stroke ceased to vibrate, he remembered the prediction of old Jacob Marley, and, lifting up his eyes, beheld a solemn Phantom, draped and hooded, coming, like a mist along the ground, towards him.

[1] **spontaneous combustion:** bursting into flame without being lighted
[2] **brawn:** a jellied loaf or sausage made from different edible parts of a pig
[3] **bilious:** sick to one's stomach
[4] **carrying their dinners to the bakers' shops:** The poor used the bakers's ovens to cook their dinners on Sundays and on Christmas Day, when bakers were legally forbidden to bake.
[5] **pudding singing in the copper:** Plum pudding was wrapped in cloth and steamed in a vat called a "copper," which was also used to boil the laundry.
[6] **rallied Bob on his credulity:** teased Bob for being so easily fooled
[7] **cant:** familiar expressions repeated unthinkingly
[8] **Baleful:** threatening evil or harm
[9] **kenned:** knew
[10] **listed:** wished, chose
[11] **blithe:** merry
[12] **execrable:** detestable, hateful
[13] **prostrate:** kneeling
[14] **Want:** extreme poverty
[15] **factious:** producing disagreement

A CLOSER LOOK

1. How has seeing Tiny Tim changed Scrooge's attitude toward him?

2. The Spirit takes Scrooge to many places in which the people, though humble, are gaily celebrating Christmas. What does the Spirit want Scrooge to learn from this?

3. Setting the scene for the Christmas festivities at Scrooge's nephew's house, the narrator observes that "there is nothing in the world so irresistibly contagious as laughter and good humor." How is Scrooge's behavior in this scene an example of this?

4. At times the Spirit repeats Scrooge's own words to show him how faulty his attitudes have been. Find two examples in Stave Three.

STAVE FOUR

The Last of the Spirits

The Phantom slowly, gravely, silently, approached. When it came near him, Scrooge bent down upon his knee; for in the very air through which this spirit moved it seemed to scatter gloom and mystery.

It was shrouded in a deep black garment, which concealed its head, its face, its form, and left nothing of it visible save one outstretched hand. But for this it would have been difficult to detach its figure from the night, and separate it from the darkness by which it was surrounded.

He felt that it was tall and stately when it came beside him, and that its mysterious presence filled him with a solemn dread. He knew no more, for the Spirit neither spoke nor moved.

"I am in the presence of the Ghost of Christmas Yet to Come?" said Scrooge.

The Spirit answered not, but pointed onward with its hand.

"You are about to show me shadows of the things that have not happened, but will happen in the time before us," Scrooge pursued. "Is that so, Spirit?"

The upper portion of the garment was contracted for an instant in its folds, as if the Spirit had inclined its head. That was the only answer he received.

Although well used to ghostly company by this time, Scrooge feared the silent shape so much that his legs trembled beneath him, and he found that he could hardly stand when he prepared to follow it. The Spirit paused a moment, as if observing his condition, and giving him time to recover.

But Scrooge was all the worse for this. It thrilled him with a vague uncertain horror, to know that, behind the dusky shroud, there were ghostly eyes intently fixed upon him, while he, though he stretched his own to the utmost, could see nothing but a spectral hand and one great heap of black.

"Ghost of the Future!" he exclaimed, "I fear you more than any specter I have seen. But, as I know your purpose is to do me good, and as I hope to live to be another man from what I was, I am prepared to bear you company, and do it with a thankful heart. Will you not speak to me?"

It gave him no reply. The hand was pointed straight before them.

"Lead on!" said Scrooge. "Lead on! The night is waning fast, and it is precious time to me, I know. Lead on, Spirit!"

The Phantom moved away as it had come towards him. Scrooge followed in the shadow of its dress, which bore him up, he thought, and carried him along.

They scarcely seemed to enter the city; for the city rather seemed to spring up about them, and encompass them of its own act. But there they were, in the heart of it, on 'Change, amongst the merchants, who hurried up and down, and chinked the money in their pockets, and conversed in groups, and looked at their watches, and trifled thoughtfully with their great gold seals, and so forth, as Scrooge had seen them often.

The Spirit stopped beside one little knot of business men. Observing that the hand was pointed to them, Scrooge advanced to listen to their talk.

"No," said a great fat man with a monstrous chin, "I don't know much about it, either way. I only know he's dead."

"When did he die?" inquired another.

"Last night, I believe."

"Why, what was the matter with him?" asked a third, taking a vast quantity of snuff[1] out of a very large snuff-box. "I thought he'd never die."

"God knows," said the first, with a yawn.

"What has he done with his money?" asked a red-faced gentleman with a pendulous excrescence[2] on the end of his nose, that shook like the gills of a turkey-cock.

"I haven't heard," said the man with the large chin, yawning again. "Left it to his company, perhaps. He hasn't left it to *me*. That's all I know."

This pleasantry was received with a general laugh.

"It's likely to be a very cheap funeral," said the same speaker, "for, upon my life, I don't know of anybody to go to it. Suppose we make up a party and volunteer?"

"I don't mind going if a lunch is provided," observed the gentleman with the excrescence on his nose. "But I must be fed, if I make one."

Another laugh.

"Well, I am the most disinterested among you, after all," said the first speaker, "for I never wear black gloves, and I never eat lunch. But I'll offer to go, if anybody else will. When I come to think of it, I'm not at all sure that I wasn't his most particular friend; for we used to stop and speak whenever we met. Bye, bye!"

Speakers and listeners strolled away, and mixed with other groups. Scrooge knew the men, and looked towards the Spirit for an explanation.

The Phantom glided on into a street. Its finger pointed to two persons meeting. Scrooge listened again, thinking that the explanation might lie here.

He knew these men, also, perfectly. They were men of business, very wealthy, and of great importance. He had made a point always of standing well in their esteem — in a business point of view, that is, strictly in a business point of view.

"How are you?" said one.

"How are you?" returned the other.

"Well!" said the first. "Old Scratch has got his own at last, hey?"

"So I am told," returned the second. "Cold, isn't it?"

"Seasonable for Christmastime. You are not a skater, I suppose?"

"No. No. Something else to think of. Good morning!"

Not another word. That was their meeting, their conversation, and their parting.

Scrooge was at first inclined to be surprised that the Spirit should attach importance to conversations apparently so trivial; but feeling assured that they must have some hidden purpose, he set himself to consider what it was likely to be. They could scarcely be supposed to have any bearing on the death of Jacob, his old partner, for that was Past, and this Ghost's province was the Future. Nor could he think of anyone immediately connected with himself, to whom he could apply them. But nothing doubting that, to whomsoever they applied, they had some latent moral for his own improvement, he resolved to treasure up every word he heard, and everything he saw, and especially to observe the shadow of himself when it appeared. For he had an expectation that the conduct of his future self would give him the clue he missed, and would render the solution of these riddles easy.

He looked about in that very place for his own image; but another man stood in his accustomed corner, and, though the clock pointed to his usual time of day for being there, he saw no likeness of himself among the multitudes that poured in through the Porch. It gave him little surprise, however; for he had been revolving in his mind a change of life, and thought and hoped he saw his newborn resolutions carried out in this.

Quiet and dark, beside him stood the Phantom, with its outstretched hand. When he roused himself from his thoughtful quest, he fancied, from the turn of the hand and its situation in reference to himself, that the Unseen Eyes were looking at him keenly. It made him shudder, and feel very cold.

They left the busy scene, and went into an obscure part of the town, where Scrooge had never penetrated before, although he recognized its situation, and its bad repute. The ways were foul and narrow, the shops and houses wretched, the people half naked, drunken, slipshod, ugly. Alleys and archways, like so many cesspools, disgorged[3] their offenses of smell, and dirt, and life, upon the straggling streets; and the whole quarter reeked with crime, with filth, and misery.

Far in this den of infamous resort, there was a low-browed, beetling shop, below a pent-house roof, where iron, old rags, bottles, bones, and greasy offal[4] were bought. Upon the floor within were piled up heaps of rusty keys, nails, chains, hinges, files, scales, weights, and refuse iron of all kinds. Secrets that few would like to scrutinize were bred and hidden in mountains of unseemly rags, masses of corrupted fat, and sepulchers[5] of bones. Sitting in among the wares he dealt in, by a charcoal stove made of old bricks, was a gray-haired rascal, nearly seventy years of age, who had screened himself from the cold air without by a frowzy curtaining of miscellaneous tatters, hung upon a line, and smoked his pipe in all the luxury of calm retirement.

Scrooge and the Phantom came into the presence of this man, just as a woman with a heavy bundle slunk into the shop. But she had scarcely entered, when another woman, similarly laden, came in too; and she was closely followed by a man in faded black, who was no less startled by the sight of them, than they had been upon the recognition of each other. After a short period of blank astonishment, in which the old man with the pipe had joined them, they all three burst into a laugh.

"Let the charwoman alone to be the first!" cried she who had entered first. "Let the laundress alone to be the second, and let the undertaker's man alone to be the third. Look here, old Joe, here's a chance! If we haven't all three met here without meaning it!"

"You couldn't have met in a better place," said old Joe, removing his pipe from his mouth. "Come into the parlor. You were made free of it long ago, you know, and the other two ain't strangers. Stop till I shut the door of the shop. Ah! How it skreeks! There ain't such a rusty bit of metal in the place as its own hinges, I believe; and I'm sure there's no such old bones here as mine. Ha, ha! We're all suitable to our calling, we're well matched. Come into the parlor. Come into the parlor."

The parlor was the space behind the screen of rags. The old man raked the fire together with an old stair-rod, and having trimmed his smoky lamp (for it was night) with the stem of his pipe, put it in his mouth again.

While he did this, the woman who had already spoken threw her bundle on the floor and sat down in a flaunting manner on a stool, crossing her elbows on her knees, and looking with a bold defiance at the other two.

"What odds, then! What odds, Mrs. Dilber?" said the woman. "Every person has a right to take care of themselves. *He* always did!"

"That's true, indeed!" said the laundress. "No man more so."

"Why, then, don't stand staring as if you was afraid, woman! Who's the wiser? We're not going to pick holes in each other's coats, I suppose?"

"No, indeed!" said Mrs. Dilber and the man together. "We should hope not."

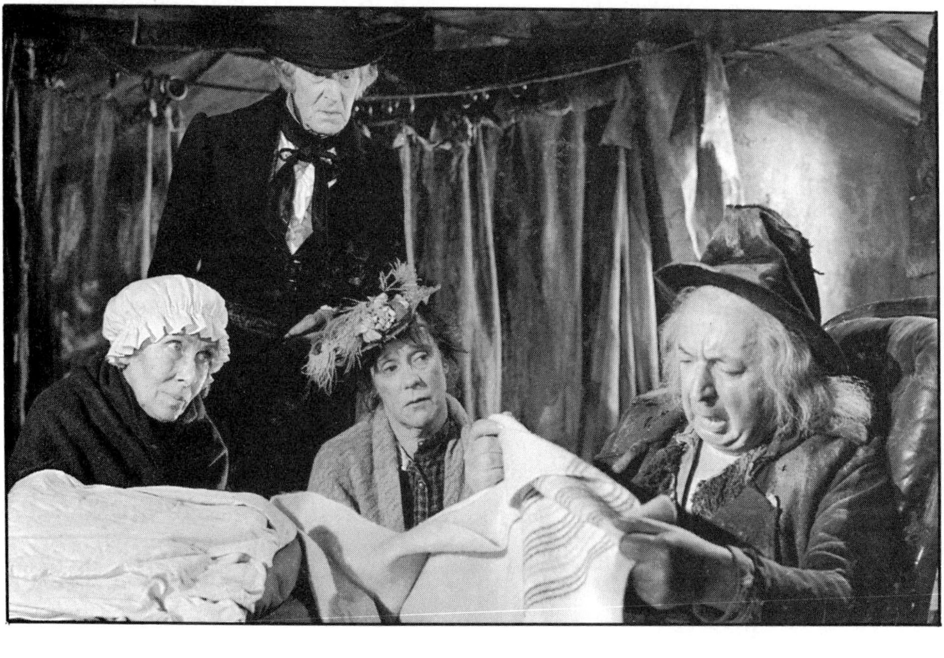

"Very well, then!" cried the woman. "That's enough. Who's the worse for the loss of a few things like these? Not a dead man, I suppose?"

"No, indeed," said Mrs. Dilber, laughing.

"If he wanted to keep 'em after he was dead, a wicked old screw," pursued the woman, "why wasn't he natural[6] in his lifetime? If he had been, he'd have had somebody to look after him when he was struck with Death, instead of lying gasping out his last there, alone by himself."

"It's the truest word that ever was spoke," said Mrs. Dilber. "It's a judgment on him."

"I wish it was a little heavier judgment," replied the woman; "and it should have been, you may depend upon it, if I could have laid my hands on anything else. Open that bundle, old Joe, and let me know the value of it. Speak out plain. I'm not afraid to be the first, nor afraid for them to see it. We knew pretty well that we were helping ourselves, before we met here, I believe. It's no sin. Open the bundle, Joe."

But the gallantry of her friends would not allow of this, and the man in faded black, mounting the breach first, produced *his* plunder.[7] It was not extensive. A seal or two, a pencil-case, a pair of sleeve-buttons, and a brooch of no great value, were all. They were severally examined and appraised by old Joe, who chalked the sums he was disposed to give for each upon the wall, and added them up into a total when he found that there was nothing more to come.

"That's your account," said Joe, "and I wouldn't give another sixpence, if I was to be boiled for not doing it. Who's next?"

Mrs. Dilber was next. Sheets and towels, a little wearing-apparel, two old-fashioned silver teaspoons, a pair of sugar tongs, and a few boots. Her account was stated on the wall in the same manner.

"I always give too much to ladies. It's a weakness of mine, and that's the way I ruin myself," said old Joe. "That's your account. If you asked me for another penny, and made it an open question, I'd repent of being so liberal, and knock off half-a-crown."

"And now undo *my* bundle, Joe," said the first woman.

Joe went down on his knees for the greater convenience of opening it, and, having unfastened a great many knots, dragged out a large and heavy roll of some dark stuff.

"What do you call this?" said Joe. "Bed-curtains!"

"Ah!" returned the woman, laughing and leaning forward on her crossed arms. "Bed-curtains!"

"You don't mean to say you took 'em down, rings and all, with him lying there?" said Joe.

"Yes I do," replied the woman. "Why not?"

"You were born to make your fortune," said Joe, "and you'll certainly do it."

"I certainly shan't hold my hand, when I can get anything in it by reaching it out, for the sake of such a man as He was, I promise you, Joe," returned the woman coolly. "Don't drop that oil upon the blankets, now."

"His blankets?" asked Joe.

"Whose else's do you think?" replied the woman. "He isn't likely to take cold without 'em, I dare say."

"I hope he didn't die of anything catching? Eh?" said old Joe, stopping in his work, and looking up.

"Don't you be afraid of that," returned the woman. "I ain't so fond of his company that I'd loiter about him for such things, if he did. Ah! You may look through that shirt till your eyes ache; but you won't find a hole in it, nor a threadbare place. It's the best he had, and a fine one too. They'd have wasted it, if it hadn't been for me."

"What do you call wasting of it?" asked old Joe.

"Putting it on him to be buried in, to be sure," replied the woman, with a laugh. "Somebody was fool enough to do it, but I took it off again. If calico ain't good enough for such a purpose, it isn't good enough for anything. It's quite as becoming to the body. He can't look uglier than he did in that one."

Scrooge listened to this dialogue in horror. As they sat grouped about their spoil,[8] in the scanty light afforded by the old man's lamp, he viewed them with a detestation and disgust, which could hardly have been greater, though they had been obscene demons, marketing the corpse itself.

"Ha, ha!" laughed the same woman, when old Joe, producing a flannel bag with money in it, told[9] out their several gains upon the ground. "This is the end of it, you see! He frightened every one away from him when he was alive, to profit us when he was dead! Ha, ha, ha!"

"Spirit!" said Scrooge, shuddering from head to foot. "I see, I see. The case of this unhappy man might be my own. My life tends that way, now. Merciful Heaven, what is this!"

He recoiled in terror, for the scene had changed, and now he almost touched a bed — a bare, uncurtained bed, on which, beneath a ragged sheet, there lay something covered up, which, though it was dumb, announced itself in awful language.

The room was very dark, too dark to be observed with any accuracy, though Scrooge glanced round it in obedience to a secret impulse, anxious to know what kind of room it was. A pale light, rising in the outer air, fell straight upon the bed; and on it, plundered and bereft, unwatched, unwept, uncared for, was the body of this man.

Scrooge glanced towards the Phantom. Its steady hand was pointed to the head. The cover was so carelessly adjusted that the slightest raising of it, the motion of a finger upon Scrooge's part, would have disclosed the face. He thought of it, felt how easy it would be to do, and longed to do it, but had no more power to withdraw the veil than to dismiss the specter at his side.

Oh cold, cold, rigid, dreadful Death, set up thine altar here, and dress it with such terrors as thou hast at thy command, for this is thy dominion! But of the loved, revered, and honored head, thou canst not turn one hair to thy dread purposes, or make one feature odious. It is not that the hand is heavy and will fall down when released; it is not that the heart and pulse are still; but that the hand WAS open, generous, and true, the heart brave, warm, and tender, and the pulse a man's. Strike, Shadow, strike! And see his good deeds springing from the wound, to sow the world with life immortal!

No voice pronounced these words in Scrooge's ears, and yet he heard them when he looked upon the bed. He thought, if this man could be raised up now, what would be his foremost thoughts? Avarice, hard dealing, griping cares? They have brought him to a rich end, truly!

He lay, in the dark empty house, with not a man, a woman, or a child to say he was kind to me in this or that, and for the memory of one kind word I will be kind to him. A cat was tearing at the door, and there was a sound of gnawing rats beneath the hearth-stone. What *they* wanted in the room of death, and why they were so restless and disturbed, Scrooge did not dare to think.

"Spirit!" he said, "this is a fearful place. In leaving it, I shall not leave its lesson, trust me. Let us go!"

Still the Ghost pointed with an unmoved finger to the head.

"I understand you," Scrooge returned, "and I would do it, if I could. But I have not the power, Spirit. I have not the power."

Again it seemed to look upon him.

"If there is any person in the town who feels emotion caused by this man's death," said Scrooge, quite agonized, "show that person to me, Spirit, I beseech you!"

The Phantom spread its dark robe before him for a moment, like a wing, and withdrawing it, revealed a room by daylight, where a mother and her children were.

She was expecting someone, and with anxious eagerness; for she walked up and down the room, started at every sound, looked out from the window, glanced at the clock, tried, but in vain, to work with her needle, and could hardly bear the voices of her children in their play.

At length the long-expected knock was heard. She hurried to the door, and met her husband, a man whose face was care-worn and depressed, though he was young. There was a remarkable expression in it now, a kind of serious delight of which he felt ashamed, and which he struggled to repress.

He sat down to the dinner that had been hoarding for him by the fire; and when she asked him faintly what news (which was not until after a long silence), he appeared embarrassed how to answer.

"Is it good," she said, "or bad?" — to help him.

"Bad," he answered.

"We are quite ruined?"

"No. There is hope yet, Caroline."

"If *he* relents,"[10] she said, amazed, "there is! Nothing is past hope, if such a miracle has happened."

"He is past relenting," said her husband. "He is dead."

She was a mild and patient creature, if her face spoke truth; but she was thankful in her soul to hear it, and she said so, with clasped hands. She prayed forgiveness the next moment, and was sorry; but the first was the emotion of her heart.

"What the half-drunken woman whom I told you of last night said to me, when I tried to see him and obtain a week's delay, and what I thought was a mere excuse to avoid me, turns out to have been quite true. He was not only very ill, but dying, then."

"To whom will our debt be transferred?"

"I don't know. But before that time we shall be ready with the money; and even though we were not, it would be bad fortune indeed to find so merciless a creditor in his successor. We may sleep tonight with light hearts, Caroline!"

Yes. Soften it as they would, their hearts were lighter. The children's faces, hushed and clustered round to hear what they so little understood, were brighter; and it was a happier house for this man's death! The only emotion that the Ghost could show him, caused by the event, was one of pleasure.

"Let me see some tenderness connected with a death," said Scrooge, "or that dark chamber, Spirit, which we left just now, will be forever present to me."

The Ghost conducted him through several streets familiar to his feet; and, as they went along, Scrooge looked here and there to find himself, but nowhere was he to be seen. They entered poor Bob Cratchit's house — the dwelling he had visited before — and found the mother and the children seated round the fire.

Quiet. Very quiet. The noisy little Cratchits were as still as statues in one corner, and sat looking up at Peter, who had a book before him. The mother and her daughters were engaged in sewing. But surely they were very quiet!

"'And He took a child, and set him in the midst of them.'"

Where had Scrooge heard those words? He had not dreamed them. The boy must have read them out, as he and the Spirit crossed the threshold. Why did he not go on?

The mother laid her work upon the table, and put her hand up to her face.

"The color hurts my eyes," she said.

The color? Ah, poor Tiny Tim!

"They're better now again," said Cratchit's wife. "It makes them weak by candlelight; and I wouldn't show weak eyes to your father when he comes home, for the world. It must be near his time."

"Past it, rather," Peter answered, shutting up his book. "But I think he has walked a little slower than he used, these few last evenings, mother."

They were very quiet again. At last she said, and in a steady cheerful voice, that only faltered once:

"I have known him walk with — I have known him walk with Tiny Tim upon his shoulder very fast indeed."

"And so have I," cried Peter. "Often."

"And so have I," exclaimed another. So had all.

"But he was very light to carry," she resumed, intent upon her work, "and his father loved him so, that it was no trouble — no trouble. And there is your father at the door!"

She hurried out to meet him, and little Bob in his comforter — he had need of it, poor fellow — came in. His tea was ready for him on the hob, and they all tried who should help him to it most. Then the two young Cratchits got upon his knees and laid, each child, a little cheek against his face, as if they said, "Don't mind it, father. Don't be grieved!"

Bob was very cheerful with them, and spoke pleasantly to all the family. He looked at the work upon the table, and praised the industry and speed of Mrs. Cratchit and the girls. They would be done long before Sunday, he said.

"Sunday! You went today then, Robert?" said his wife.

"Yes, my dear," returned Bob. "I wish you could have gone. It would have done you good to see how green a place it is. But you'll see it often. I promised him that I would walk there on a Sunday. My little, little child!" cried Bob. "My little child!"

He broke down all at once. He couldn't help it. If he could have helped it, he and his child would have been farther apart, perhaps, than they were.

He left the room, and went upstairs into the room above, which was lighted cheerfully, and hung with Christmas. There was a chair set close beside the child, and there were signs of someone having been there lately. Poor Bob sat down in it, and when he had thought a little and composed himself, he kissed the little face. He was reconciled to what had happened, and went down again quite happy.

They drew about the fire, and talked; the girls and mother working still. Bob told them of the extraordinary kindness of Mr. Scrooge's nephew, whom he had scarcely seen but once, and who, meeting him in the street that day, and seeing that he looked a little — "just a little down, you know," said Bob, inquired what had happened to distress him. "On which," said Bob, "for he is the pleasantest-spoken gentleman you ever heard, I told him. 'I am heartily sorry for it, Mr. Cratchit,' he said, 'and heartily sorry for your good wife.' By the by, how he ever knew *that,* I don't know."

"Knew what, my dear?"

"Why, that you were a good wife," replied Bob.

"Everybody knows that," said Peter.

"Very well observed, my boy!" cried Bob. "I hope they do. 'Heartily sorry,' he said, 'for your good wife. If I can be of service to you in any way,' he said, giving me his card, 'that's where I live. Pray come to me.' Now it wasn't," cried Bob, "for the sake of anything he might be able to do for us, so much as for his kind way, that this was quite delightful. It really seemed as if he had known our Tiny Tim, and felt with us."

"I'm sure he's a good soul!" said Mrs. Cratchit.

"You would be surer of it, my dear," returned Bob, "if you saw and spoke to him. I shouldn't be at all surprised, mark what I say, if he got Peter a better situation."

"Only hear that, Peter," said Mrs. Cratchit.

"And then," cried one of the girls, "Peter will be keeping company with someone, and setting up for himself."

"Get along with you!" retorted Peter, grinning.

"It's just as likely as not," said Bob, "one of these days, though there's plenty of time for that, my dear. But, however and whenever we part from one another, I am sure we shall none of us forget poor Tiny Tim — shall we — or this first parting that there was among us?"

"Never, father!" cried they all.

"And I know," said Bob, "I know, my dears, that when we recollect how patient and how mild he was, although he was a little, little child, we shall not quarrel easily among ourselves, and forget poor Tiny Tim in doing it."

"No, never, father!" they all cried again.

"I am very happy," said little Bob, "I am very happy!"

Mrs. Cratchit kissed him, his daughters kissed him, the two young Cratchits kissed him, and Peter and himself shook hands. Spirit of Tiny Tim, thy childish essence was from God!

"Specter," said Scrooge, "something informs me that our parting moment is at hand. I know it, but I know not how. Tell me what man that was whom we saw lying dead?"

The Ghost of Christmas Yet to Come conveyed him, as before — though at a different time, he thought; indeed, there seemed no order in these later visions, save that they were in the Future — into the resorts of business men, but showed him not himself. Indeed, the Spirit did not stay for anything, but went straight on, as to the end just now desired, until besought by Scrooge to tarry for a moment.

"This court," said Scrooge, "through which we hurry now, is where my place of occupation is, and has been for a length of time. I see the house. Let me behold what I shall be, in days to come!"

The Spirit stopped; the hand was pointed elsewhere.

"The house is yonder," Scrooge exclaimed. "Why do you point away?"

The inexorable[11] finger underwent no change.

Scrooge hastened to the window of his office, and looked in. It was an office still, but not his. The furniture was not the same, and the figure in the chair was not himself. The Phantom pointed as before.

He joined it once again, and, wondering why and whither he had gone, accompanied it until they reached an iron gate. He paused to look round before entering.

A churchyard. Here, then, the wretched man whose name he had now to learn, lay underneath the ground. It was a worthy place: walled in by houses; overrun by grass and weeds, the growth of vegetation's death, not life; choked up with too much burying; fat with repleted appetite. A worthy place!

The Spirit stood among the graves, and pointed down to One. He advanced towards it, trembling. The Phantom was exactly as it had been, but he dreaded that he saw new meaning in its solemn shape.

"Before I draw nearer to that stone to which you point," said Scrooge, "answer me one question. Are these the shadows of the things that *will* be, or are they shadows of the things that *may* be, only?"

Still the Ghost pointed downward to the grave by which it stood.

"Men's courses will foreshadow certain ends, to which, if persevered in, they must lead," said Scrooge. "But if the courses be departed from, the ends will change. Say it is thus with what you show me!"

The Spirit was immovable as ever.

Scrooge crept towards it, trembling as he went, and following the finger, read upon the stone of the neglected grave his own name, EBENEZER SCROOGE.

"Am *I* that man who lay upon the bed?" he cried, upon his knees.

The finger pointed from the grave to him, and back again.

"No, Spirit! Oh, no, no!"

The finger still was there.

"Spirit!" he cried, tight clutching at its robe, "hear me! I am not the man I was. I will not be the man I must have been but for this intercourse. Why show me this, if I am past all hope?"

For the first time the hand appeared to shake.

"Good Spirit," he pursued, as down upon the ground he fell before it, "your nature intercedes for me, and pities me. Assure me that I yet may change these shadows you have shown me, by an altered life!"

The kind hand trembled.

"I will honor Christmas in my heart, and try to keep it all the year. I will live in the Past, the Present, and the Future. The Spirits of all Three shall strive within me. I will not shut out the lessons that they teach. Oh, tell me I may sponge away the writing on this stone!"

In his agony, he caught the spectral hand. It sought to free itself, but he was strong in his entreaty, and detained it. The Spirit, stronger yet, repulsed him.

Holding up his hands in one last prayer to have his fate reversed, he saw an alteration in the Phantom's hood and dress. It shrunk, collapsed, and dwindled down into a bedpost.

[1] **snuff:** powdered tobacco that is inhaled through the nostrils
[2] **pendulous excrescence:** a hanging wart
[3] **disgorged:** poured forth; vomited
[4] **offal:** waste parts, especially of a butchered animal
[5] **sepulchers:** burial places; tombs
[6] **natural:** kinder, more human
[7] **plunder:** stolen goods, loot
[8] **spoil:** stolen goods, loot
[9] **told:** counted
[10] **relents:** becomes less harsh, gives in
[11] **inexorable:** not capable of being moved by persuasion; inflexible

A CLOSER LOOK

1. How do Scrooge's business acquaintances react to his death?

2. Why does the charwoman feel justified in stealing Scrooge's bed-curtains and other things? Find an example of a statement in which she justifies her actions.

3. When Scrooge asks to see anyone "who feels emotion caused by this man's death," the Spirit shows him the young couple who owe him money. What emotion do they feel?

STAVE FIVE

The End of It

Yes! And the bedpost was his own. The bed was his own, the room was his own. Best and happiest of all, the Time before him was his own, to make amends in!

"I will live in the Past, the Present, and the Future!" Scrooge repeated, as he scrambled out of bed. "The Spirits of all Three shall strive within me. O Jacob Marley! Heaven and the Christmastime be praised for this! I say it on my knees, old Jacob, on my knees!"

He was so fluttered and so glowing with his good intentions, that his broken voice would scarcely answer to his call. He had been sobbing violently in his conflict with the Spirit, and his face was wet with tears.

"They are not torn down," cried Scrooge, folding one of his bed-curtains in his arms, "they are not torn down, rings and all. They are here — I am here — the shadows of the things that would have been may be dispelled. They will be. I know they will!"

His hands were busy with his garments all this time: turning them inside out, putting them on upside down, tearing them, mislaying them, making them parties to every kind of extravagance.

"I don't know what to do!" cried Scrooge, laughing and crying in the same breath, and making a perfect Laocoön[1] of himself with his stockings. "I am as light as a feather, I am as happy as an angel, I am as merry as a schoolboy. I am as giddy as a drunken man. A merry Christmas to everybody! A happy New Year to all the world. Hallo here! Whoop! Hallo!"

He had frisked into the sitting room, and was now standing there, perfectly winded.

"There's the saucepan that the gruel was in!" cried Scrooge, starting off again, and going round the fireplace. "There's the door by which the Ghost of Jacob Marley entered! There's the corner where the Ghost of Christmas Present sat! There's the window where I saw the wandering Spirits! It's all right, it's all true, it all happened. Ha, ha, ha!"

Really, for a man who had been out of practice for so many years, it was a splendid laugh, a most illustrious laugh. The father of a long, long line of brilliant laughs.

"I don't know what day of the month it is!" said Scrooge. "I don't know how long I've been among the Spirits. I don't know anything. I'm quite a baby. Never mind. I don't care. I'd rather be a baby. Hallo! Whoop! Hallo here!"

He was checked in his transports by the churches ringing out the lustiest peals he had ever heard. Clash, clang, hammer, ding, dong, bell. Bell, dong, ding, hammer, clang, clash! Oh, glorious, glorious!

Running to the window, he opened it, and put out his head. No fog, no mist; clear, bright, jovial, stirring, cold; cold, piping for the blood to dance to; golden sunlight; heavenly sky; sweet fresh air; merry bells. Oh, glorious! Glorious!

"What's today?" cried Scrooge, calling downward to a boy in Sunday clothes, who perhaps had loitered in to look about him.

"EH?" returned the boy, with all his might of wonder.

"What's today, my fine fellow?" said Scrooge.

"Today!" replied the boy. "Why, CHRISTMAS DAY."

"It's Christmas Day!" said Scrooge to himself. "I haven't missed it. The Spirits have done it all in one night. They can do anything they like. Of course they can. Of course they can. Hallo, my fine fellow!"

"Hallo!" returned the boy.

"Do you know the poulterer's, in the next street but one, at the corner?" Scrooge inquired.

"I should hope I did," replied the lad.

"An intelligent boy!" said Scrooge. "A remarkable boy! Do you know whether they've sold the prize Turkey that was hanging up there? Not the little prize Turkey, the big one?"

"What, the one as big as me?" returned the boy.

"What a delightful boy!" said Scrooge. "It's a pleasure to talk to him. Yes, my buck!"

"It's hanging there now," replied the boy.

"Is it?" said Scrooge. "Go and buy it."

"Walk-ER!"[2] exclaimed the boy.

"No, no," said Scrooge, "I am in earnest. Go and buy it, and tell 'em to bring it here, that I may give them the directions where to take it. Come back with the man, and I'll give you a shilling. Come back with him in less than five minutes, and I'll give you half-a-crown!"

The boy was off like a shot. He must have had a steady hand at a trigger who could have got a shot off half so fast.

"I'll send it to Bob Cratchit's!" whispered Scrooge, rubbing his hands, and splitting with a laugh. "He shan't know who sends it. It's twice the size of Tiny Tim. Joe Miller never made such a joke as sending it to Bob's will be!"

The hand in which he wrote the address was not a steady one, but write it he did, somehow, and went downstairs to open the street door, ready for the coming of the poulterer's man. As he stood there, waiting his arrival, the knocker caught his eye.

"I shall love it, as long as I live!" cried Scrooge, patting it with his hand. "I scarcely ever looked at it before. What an honest expression it has in its face! It's a wonderful knocker! — Here's the Turkey. Hallo! Whoop! How are you? Merry Christmas!"

It *was* a Turkey! He never could have stood upon his legs, that bird. He would have snapped 'em short off in a minute, like sticks of sealing wax.

"Why, it's impossible to carry that to Camden Town," said Scrooge. "You must have a cab."

The chuckle with which he said this, and the chuckle with which he paid for the Turkey, and the chuckle with which he paid for the cab, and the chuckle with which he recompensed[3] the boy were only to be exceeded by the chuckle with which he sat down breathless in his chair again, and chuckled till he cried.

Shaving was not an easy task, for his hand continued to shake very much, and shaving requires attention, even when you don't dance while you are at it. But if he had cut the end of his nose off, he would have put a piece of sticking-plaster over it, and been quite satisfied.

He dressed himself "all in his best," and at last got out into the streets. The people were by this time pouring forth, as he had seen them with the Ghost of Christmas Present; and walking with his hands behind him, Scrooge regarded everyone with a delighted smile. He looked so irresistibly pleasant, in a word, that three or four good-humored fellows said, "Good morning, sir! A merry Christmas to you!" And Scrooge said often afterwards, that of all the blithe sounds he had ever heard, those were the blithest in his ears.

He had not gone far, when, coming on towards him he beheld the portly gentleman who had walked into his counting-house the day before and said, "Scrooge and Marley's, I believe?" It sent a pang across his heart to think how this old gentleman would look upon him when they met; but he knew what path lay straight before him, and he took it.

"My dear sir," said Scrooge, quickening his pace, and taking the old gentleman by both his hands. "How do you do? I hope you succeeded yesterday. It was very kind of you. A merry Christmas to you, sir!"

"Mr. Scrooge?"

"Yes," said Scrooge. "That is my name, and I fear it may not be pleasant to you. Allow me to ask your pardon. And will you have the goodness" — here Scrooge whispered in his ear.

"Lord bless me!" cried the gentleman, as if his breath were gone. "My dear Mr. Scrooge, are you serious?"

"If you please," said Scrooge. "Not a farthing less. A great many back-payments are included in it, I assure you. Will you do me that favor?"

"My dear sir," said the other, shaking hands with him, "I don't know what to say to such munifi—"[4]

"Don't say anything, please," retorted Scrooge. "Come and see me. Will you come and see me?"

"I will!" cried the old gentleman. And it was clear he meant to do it.

"Thank'ee," said Scrooge. "I am much obliged to you. I thank you fifty times. Bless you!"

He went to church, and walked about the streets, and watched the people hurrying to and fro, and patted children on the head, and questioned beggars, and looked down into the kitchens of houses, and up to the windows, and found that everything could yield him pleasure. He had never dreamed that any walk — that anything — could give him so much happiness. In the afternoon, he turned his steps towards his nephew's house.

He passed the door a dozen times, before he had the courage to go up and knock. But he made a dash, and did it:

"Is your master home, my dear?" said Scrooge to the girl. Nice girl! Very.

"Yes, sir."

"Where is he, my love?" said Scrooge.

"He's in the dining room, along with mistress. I'll show you upstairs, if you please."

"Thank'ee. He knows me," said Scrooge, with his hand already on the dining-room lock. "I'll go in here, my dear."

He turned it gently, and sidled his face in, round the door. They were looking at the table (which was spread out in great array); for these young housekeepers are always nervous on such points, and like to see that everything is right.

"Fred!" said Scrooge.

Dear heart alive, how his niece by marriage started! Scrooge had forgotten, for the moment, about her sitting in the corner with the footstool, or he wouldn't have done it, on any account.

"Why bless my soul!" cried Fred, "who's that?"

"It's I. Your uncle Scrooge. I have come to dinner. Will you let me in, Fred?"

Let him in! It is a mercy he didn't shake his arm off. He was at home in five minutes. Nothing could be heartier. His niece looked

just the same. So did Topper when *he* came. So did the plump sister when *she* came. So did everyone when *they* came. Wonderful party, wonderful games, wonderful unanimity, won-der-ful happiness!

But he was early at the office next morning. Oh he was early there. If he could only be there first, and catch Bob Cratchit coming late! That was the thing he had set his heart upon.

And he did it, yes he did! The clock struck nine. No Bob. A quarter past. No Bob. He was full eighteen minutes and a half behind his time. Scrooge sat with his door wide open, that he might see him come into the tank.

His hat was off before he opened the door, his comforter, too. He was on his stool in a jiffy, driving away his pen, as if he were trying to overtake nine o'clock.

"Hallo!" growled Scrooge, in his accustomed voice as near as he could feign[5] it. "What do you mean by coming here at this time of day?"

"I am very sorry, sir," said Bob. "I *am* behind my time."

"You are?" replied Scrooge. "Yes. I think you are. Step this way, if you please."

"It's only once a year, sir," pleaded Bob, appearing from the tank. "It shall not be repeated. I was making rather merry yesterday, sir."

"Now, I'll tell you what, my friend," said Scrooge, "I am not going to stand this sort of thing any longer. And therefore," he continued, leaping from his stool, and giving Bob such a dig in the waistcoat that he staggered back into the tank again — "and therefore, I am about to raise your salary!"

Bob trembled, and got a little nearer to the ruler. He had a momentary idea of knocking Scrooge down with it, holding him, and calling to the people in the court for help and a straight-waistcoat.[6]

"A merry Christmas, Bob!" said Scrooge, with an earnestness that could not be mistaken, as he clapped him on the back. "A merrier Christmas, Bob, my good fellow, than I have given you for many a year! I'll raise your salary, and endeavor to assist your struggling family, and we will discuss your affairs this very afternoon, over a Christmas bowl of smoking bishop, Bob! Make up the fires, and buy another coal-scuttle before you dot another *i*, Bob Cratchit!"

Scrooge was better than his word. He did it all, and infinitely more; and to Tiny Tim, who did NOT die, he was a second father. He became as good a friend, as good a master, and as good a man as the good old city knew, or any other good old city, town, or borough in the good old world. Some people laughed to see the alteration in him, but he let them laugh, and little heeded them; for he was wise enough to know that nothing ever happened on this globe, for good, at which some people did not have their fill of laughter in the outset; and knowing that such as these would be blind anyway, he thought it quite as well that they should wrinkle up their eyes in grins, as have the malady in less attractive forms. His own heart laughed, and that was quite enough for him.

He had no further intercourse with Spirits, but lived upon the Total Abstinence Principle ever afterwards; and it was always said of him, that he knew how to keep Christmas well, if any man alive possessed the knowledge. May that be truly said of us, and all of us! And so, as Tiny Tim observed, God Bless Us, Every One!

[1] **Laocoön:** According to Greek mythology, Laocoön was a Trojan priest who was strangled to death with his two sons by huge sea serpents. Dickens had probably seen copies of the famous sculpture in the Vatican of Laocoön and his sons tangled in the serpents' coils.

[2] **Walk-ER:** a cockney expression of the day indicating surprise or disbelief

[3] **recompensed:** paid

[4] **munifi—:** The gentleman was going to say *munificence,* which means "great generosity."

[5] **feign:** fake, pretend

[6] **straight-waistcoat:** a straitjacket: a jacketlike garment used to bind the arms of a violent person

A CLOSER LOOK

1. Why does Scrooge say he will love the knocker as long as he lives?

2. What is the significance of the fact that Scrooge chuckles as he pays for the turkey and the cab, and as he pays the boy for his work?

3. What specific actions does Scrooge take to make amends for his previous behavior? Give three examples.

The photographs used to illustrate **Dr. Jekyll and Mr. Hyde** *are stills from the 1932 version of the movie, starring Fredric March. You will notice that March wears heavy make-up to make Mr. Hyde look physically hideous.*

Robert Louis Stevenson

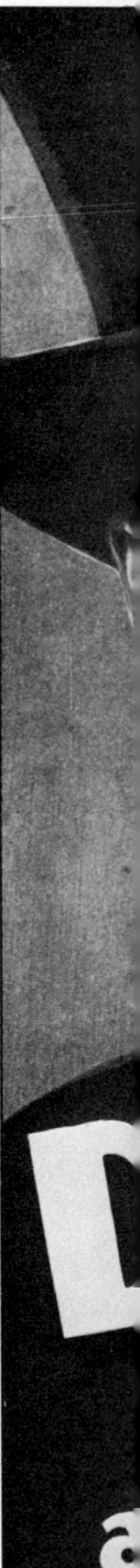

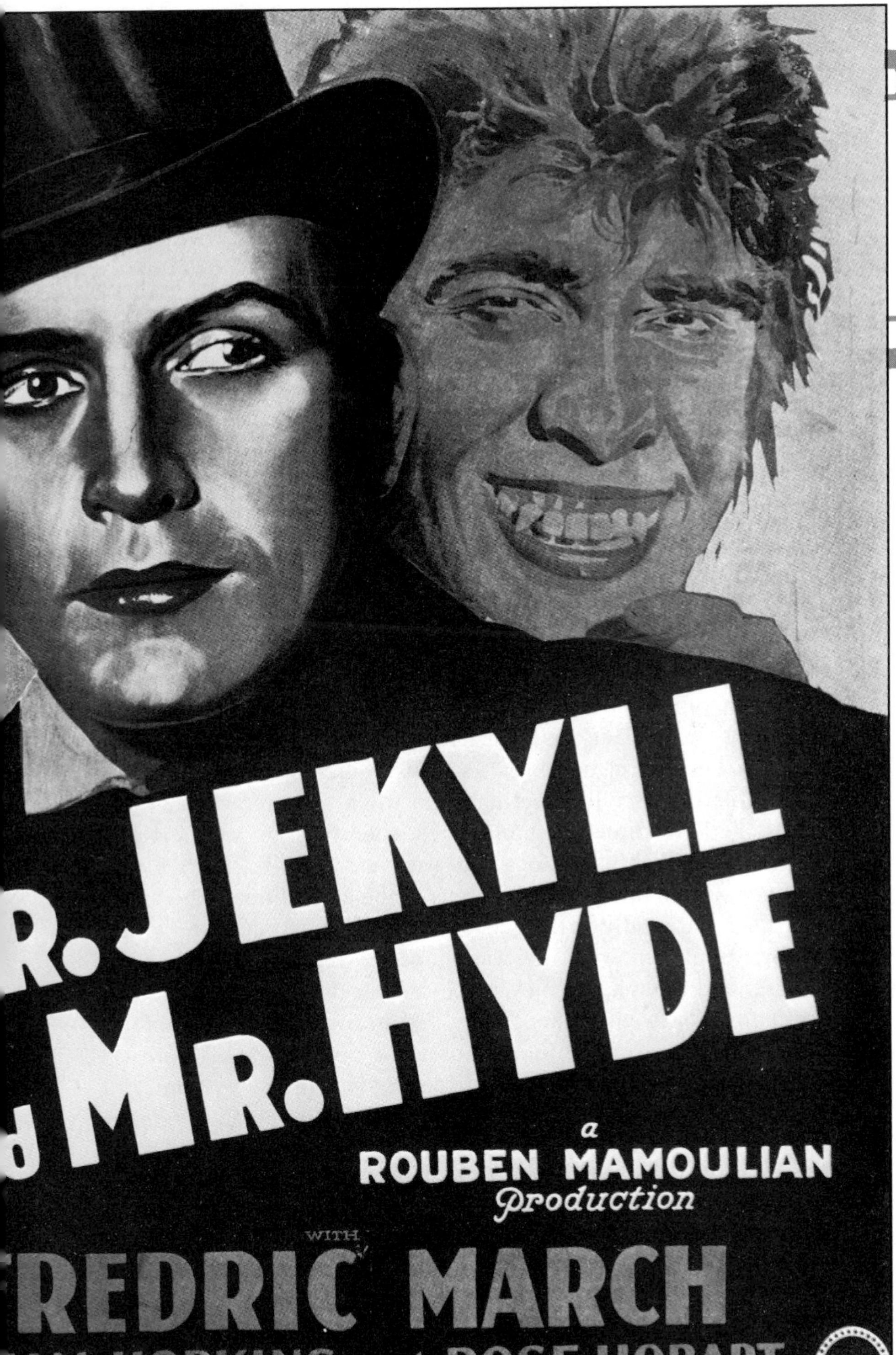
R. JEKYLL
d MR. HYDE
a
ROUBEN MAMOULIAN
Production
WITH
REDRIC MARCH
IAM HOPKINS and ROSE HOBART

• This famous novel by Robert Louis Stevenson tells the story of Dr. Henry Jekyll, a man who maintains a wholesome life-style and an impeccable reputation. The doctor is well liked and well respected—that is, until his name is mysteriously linked with that of Edward Hyde, a character known for his cruelty and depravity.

Robert Louis Stevenson

DR. JEKYLL AND MR. HYDE

CHAPTER ONE

Story of the Door

MR. UTTERSON THE LAWYER WAS A MAN OF A rugged countenance that was never lighted by a smile; cold, scanty and embarrassed in discourse;[1] backward in sentiment; lean, long, dusty, dreary, and yet somehow lovable. At friendly meetings, and when the wine was to his taste, something eminently human beaconed from his eye; something indeed which never found its way into his talk, but which spoke not only in these silent symbols of the after-dinner face, but more often and loudly in the acts of his life. He was austere[2] with himself; drank gin when he was alone, to mortify[3] a taste for vintages; and though he enjoyed the theater, had not crossed the doors of one for twenty years. But he had an approved tolerance for others; sometimes wondering, almost with envy, at the high pressure of spirits involved in their misdeeds; and in any extremity[4] inclined to help rather than to reprove.[5] "I incline to Cain's heresy,"[6] he used to say quaintly: "I let my brother go to the devil in his own way." In this character, it was frequently his fortune to be the last reputable acquaintance and the last good influence in the lives of downgoing men. And to such as these, so long as they came about his chambers, he never marked a shade of change in his demeanor.[7]

No doubt the feat was easy to Mr. Utterson; for he was undemonstrative at the best, and even his friendships seemed to be founded in a similar catholicity[8] of good nature. It is the mark of a modest man to accept his friendly circle ready-made from the hands of opportunity, and that was the lawyer's way. His friends were those of his own blood, or those whom he had known the longest; his affections, like ivy, were the growth of time, they implied no aptness in the object. Hence, no doubt, the bond that united him to Mr. Richard Enfield, his distant kinsman, the well-known man about town. It was a nut to crack for many, what these two could see in each other, or what subject they could find in common. It was reported by those who encountered them in their Sunday walks that they said nothing, looked singularly dull, and would hail with obvious relief the appearance of a friend. For all that, the two men put the greatest store by these excursions, counted them the chief jewel of each week, and not only set aside occasions of pleasure but even resisted the calls of business, that they might enjoy them uninterrupted.

It chanced on one of these rambles that their way led them down a by-street[9] in a busy quarter of London. The street was small and what is called quiet, but it drove a thriving trade on the weekdays. The inhabitants were all doing well, it seemed, and all emulously[10] hoping to do better still, and laying out the surplus of their gains in coquetry; so that the shop fronts stood along that thoroughfare with an air of invitation, like rows of smiling saleswomen. Even on Sunday, when it veiled its more florid[11] charms and lay comparatively empty of passage, the street shone out in contrast to its dingy neighborhood, like a fire in a forest; and with its freshly painted shutters, well-polished brasses, and general cleanliness and gaiety of note, instantly caught and pleased the eye of the passenger.

Two doors from one corner, on the left hand going east, the line was broken by the entry of a court; and just at that point, a certain sinister block of building thrust forward its gable on the street. It was two stories high; showed no window, nothing but a door on the lower story and a blind forehead of discolored wall on the upper; and bore in every feature the marks of prolonged and sordid negligence. The door, which was equipped with neither bell nor knocker, was blistered and distained.[12] Tramps slouched into the recess and struck matches on the panels; children kept shop upon the steps; the schoolboy had tried his knife on the mouldings; and for close on a generation, no one had appeared to drive away these random visitors or to repair their ravages.

Mr. Enfield and the lawyer were on the other side of the by-street; but when they came abreast of the entry, the former lifted up his cane and pointed.

"Did you ever remark that door?" he asked; and when his companion had replied in the affirmative, "It is connected in my mind," added he, "with a very odd story."

"Indeed!" said Mr. Utterson, with a slight change of voice, "and what was that?"

"Well, it was this way," returned Mr. Enfield: "I was coming home from some place at the end of the world, about three o'clock of a black winter morning, and my way lay through a part of town where there was literally nothing to be seen but lamps. Street after street, and all the folks asleep—street after street, all lighted up as if for a procession, and all as empty as a church—till at last I got into that state of mind when a man listens and listens, and begins to long for the sight of a policeman. All at once I saw two figures: one a little man who was stumping along eastward at a good walk,

and the other a girl of maybe eight or ten who was running as hard as she was able down a cross street. Well, sir, the two ran into one another naturally enough at the corner; and then came the horrible part of the thing; for the man trampled calmly over the child's body and left her screaming on the ground. It sounds nothing to hear, but it was hellish to see. It wasn't like a man; it was like some Juggernaut.[13] I gave a view halloa,[14] took to my heels, collared[15] my gentleman, and brought him back to where there was already quite a group about the screaming child. He was perfectly cool and made no resistance, but gave me one look, so ugly that it brought out the sweat on me like running. The people who had turned out were the girl's own family; and pretty soon the doctor, for whom she had been sent, put in his appearance. Well, the child was not much the worse—more frightened, according to the Sawbones; and there you might have supposed would be an end to it. But there was one curious circumstance. I had taken a loathing to my gentleman at first sight. So had the child's family, which was only natural. But the doctor's case was what struck me. He was the usual cut and dry apothecary,[16] of no particular age and color, with a strong Edinburgh accent, and about as emotional as a bagpipe. Well sir, he was like the rest of us; every time he looked at my prisoner, I saw that Sawbones turned sick and white with the desire to kill him. I knew what was in his mind, just as he knew what was in mine; and killing being out of the question, we did the next best. We told the man we could and would make such a scandal out of this as should make his name stink from one end of London to the other. If he had any friends or any credit, we undertook that he should lose them. And all the time, as we were pitching it in red hot, we were keeping the women off him as best we could, for they were as wild as harpies.[17] I never saw a circle of such hateful faces; and there was the man in the middle, with a kind of black, sneering coolness—frightened too, I could see that—but carrying it off, sir, really like Satan. 'If you choose to make capital[18] out of this accident,' said he, 'I am naturally helpless. No gentleman but wishes to avoid a scene,' says he. 'Name your figure.' Well, we screwed him up[19] to a hundred pounds for the child's family; he would have clearly liked to stick out;[20] but there was something about the lot of us that meant mischief, and at last he struck.[21] The next thing was to get the money; and where do you think he carried us but to that place with the door?—whipped out a key, went in, and presently came back with the matter of ten pounds in gold and a check for the balance on Coutts's, drawn payable to bearer, and signed with a name that I can't mention, though it's one of the points of my story, but it was a name at least very well known and often printed. The figure was stiff; but the signature was good for more than that, if it was only genuine. I took the liberty of pointing out to my gentleman that the whole business looked apocryphal;[22] and that a man does not, in real life, walk into a cellar door at four in the morning and come out of it with another man's check for close upon a hundred pounds. But he was quite easy and sneering. 'Set your mind at rest,' says he; 'I will stay with you till the banks open, and cash the check myself.' So we all set off, the doctor, and the child's father, and our friend and myself, and passed the rest of the night in my chambers; and next day, when we had breakfasted, went in a body to the bank. I gave in the check myself, and said I had every reason to believe it was a forgery. Not a bit of it. The check was genuine."

"Tut-tut!" said Mr. Utterson.

"I see you feel as I do," said Mr. Enfield. "Yes, it's a bad story. For my man was a fellow that nobody could have to do with, a really damnable man; and the person that drew the check is the very pink of the proprieties, celebrated too, and (what makes it worse) one of your fellows who do what they call good. Blackmail, I suppose; an honest man paying through the nose for some of the capers[23] of his youth. Blackmail House is what I call that place with the door, in consequence. Though even that, you know, is far from explaining all," he added; and with the words fell into a vein of musing.

From this he was recalled by Mr. Utterson asking rather suddenly: "And you don't know if the drawer[24] of the check lives there?"

"A likely place, isn't it?" returned Mr. Enfield. "But I happen to have noticed his address; he lives in some square or other."

"And you never asked about—the place with the door?" said Mr. Utterson.

"No, sir: I had a delicacy," was the reply. "I feel very strongly about putting questions; it partakes too much of the style of the day of judgment. You start a question, and it's like starting a stone. You sit quietly on the top of a hill; and away the stone goes, starting others; and presently some bland old bird (the last you would have thought of) is knocked on the head in his own back garden, and the family have to change their name. No, sir, I make it a rule of mine: the more it looks like Queer Street, the less I ask."

"A very good rule, too," said the lawyer.

"But I have studied the place for myself," continued Mr. Enfield. "It seems scarcely a house. There is no other door, and nobody goes in or out of that one, but, once in a great while, the gentleman of my adventure. There are three windows looking on the court on the first floor; none below; the windows are always shut, but they're clean. And then there is a chimney, which is generally smoking; so somebody must live there. And yet it's not so sure; for the buildings are so packed together about that court that it's hard to say where one ends and another begins."

The pair walked on again for a while in silence; and then—"Enfield," said Mr. Utterson, "that's a good rule of yours."

"Yes, I think it is," returned Enfield.

"But for all that," continued the lawyer, "there's one point I want to ask: I want to ask the name of that man who walked over the child."

"Well," said Mr. Enfield, "I can't see what harm it would do. It was a man of the name of Hyde."

"H'm," said Mr. Utterson. "What sort of a man is he to see?"

"He is not easy to describe. There is something wrong with his appearance; something displeasing, something downright detestable. I never saw a man I so disliked, and yet I scarce know why. He must be deformed somewhere; he gives a strong feeling of deformity, although I couldn't specify the point. He's an extraordinary-looking man, and yet I really can name nothing out of the way. No, sir; I can make no hand of it; I can't describe him. And it's not want of memory, for I declare I can see him this moment."

Mr. Utterson again walked some way in silence, and obviously under a weight of consideration. "You are sure he used a key?" he inquired at last.

"My dear sir . . ." began Enfield, surprised out of himself.

"Yes, I know," said Utterson; "I know it must seem strange. The fact is, if I do not ask you the name of the other party, it is because I know it already. You see, Richard, your tale has gone home. If you have been inexact in any point, you had better correct it."

"I think you might have warned me," returned the other, with a touch of sullenness. "But I have been pedantically exact, as you call it. The fellow had a key; and, what's more, he has it still. I saw him use it not a week ago."

Mr. Utterson sighed deeply, but said never a word; and the young man presently resumed. "Here is another lesson to say nothing," said he. "I am ashamed of my long tongue. Let us make a bargain never to refer to this again."

"With all my heart," said the lawyer. "I shake hands on that, Richard."

[1] **discourse:** talk, conversation
[2] **austere:** stern
[3] **mortify:** to subdue or deaden
[4] **extremity:** a time of very great danger or need
[5] **reprove:** to express disapproval of
[6] **Cain's heresy:** the idea that individuals are not responsible for their fellow men. Cain is the Biblical figure who said, ". . . Am I my brother's keeper?"
[7] **demeanor:** manner; outward behavior
[8] **catholicity:** universality
[9] **by-street:** side street
[10] **emulously:** ambitiously
[11] **florid:** heavily decorated
[12] **distained:** discolored
[13] **Juggernaut:** a massive force or object that crushes whatever is in its path
[14] **view halloa:** a loud call made by a hunter upon seeing a fox break cover
[15] **collared:** grabbed; stopped
[16] **apothecary:** earlier name for a druggist. From about 1700, apothecaries began to serve as doctors.
[17] **harpies:** shrewish, ill-tempered women
[18] **capital:** advantage; gain; money
[19] **screwed him up:** forced him to agree
[20] **stick out:** to hold out for a better price
[21] **struck:** agreed to the terms
[22] **apocryphal:** of questionable authenticity; phony
[23] **capers:** adventures; pranks
[24] **drawer:** person who draws an order for the payment of money (person who writes a check)

CHAPTER TWO

Search for Mr. Hyde

That evening Mr. Utterson came home to his bachelor house in somber spirits, and sat down to dinner without relish. It was his custom of a Sunday, when this meal was over, to sit close by the fire, a volume of some dry divinity[1] on his reading desk, until the clock of the neighboring church rang out the hour of twelve, when he would go soberly and gratefully to bed. On this night, however, as soon as the cloth was taken away, he took up a candle and went into his business room. There he opened his safe, took from the most private part of it a document endorsed on the envelope as Dr. Jekyll's Will, and sat down with a clouded brow to study its contents. The will was holograph;[2] for Mr. Utterson, though he took charge of it now that it was made, had refused to lend the least assistance in the making of it; it provided not only that, in case of the decease of Henry Jekyll, M.D., D.C.L., LL.D., F.R.S., etc., all his possessions were to pass into the hands of his "friend and benefactor Edward Hyde"; but that in case of Dr. Jekyll's "disappearance or unexplained absence for any period exceeding three calendar months," the said Edward Hyde should step into the said Henry Jekyll's shoes without further delay, and free from any burthen or obligation, beyond the payment of a few small sums to the members of the doctor's household. This document had long been the lawyer's eyesore. It offended him both as a lawyer and as a lover of the sane and customary sides of life, to whom the fanciful was the immodest.[3] And hitherto it was his ignorance of Mr. Hyde that had swelled his indignation; now, by a sudden turn, it was his knowledge. It was already bad enough when the name was but a name of which he could learn no more. It was worse when it began to be clothed upon with detestable attributes; and out of the shifting, insubstantial mists that had so long baffled his eye, there leaped up the sudden, definite presentment[4] of a fiend.

"I thought it was madness," he said, as he replaced the obnoxious paper in the safe, "and now I begin to fear it is disgrace."

With that he blew out his candle, put on a greatcoat, and set forth in the direction of Cavendish Square, that citadel of medicine, where his friend, the great Dr. Lanyon, had his house and received his crowding patients. "If anyone knows, it will be Lanyon," he had thought.

The solemn butler knew and welcomed him; he was subjected to no stage of delay, but ushered direct from the door to the dining room, where Dr. Lanyon sat alone over his wine. This was a hearty, healthy, dapper, red-faced gentleman, with a shock of hair prematurely white, and a boisterous and decided manner. At sight of Mr. Utterson, he sprang up from his chair and welcomed him with both hands. The geniality, as was the way of the man, was somewhat theatrical to the eye, but it reposed[5] on genuine feeling. For these two were old friends, old mates both at school and college, both thorough respecters of themselves and of each other, and, what does not always follow, men who thoroughly enjoyed each other's company.

After a little rambling talk, the lawyer led up to the subject which so disagreeably preoccupied his mind.

"I suppose, Lanyon," said he, "you and I must be the two oldest friends that Henry Jekyll has?"

"I wish the friends were younger," chuckled Dr. Lanyon. "But I suppose we are. And what of that? I see little of him now."

"Indeed!" said Utterson. "I thought you had a bond of common interest."

"We had," was the reply. "But it is more than ten years since Henry Jekyll became too fanciful for me. He began to go wrong—wrong in mind; and though, of course, I continue to take an interest in him for old time's sake as they say, I see and I have seen devilish little of the man. Such unscientific balderdash,"[6] added the doctor, flushing suddenly purple, "would have estranged Damon and Pythias."[7]

This little spirit of temper was somewhat of a relief to Mr. Utterson. "They have only differed on some point of science," he thought, and being a man of no scientific passions (except in the matter of conveyancing[8]) he even added: "It is nothing worse than that!" He gave his friend a few seconds to recover his composure, and then approached the question he had come to put.

"Did you ever come across a protégé of his—one Hyde?" he asked.

"Hyde?" repeated Lanyon. "No. Never heard of him. Since my time."

That was the amount of information that the lawyer carried back with him to the great, dark bed on which he tossed to and fro until the small hours of the morning began to grow large. It was a night of little ease to his toiling mind, toiling in mere darkness and besieged by questions.

Six o'clock struck on the bells of the church that was so conveniently near to Mr. Utterson's dwelling, and still he was digging at the problem. Hitherto it had touched him on the intellectual side alone, but now his imagination also was engaged, or rather enslaved; and as he lay and tossed in the gross darkness of the night and the curtained room, Mr. Enfield's tale went by before his mind in a scroll of lighted pictures. He would be aware of the great field of lamps of a nocturnal city; then of the figure of a man walking swiftly; then of a child running from the doctor's; and then these met, and that human Juggernaut trod the child down and passed on regardless of her screams. Or else he would see a room in a rich house, where his friend lay asleep, dreaming and smiling at his dreams; and then the door of that room would be opened, the curtains of the bed plucked apart, the sleeper recalled, and, lo! there would stand by his side a figure to whom power was given, and even at that dead hour he must rise and do its bidding. The figure in these two phases haunted the lawyer all night; and if at any time he dozed over, it was but to see it glide more stealthily through sleeping houses, or move the more swiftly and still the more swiftly, even to dizziness, through wider labyrinths[9] of lamp-lighted city, and at every street corner crush a child and leave her screaming. And still the figure had no face by which he might know it; even in his dreams, it had no face, or one that baffled him and melted before his eyes; and thus it was that there sprang up and grew apace[10] in the lawyer's mind a singularly strong, almost an inordinate,[11] curiosity to behold the features of the real Mr. Hyde. If he could but once set eyes on him, he thought the mystery would lighten and perhaps roll altogether away, as was the habit of mysterious things when well examined. He might see a reason for his friend's strange preference or bondage (call it which you please), and even for the startling clauses of the will. And at least it would be a face worth seeing: the face of a man who was without bowels of mercy—a face which had but to show itself to raise up, in the mind of the unimpressionable Enfield, a spirit of enduring hatred.

From that time forward Mr. Utterson began to haunt the door in the by-street of shops. In the morning before office hours, at noon when business was plenty and time scarce, at night under the face of the fogged city moon, by all lights and at all hours of solitude or concourse,[12] the lawyer was to be found on his chosen post.

"If he be Mr. Hyde," he had thought, "I shall be Mr. Seek."

And at last his patience was rewarded. It was a fine dry night; frost in the air; the streets as clean as a ballroom floor; the lamps, unshaken by any wind, drawing a regular pattern of light and shadow. By ten o'clock, when the shops were closed, the by-street was very solitary and, in spite of the low growl of London from all round, very silent. Small sounds carried far; domestic sounds out of the houses were clearly audible on either side of the roadway; and the rumor of the approach of any passenger preceded him by a long time. Mr. Utterson had been some minutes at his post when he was aware of an odd, light footstep drawing near. In the course of his nightly patrols he had long grown accustomed to the quaint effect with which the footfalls of a single person, while he is still a great way off, suddenly spring out distinct from the vast hum and clatter of the city. Yet his attention had never before been so sharply and decisively arrested; and it was with a strong, superstitious prevision of success that he withdrew into the entry of the court.

The steps drew swiftly nearer and swelled out suddenly louder as they turned the end of the street. The lawyer, looking forth from the entry, could soon see what manner of man he had to deal with. He was small, and very plainly dressed; and the look of him, even at that distance, went somehow strongly against the watcher's inclination. But he made straight for the door, crossing the roadway to save time; and as he came, he drew a key from his pocket, like one approaching home.

Mr. Utterson stepped out and touched him on the shoulder as he passed. "Mr. Hyde, I think?"

Mr. Hyde shrank back with a hissing intake of the breath. But his fear was only momentary; and though he did not look the lawyer in the face, he answered coolly enough: "That is my name. What do you want?"

"I see you are going in," returned the lawyer. "I am an old friend of Dr. Jekyll's—Mr. Utterson, of Gaunt Street—you must have heard my name; and meeting you so conveniently, I thought you might admit me."

"You will not find Dr. Jekyll; he is from home," replied Mr. Hyde, blowing in the key. And then suddenly, but still without looking up, "How did you know me?" he asked.

"On your side," said Mr. Utterson, "will you do me a favor?"

"With pleasure," replied the other. "What shall it be?"

"Will you let me see your face?" asked the lawyer.

Mr. Hyde appeared to hesitate; and then, as if upon some sudden reflection, fronted about with an air of defiance; and the pair stared at each other pretty fixedly for a few seconds. "Now I shall know you again," said Mr. Utterson. "It may be useful."

"Yes," returned Mr. Hyde, "it is as well we have met; and apropos,[13] you should have my address." And he gave a number of a street in Soho.

"Good God!" thought Mr. Utterson, "can he too have been thinking of the will?" But he kept his feelings to himself, and only grunted in acknowledgment of the address.

"And now," said the other, "how did you know me?"

"By description," was the reply.

"Whose description?"

"We have common friends," said Mr. Utterson.

"Common friends!" echoed Mr. Hyde, a little hoarsely. "Who are they?"

"Jekyll, for instance," said the lawyer.

"He never told you," cried Mr. Hyde, with a flush of anger. "I did not think you would have lied."

"Come," said Mr. Utterson, "that is not fitting language."

The other snarled aloud into a savage laugh; and the next moment, with extraordinary quickness, he had unlocked the door and disappeared into the house.

The lawyer stood awhile when Mr. Hyde had left him, the picture of disquietude.[14] Then he began slowly to mount the street, pausing every step or two, and putting his hand to his brow like a man in mental perplexity. The problem he was thus debating as he walked was one of a class that is rarely solved. Mr. Hyde was pale and dwarfish; he gave an impression of deformity without any nameable malformation; he had a displeasing smile, he had borne himself to the lawyer with a sort of murderous mixture of timidity and boldness; and he spoke with a husky, whispering, and somewhat broken voice—all these were points against him. But not all of these together could explain the hitherto unknown disgust, loathing, and fear with which Mr. Utterson regarded him. "There must be something else," said the perplexed gentleman. "There *is* something more, if I could find a name for it. God bless me, the man seems hardly human! Something troglodytic,[15] shall we say? or can it be the old story of Dr. Fell?[16] or is it the mere radiance of a foul soul that thus transpires[17] through, and transfigures, its clay continent?[18] The last, I think; for, O my poor old Harry Jekyll, if ever I read Satan's signature upon a face, it is on that of your new friend."

Round the corner from the by-street there was a square of ancient, handsome houses, now for the most part decayed from their high estate, and let in flats and chambers to all sorts and conditions of men: map engravers, architects, shady lawyers, and the agents of obscure enterprises. One house, however, second from the corner, was still occupied entire; and at the door of this, which wore a great air of wealth and comfort, though it was now plunged in darkness except for the fanlight, Mr. Utterson stopped and knocked. A well-dressed, elderly servant opened the door.

"Is Dr. Jekyll at home, Poole?" asked the lawyer.

"I will see, Mr. Utterson," said Poole, admitting the visitor as he spoke, into a large, low-roofed, comfortable hall, paved with flags, warmed (after the fashion of a country house) by a bright, open fire, and furnished with costly cabinets of oak. "Will you wait here by the fire, sir, or shall I give you a light in the dining room?"

"Here, thank you," said the lawyer, and he drew near and leaned on the tall fender.[19] This hall, in which he was now left alone, was a pet fancy of his friend the doctor's, and Utterson himself was wont to speak of it as the pleasantest room in London. But tonight there was a shudder in his blood; the face of Hyde sat heavy on his memory; he felt (what was rare with him) a nausea and distaste of life; and in the gloom of his spirits, he seemed to read a menace in the flickering of the firelight on the polished cabinets and the uneasy starting of the shadow on the roof. He was ashamed of his relief when Poole presently returned to announce that Dr. Jekyll was gone out.

"I saw Mr. Hyde go in by the old dissecting-room door, Poole," he said. "Is that right, when Dr. Jekyll is from home?"

"Quite right, Mr. Utterson, sir," replied the servant. "Mr. Hyde has a key."

"Your master seems to repose a great deal of trust in that young man, Poole," resumed the other musingly.

"Yes, sir, he do indeed," said Poole. "We have all orders to obey him."

"I do not think I ever met Mr. Hyde?" asked Utterson.

"Oh dear no, sir. He never *dines* here," replied the butler. "Indeed, we see very little of him on this side of the house; he mostly comes and goes by the laboratory."

"Well, good night, Poole."

"Good night, Mr. Utterson."

And the lawyer set out homeward with a very heavy heart. "Poor Harry Jekyll," he thought, "my mind misgives me he is in deep waters! He was wild when he was young—a long while ago, to be sure—but in the law of God, there is no statute of limitations.[20] Ah, it must be that: the ghost of some old sin, the cancer of some concealed disgrace; punishment coming, *pede claudo,*[21] years after memory has forgotten and self-love condoned the fault." And the lawyer, scared by the thought, brooded awhile on his own past, groping in all the corners of memory, lest by chance some Jack-in-the-Box of an old iniquity[22] should leap to light there. His past was fairly blameless; few men could read the rolls of their life with less apprehension; yet he was humbled to the dust by the many ill things he had done, and raised up again into a sober and fearful gratitude by the many that he had come so near to doing, yet avoided. And then by a return on his former subject, he conceived a spark of hope. "This Master Hyde, if he were studied," thought he, "must have secrets of his own: black secrets, by the look of him; secrets compared to which poor Jekyll's worst would be like sunshine. Things cannot continue as they are. It turns me cold to think of this creature stealing like a thief to Harry's bedside; poor Harry, what a wakening! And the danger of it! For if this Hyde suspects the existence of the will, he may grow impatient to inherit. Ah, I must put my shoulder to the wheel—if Jekyll will but let me," he added, "if Jekyll will only let me." For once more he saw before his mind's eye, as clear as a transparency, the strange clauses of the will.

[1] **divinity:** book of religious essays
[2] **holograph:** a document written entirely in the handwriting of its author
[3] **immodest:** immoderate; excessive
[4] **presentment:** the act of presenting to view or consciousness
[5] **reposed:** rested
[6] **balderdash:** nonsense
[7] **Damon and Pythias:** two inseparable friends of Greek legend
[8] **conveyancing:** the act of drawing deeds, leases, and other documents
[9] **labyrinths:** mazes
[10] **apace:** swiftly
[11] **inordinate:** excessive
[12] **concourse:** crowd
[13] **apropos:** pertinently; "as a matter of fact"
[14] **disquietude:** anxiety
[15] **troglodytic:** brutish; like a primitive cave-dweller
[16] **Dr. Fell:** the subject of a famous poem in which the narrator cannot say why he feels the way he does
[17] **transpires:** breathes through
[18] **clay continent:** body
[19] **fender:** a metal screen placed before a fireplace
[20] **statute of limitations:** law setting a time limit after which offenses cannot be punished
[21] ***pede claudo:*** (Latin) with a limping foot
[22] **iniquity:** sin

CHAPTER THREE

Dr. Jekyll Was Quite at Ease

A fortnight[1] later, by excellent good fortune, the doctor gave one of his pleasant dinners to some five or six old cronies, all intelligent, reputable men, and all judges of good wine; and Mr. Utterson so contrived that he remained behind after the others had departed. This was no new arrangement, but a thing that had befallen many scores of time. Where Utterson was liked, he was liked well. Hosts loved to detain the dry lawyer, when the light-hearted and the loose-tongued had already their foot on the threshold; they liked to sit awhile in his unobtrusive[2] company, practicing for solitude, sobering their minds in the man's rich silence, after the expense and strain of gaiety. To this rule, Dr. Jekyll was no exception; and as he now sat on the opposite side of the fire—a large, well-made, smooth-faced man of fifty, with something of a slyish cast perhaps, but every mark of capacity and kindness—you could see by his looks that he cherished for Mr. Utterson a sincere and warm affection.

"I have been wanting to speak to you, Jekyll," began the latter. "You know that will of yours?"

A close observer might have gathered that the topic was distasteful, but the doctor carried it off gaily. "My poor Utterson," said he, "you are unfortunate in such a client. I never saw a man so distressed as you were by my will, unless it were that hide-bound[3] pedant,[4] Lanyon, at what he called my scientific heresies. Oh, I know he's a good fellow—you needn't frown—an excellent fellow, and I always mean to see more of him; but a hide-bound pedant for all that; an ignorant, blatant pedant. I was never more disappointed in any man than Lanyon."

"You know that I never approved of it," pursued Utterson, ruthlessly disregarding the fresh topic.

"My will? Yes, certainly, I know that," said the doctor, a trifle sharply. "You have told me so."

"Well, I tell you so again," continued the lawyer. "I have been learning something of young Hyde."

The large, handsome face of Dr. Jekyll grew pale to the very lips, and there came a blackness about his eyes. "I do not care to hear more," said he. "This is a matter I thought we had agreed to drop."

"What I heard was abominable," said Utterson.

"It can make no change. You do not understand my position," returned the doctor, with a certain incoherency[5] of manner. "I am painfully situated, Utterson; my position is a very strange one—a very strange one. It is one of those affairs that cannot be mended by talking."

"Jekyll," said Utterson, "you know me: I am a man to be trusted. Make a clean breast of this in confidence, and I make no doubt I can get you out of it."

"My good Utterson," said the doctor, "this is very good of you; this is downright good of you, and I cannot find words to thank you in. I believe you fully; I would trust you before any man alive—ay, before myself, if I could make the choice; but indeed it isn't what you fancy; it is not so bad as that; and just to put your good heart at rest, I will tell you one thing: the moment I choose, I can be rid of Mr. Hyde. I give you my hand upon that; and I thank you again and again; and I will just add one little word, Utterson, that I'm sure you'll take in good part: this is a private matter, and I beg of you to let it sleep."

Utterson reflected a little, looking in the fire.

"I have no doubt you are perfectly right," he said at last, getting to his feet.

"Well, but since we have touched upon this business, and for the last time I hope," continued the doctor, "there is one point I should like you to understand. I have really a very great interest in poor Hyde. I know you have seen him—he told me so—and I fear he was rude. But I do sincerely take a great, a very great interest in that young man; and if I am taken away, Utterson, I wish you to promise me that you will bear with him and get his rights for him. I think you would, if you knew all; and it would be a weight off my mind if you would promise."

"I can't pretend that I shall ever like him," said the lawyer.

"I don't ask that," pleaded Jekyll, laying his hand upon the other's arm; "I only ask for justice; I only ask you to help him for my sake, when I am no longer here."

Utterson heaved an irrepressible sigh. "Well," said he, "I promise."

[1] **fortnight:** two weeks
[2] **unobtrusive:** not readily noticed
[3] **hide-bound:** inflexible
[4] **pedant:** one who is unimaginative or narrow-minded in the use of knowledge
[5] **incoherency:** the condition of being unconnected, disordered

A CLOSER LOOK

1. Mr. Hyde is seen coming and going through a certain door in a by-street (side street) of shops. Where does the door lead?

2. What does Utterson know about Mr. Hyde before he hears Enfield's story? Why is Utterson disturbed by the story?

3. Stevenson makes it clear that both Enfield and the apothecary are men who are not easily affected, yet they both have a violent reaction to Hyde. What do they both want to do to him? What does this fact tell us about Hyde?

4. Describe Mr. Hyde's physical appearance.

5. Describe Dr. Jekyll's physical appearance.

6. Why does Utterson think that Dr. Jekyll must be the victim of blackmail?

7. What does Mr. Utterson try to get Dr. Jekyll to confess? How does Jekyll respond to Utterson's offer to help?

CHAPTER FOUR

The Carew Murder Case

Nearly a year later, in the month of October 18—, London was startled by a crime of singular ferocity, and rendered all the more notable by the high position of the victim. The details were few and startling. A maidservant living alone in a house not far from the river had gone upstairs to bed about eleven. Although a fog rolled over the city in the small hours, the early part of the night was cloudless, and the lane, which the maid's window overlooked, was brilliantly lit by the full moon. It seems she was romantically given; for she sat down upon her box, which stood immediately under the window, and fell into a dream of musing. Never (she used to say, with streaming tears when she narrated that experience), never had she felt more at peace with all men or thought more kindly of the world. And as she so sat she became aware of an aged and beautiful gentleman with white hair, drawing near along the lane; and advancing to meet him, another and very small gentleman, to whom at first she paid less attention. When they had come within speech (which was just under the maid's eyes), the older man bowed and accosted[1] the other with a very pretty manner of politeness. It did not seem as if the subject of his address were of great importance; indeed, from his pointing, it sometimes appeared as if he were only inquiring his way; but the moon shone on his face as he spoke, and the girl was pleased to watch it, it seemed to breathe such an innocent and Old World kindness of disposition, yet with something high too, as of a well-founded self-content. Presently her eye wandered to the other, and she was surprised to recognize in him a certain Mr. Hyde, who had once visited her master, and for whom she had conceived a dislike. He had in his hand a heavy cane, with which he was trifling; but he answered never a word, and seemed to listen with an ill-contained impatience. And then all of a sudden he broke out in a great flame of anger, stamping with his foot, brandishing the cane, and carrying on (as the maid described it) like a madman. The old gentleman took a step back, with the air of one very much surprised and a trifle hurt; and at that Mr. Hyde broke out of all bounds and clubbed him to the earth. And next moment with apelike fury, he was trampling his victim under foot, and hailing down a storm of blows, under which the bones were audibly shattered and the body jumped upon the roadway. At the horror of these sights and sounds, the maid fainted.

It was two o'clock when she came to herself and called for the police. The murderer was gone long ago; but there lay his victim in the middle of the lane, incredibly mangled. The stick with which the deed had been done, although it was of some rare and very tough and heavy wood, had broken in the middle under the stress of this insensate[2] cruelty; and one splintered half had rolled in the neighboring gutter—the other, without doubt, had been carried away by the murderer. A purse and a gold watch were found upon the victim; but no cards or papers, except a sealed and stamped envelope, which he had been probably carrying to the post, and which bore the name and address of Mr. Utterson.

This was brought to the lawyer the next morning, before he was out of bed; and he had no sooner seen it, and been told the circumstances, than he shot out a solemn lip. "I shall say nothing till I have seen the body," said he; "this may be very serious. Have the kindness to wait while I dress." And with the same grave countenance he hurried through his breakfast and drove to the police station, whither the body had been carried. As soon as he came into the cell, he nodded.

"Yes," said he, "I recognize him. I am sorry to say that this is Sir Danvers Carew."

"Good God, sir," exclaimed the officer, "is it possible?" And the next moment his eye lighted up with professional ambition. "This will make a deal of noise," he said. "And perhaps you can help us to the man." And he briefly narrated what the maid had seen, and showed the broken stick.

Mr. Utterson had already quailed[3] at the name of Hyde; but when the stick was laid before him, he could doubt no longer: broken and battered as it was, he recognized it for one that he had himself presented many years before to Henry Jekyll.

"Is this Mr. Hyde a person of small stature?" he inquired.

"Particularly small and particularly wicked-looking, is what the maid calls him," said the officer.

Mr. Utterson reflected; and then, raising his head, "If you will come with me in my cab," he said, "I think I can take you to his house."

It was by this time about nine in the morning, and the first fog of the season. A great chocolate-colored pall[4] lowered over heaven, but the wind was continually charging and routing these embattled vapors; so that as the cab crawled from street to street, Mr. Utterson beheld a marvelous number of degrees and hues of twilight; for here it would be dark like the back end of evening; and there would be a glow of a rich, lurid[5] brown, like the light of some strange conflagration;[6] and here, for a moment, the fog would be quite broken up, and a haggard shaft of daylight would glance in between the swirling wreaths. The dismal quarter of Soho seen under these changing glimpses, with its muddy ways and slatternly[7] passengers, and its lamps, which had never been extinguished or had been kindled afresh to combat this mournful reinvasion of darkness, seemed, in the lawyer's eyes, like a district of some city in a nightmare. The thoughts of his mind, besides, were of the gloomiest dye; and when he glanced at the companion of his drive, he was conscious of some touch of that terror of the law and the law's officers which may at times assail the most honest.

As the cab drew up before the address indicated, the fog lifted a little and showed him a dingy street, a gin palace, a low French eating house, a shop for the retail of penny numbers and twopenny salads, many ragged children huddled in the doorways, and many women of many different nationalities passing out, key in hand, to have a morning glass; and the next moment the fog settled down again upon that part, as brown as umber, and cut him off from his blackguardly[8] surroundings. This was the home of Henry Jekyll's favorite—of a man who was heir to a quarter of a million sterling.

An ivory-faced and silvery-haired old woman opened the door. She had an evil face, smoothed by hypocrisy, but her manners were excellent. Yes, she said, this was Mr. Hyde's, but he was not at home; he had been in that night very late, but had gone away again in less than an hour: there was nothing strange in that; his habits were very irregular, and he was often absent; for instance, it was nearly two months since she had seen him till yesterday.

"Very well then, we wish to see his rooms," said the lawyer; and when the woman began to declare it was impossible, "I had better tell you who this person is," he added. "This is Inspector Newcomen, of Scotland Yard."

A flash of odious[9] joy appeared upon the woman's face. "Ah!" said she, "he is in trouble! What has he done?"

Mr. Utterson and the inspector exchanged glances. "He don't seem a very popular character," observed the latter. "And now, my good woman, just let me and this gentleman have a look about us."

In the whole extent of the house, which but for the old woman remained otherwise empty, Mr. Hyde had only used a couple of rooms; but these were furnished with luxury and good taste. A closet was filled with wine; the plate was of silver, the napery[10] elegant; a good picture hung upon the walls, a gift (as Utterson supposed) from Henry Jekyll, who was much of a connoisseur; and the carpets were of many plies[11] and agreeable in color. At this moment, however, the rooms bore every mark of having been recently and hurriedly ransacked: clothes lay about the floor, with their pockets inside out; lockfast drawers stood open; and on the hearth there lay a pile of gray ashes, as though many papers had been burned. From these embers the inspector disinterred[12] the butt end of a green check book, which had resisted the action of the fire; the other half of the stick was found behind the door; and as this clinched his suspicions, the officer declared himself delighted. A visit to the bank, where several thousand pounds were found to be lying to the murderer's credit, completed his gratification.

"You may depend upon it, sir," he told Mr. Utterson: "I have him in my hand. He must have lost his head, or he never would have left the stick, or, above all, burned the check book. Why, money's life to the man. We have nothing to do but wait for him at the bank and get out the handbills."

This last, however, was not so easy of accomplishment; for Mr. Hyde had numbered few familiars—even the master of the servant maid had only seen him twice; his family could nowhere be traced; he had never been photographed; and the few who could describe him differed widely, as common observers will. Only on one point were they agreed, and that was the haunting sense of unexpressed deformity with which the fugitive impressed his beholders.

1 **accosted:** greeted
2 **insensate:** unfeeling
3 **quailed:** drawn back in fear
4 **pall:** dark or gloomy covering
5 **lurid:** shining with the glow of fire seen through smoke or cloud
6 **conflagration:** large fire
7 **slatternly:** dirty; slovenly
8 **blackguardly:** vulgar; low
9 **odious:** exciting hatred; offensive
10 **napery:** tablecloths and napkins
11 **plies:** layers
12 **disinterred:** dug up

CHAPTER FIVE

Incident of the Letter

It was late in the afternoon when Mr. Utterson found his way to Dr. Jekyll's door, where he was at once admitted by Poole, and carried down by the kitchen offices and across a yard which had once been a garden, to the building which was indifferently known as the laboratory or the dissecting rooms. The doctor had bought the house from the heirs of a celebrated surgeon; and his own tastes being rather chemical than anatomical, had changed the destination[1] of the block at the bottom of the garden. It was the first time that the lawyer had been received in that part of his friend's quarters; and he eyed the dingy windowless structure with curiosity, and gazed round with a distasteful sense of strangeness as he crossed the theater, once crowded with eager students and now lying gaunt[2] and silent, the tables laden with chemical apparatus, the floor strewn with crates and littered with packing straw, and the light falling dimly through the foggy cupola. At the farther end, a flight of stairs mounted to a door covered with red baize;[3] and through this, Mr. Utterson was at last received into the doctor's cabinet.[4] It was a large room, fitted round with glass presses,[5] furnished, among other things, with a cheval glass[6] and a business table, and looking out upon the court by three dusty windows barred with iron. The fire burned in the grate; a lamp was set lighted on the chimney shelf, for even in the houses the fog began to lie thickly; and there, close up to the warmth, sat Dr. Jekyll, looking deadly sick. He did not rise to meet his visitor, but held out a cold hand and bade him welcome in a changed voice.

"And now," said Mr. Utterson, as soon as Poole had left them, "you have heard the news?"

The doctor shuddered. "They were crying it in the square," he said. "I heard them in my dining room."

"One word," said the lawyer. "Carew was my client, but so are you; and I want to know what I am doing. You have not been mad enough to hide this fellow?"

"Utterson, I swear to God," cried the doctor, "I swear to God I will never set eyes on him again. I bind my honor to you that I am done with him in this world. It is all at an end. And indeed he does not want my help; you do not know him as I do; he is safe, he is quite safe; mark my words, he will never more be heard of."

The lawyer listened gloomily; he did not like his friend's feverish manner. "You seem pretty sure of him," said he; "and for your sake, I hope you may be right. If it came to a trial, your name might appear."

"I am quite sure of him," replied Jekyll; "I have grounds for certainty that I cannot share with anyone. But there is one thing on which you may advise me. I have—I have received a letter; and I am at a loss whether I should show it to the police. I should like to leave it in your hands, Utterson; you would judge wisely, I am sure; I have so great a trust in you."

"You fear, I suppose, that it might lead to his detection?" asked the lawyer.

"No," said the other. "I cannot say that I care what becomes of Hyde; I am quite done with him. I was thinking of my own character, which this hateful business has rather exposed."

Utterson ruminated awhile; he was surprised at his friend's selfishness, and yet relieved by it. "Well," said he, at last, "let me see the letter."

The letter was written in an odd, upright hand and signed "Edward Hyde"; and it signified, briefly enough, that the writer's benefactor, Dr. Jekyll, whom he had long so unworthily repaid for a thousand generosities, need labor under no alarm for his safety, as he had means of escape on which he placed a sure dependence. The lawyer liked this letter well enough: it put a better color on the intimacy than he had looked for, and he blamed himself for some of his past suspicions.

"Have you the envelope?" he asked.

"I burned it," replied Jekyll, "before I thought what I was about. But it bore no postmark. The note was handed in."

"Shall I keep this and sleep upon it?" asked Utterson.

"I wish you to judge for me entirely," was the reply. "I have lost confidence in myself."

"Well, I shall consider," returned the lawyer. "And now one word more: it was Hyde who dictated the terms in your will about that disappearance?"

The doctor seemed seized with a qualm of faintness; he shut his mouth tight and nodded.

"I knew it," said Utterson. "He meant to murder you. You have had a fine escape."

"I have had what is far more to the purpose," returned the doctor solemnly: "I have had a lesson—O God, Utterson, what a lesson I have had!" And he covered his face for a moment with his hands.

On his way out, the lawyer stopped and had a word or two with Poole. "By the by," said he, "there was a letter handed in today: what was the messenger like?" But Poole was positive nothing had come except by post, "and only circulars by that," he added.

This news sent off the visitor with his fears renewed. Plainly the letter had come by the laboratory door; possibly, indeed, it had been written in the cabinet; and, if that were so, it must be differently judged, and handled with the more caution. The newsboys, as he went, were crying themselves hoarse along the footways: "Special edition! Shocking murder of an M.P.!"[7] That was the funeral oration of one friend and client, and he could not help a certain apprehension lest the good name of another should be sucked down in the eddy of the scandal. It was, at least, a ticklish decision that he had to make; and, self-reliant as he was by habit, he began to cherish a longing for advice. It was not to be had directly; but perhaps, he thought, it might be fished for.

Presently after, he sat on one side of his own hearth, with Mr. Guest, his head clerk, upon the other; and midway between, at a nicely calculated distance from the fire, a bottle of particular old wine that had long dwelt unsunned in the foundations of his house. The fog still slept on the wind above the drowned city, where the lamps glimmered like carbuncles;[8] and through the muffle and smother of these fallen clouds, the procession of the town's life was still rolling in through the great arteries with a sound as of a mighty wind. But the room was gay with firelight. In the bottle, the acids were long ago resolved; the imperial dye had softened with time, as the color grows richer in stained windows; and the glow of hot autumn afternoons on hillside vineyards was ready to be set free and to disperse the fogs of London. Insensibly the lawyer melted. There was no man from whom he kept fewer secrets than Mr. Guest, and he was not always sure that he kept as many as he meant. Guest had often been on business to the doctor's: he knew Poole; he could scarce have failed to hear of Mr. Hyde's familiarity about the house; he might draw conclusions. Was it not as well, then, that he should see a letter which put that mystery to right?—and, above all, since Guest, being a great student and critic of handwriting, would consider the step natural and obliging? The clerk, besides, was a man of counsel; he would scarce read so strange a document without dropping a remark; and by that remark Mr. Utterson might shape his future course.

"This is a sad business about Sir Danvers," he said.

"Yes, sir, indeed. It has elicited a great deal of public feeling," returned Guest. "The man, of course, was mad."

"I should like to hear your views on that," replied Utterson. "I have a document here in his handwriting; it is between ourselves, for I scarce know what to do about it; it is an ugly business at the best. But there it is; quite in your way: a murderer's autograph."

Guest's eyes brightened, and he sat down at once and studied it with passion. "No, sir," he said; "not mad, but it is an odd hand."

"And by all accounts a very odd writer," added the lawyer.

Just then the servant entered with a note.

"Is that from Dr. Jekyll, sir?" inquired the clerk. "I thought I knew the writing. Anything private, Mr. Utterson?"

"Only an invitation to dinner. Why? Do you want to see it?"

"One moment. I thank you, sir"; and the clerk laid the two sheets of paper alongside and sedulously compared their contents. "Thank you, sir," he said at last, returning both; "it's a very interesting autograph."

There was a pause during which Mr. Utterson struggled with himself. "Why did you compare them, Guest?" he inquired suddenly.

"Well, sir," returned the clerk, "there's a rather singular resemblance; the two hands are in many points identical: only differently sloped."

"Rather quaint,"[9] said Utterson.

"It is, as you say, rather quaint," returned Guest.

"I wouldn't speak of this note, you know," said the master.

"No, sir," said the clerk. "I understand."

But no sooner was Mr. Utterson alone that night than he locked the note into his safe, where it reposed from that time forward. "What!" he thought. "Henry Jekyll forge for a murderer!" And his blood ran cold in his veins.

[1] **destination:** the purpose for which something is intended
[2] **gaunt:** barren
[3] **baize:** felt-like material, often used to cover pool tables
[4] **cabinet:** small private room set aside for some specific activity
[5] **glass presses:** upright cases used for storing books or other articles
[6] **cheval glass:** a full-length mirror mounted so that it can be tilted in a frame
[7] **M.P.:** Member of Parliament
[8] **carbuncles:** mythical red gems believed to give off their own light
[9] **quaint:** strange

CHAPTER SIX

Remarkable Incident of Dr. Lanyon

Time ran on; thousands of pounds were offered in reward, for the death of Sir Danvers was resented as a public injury; but Mr. Hyde had disappeared out of the ken[1] of the police as though he had never existed. Much of his past was unearthed, indeed, and all disreputable:[2] tales came out of the man's cruelty, at once so callous and violent, of his vile life, of his strange associates, of the hatred that seemed to have surrounded his career; but of his present whereabouts, not a whisper. From the time he had left the house in Soho on the morning of the murder, he was simply blotted out; and gradually, as time drew on, Mr. Utterson began to recover from the hotness of his alarm and to grow more at quiet with himself. The death of Sir Danvers was, to his way of thinking, more than paid for by the disappearance of Mr. Hyde. Now that that evil influence had been withdrawn, a new life began for Dr. Jekyll. He came out of his seclusion, renewed relations with his friends, became once more their familiar guest and entertainer; and whilst he had always been known for charities, he was now no less distinguished for religion. He was busy, he was much in the open air, he did good; his face seemed to open and brighten, as if with an inward consciousness of service; and for more than two months, the doctor was at peace.

On the 8th of January, Utterson had dined at the doctor's with a small party. Lanyon had been there, and the face of the host had looked from one to the other as in the old days, when the trio were inseparable friends. On the 12th, and again on the 14th, the door was shut against the lawyer. "The doctor was confined to the house," Poole said, "and saw no one." On the 15th, he tried again, and was again refused; and having now been used for the last two months to see his friend almost daily, he found this return of solitude to weigh upon his spirits. The fifth night he had Guest in to dine with him, and the sixth he betook himself to Dr. Lanyon's.

There at least he was not denied admittance; but when he came in, he was shocked at the change which had taken place in the doctor's appearance. He had his death warrant written legibly upon his face. The rosy man had grown pale, his flesh had fallen away, he was visibly balder and older; and yet it was not so much these tokens of a swift physical decay that arrested the lawyer's notice as a look in the eye and quality of manner that seemed to testify to some deep-seated terror of the mind. It was unlikely that the doctor should fear death, and yet that was what Utterson was tempted to suspect. "Yes," he thought, "he is a doctor; he must know his own state and that his days are counted, and the knowledge is more than he can bear." And yet when Utterson remarked on his ill looks, it was with an air of great firmness that Lanyon declared himself a doomed man.

"I have had a shock," he said, "and I shall never recover. It is a question of weeks. Well, life has been pleasant. I liked it; yes, sir, I used to like it. I sometimes think if we knew all, we should be more glad to get away."

"Jekyll is ill, too," observed Utterson. "Have you seen him?"

But Lanyon's face changed, and he held up a trembling hand. "I wish to see or hear no more of Dr. Jekyll," he said, in a loud, unsteady voice. "I am quite done with that person, and I beg that you will spare me any allusion[3] to one whom I regard as dead."

"Tut, tut!" said Mr. Utterson; and then, after a considerable pause, "Can't I do anything?" he inquired. "We are three very old friends, Lanyon; we shall not live to make others."

"Nothing can be done," returned Lanyon; "ask himself."

"He will not see me," said the lawyer.

"I am not surprised at that," was the reply. "Some day, Utterson, after I am dead, you may perhaps come to learn the right and wrong of this. I cannot tell you. And in the meantime, if you can sit and talk with me of other things, for God's sake, stay and do so; but if you cannot keep clear of this accursed topic, then, in God's name, go, for I cannot bear it."

As soon as he got home, Utterson sat down and wrote to Jekyll, complaining of his exclusion from the house, and asking the cause of this unhappy break with Lanyon; and the next day brought him a long answer, often very pathetically worded and sometimes darkly mysterious in drift. The quarrel with Lanyon was incurable. "I do not blame our old friend," Jekyll wrote, "but I share his view that we must never meet. I mean from henceforth to lead a life of extreme seclusion; you must not be surprised, nor must you doubt my friendship, if my door is often shut even to you. You must suffer me to go my own dark way. I have brought on myself a punishment and a danger that I cannot name. If I am the chief of sinners; I am the chief of sufferers also. I could not think that this earth contained a place for sufferings and terrors so unmanning;[4]

and you can do but one thing, Utterson, to lighten this destiny, and that is to respect my silence." Utterson was amazed; the dark influence of Hyde had been withdrawn, the doctor had returned to his old tasks and amities;[5] a week ago, the prospect had smiled with every promise of a cheerful and an honored age; and now, in a moment, friendship and peace of mind and the whole tenor[6] of his life were wrecked. So great and unprepared a change pointed to madness; but in view of Lanyon's manner and words, there must lie for it some deeper ground.

A week afterward Dr. Lanyon took to his bed, and in something less than a fortnight he was dead. The night after the funeral, at which he had been sadly affected, Utterson locked the door of his business room, and sitting there by the light of a melancholy candle, drew out and set before him an envelope addressed by the hand and sealed with the seal of his dead friend. "PRIVATE: for the hands of J. G. Utterson *alone,* and in case of his predecease *to be destroyed unread,*" so it was emphatically superscribed; and the lawyer dreaded to behold the contents. "I have buried one friend today," he thought; "what if this should cost me another?" And then he condemned the fear as a disloyalty, and broke the seal. Within there was another enclosure, likewise sealed, and marked upon the cover as "Not to be opened till the death or disappearance of Dr. Henry Jekyll." Utterson could not trust his eyes. Yes, it was disappearance; here again, as in the mad will, which he had long ago restored to its author, here again were the idea of a disappearance and the name of Henry Jekyll bracketed. But in the will, that idea had sprung from the sinister suggestion of the man Hyde; it was set there with a purpose all too plain and horrible. Written by the hand of Lanyon, what should it mean? A great curiosity came to the trustee, to disregard the prohibition, and dive at once to the bottom of these mysteries; but professional honor and faith to his dead friend were stringent obligations, and the packet slept in the inmost corner of his private safe.

It is one thing to mortify curiosity, another to conquer it; and it may be doubted if, from that day forth, Utterson desired the society of his surviving friend with the same eagerness. He thought of him kindly, but his thoughts were disquieted and fearful. He went to call indeed, but he was perhaps relieved to be denied admittance; perhaps, in his heart, he preferred to speak with Poole upon the doorstep, and surrounded by the air and sounds of the open city, rather than to be admitted into that house of voluntary bondage, and to sit and speak with its inscrutable[7] recluse. Poole had, indeed, no very pleasant news to communicate. The doctor, it appeared, now more than ever confined himself to the cabinet over the laboratory, where he would sometimes even sleep: he was out of spirits, he had grown very silent, he did not read; it seemed as if he had something on his mind. Utterson became so used to the unvarying character of these reports, that he fell off little by little in the frequency of his visits.

[1] **ken:** range of vision
[2] **disreputable:** disgraceful; dishonorable
[3] **allusion:** indirect reference to
[4] **unmanning:** causing to lose courage
[5] **amities:** friendships
[6] **tenor:** general course; quality
[7] **inscrutable:** mysterious; impossible to understand

A CLOSER LOOK

1. How do the police know that it was Hyde who murdered Sir Danvers Carew?

2. Descriptions of Mr. Hyde differ widely, except on one point. What impression does Hyde give to everyone who sees him?

3. Jekyll shows Utterson a letter from Mr. Hyde. Why is Utterson relieved when he first reads the letter? Why does Poole's report that no messenger had come that day renew Utterson's fears?

4. What does Mr. Guest discover when he compares Hyde's letter to Jekyll's note? What does this discovery lead Utterson to believe?

5. How does Dr. Jekyll change after the disappearance of Mr. Hyde?

6. What has caused Dr. Lanyon's health to fail so suddenly? What are his feelings towards Dr. Jekyll?

7. Dr. Lanyon leaves Utterson a sealed document marked "not to be opened till the death or disappearance of Dr. Henry Jekyll." On what other document has the word "disappearance" appeared? What is surprising about Lanyon's use of the word?

CHAPTER SEVEN

Incident at the Window

It chanced on Sunday, when Mr. Utterson was on his usual walk with Mr. Enfield, that their way lay once again through the by-street; and that when they came in front of the door, both stopped to gaze on it.

"Well," said Enfield, "that story's at an end, at least. We shall never see more of Mr. Hyde."

"I hope not," said Utterson. "Did I ever tell you that I once saw him and shared your feeling of repulsion?"

"It was impossible to do the one without the other," returned Enfield. "And, by the way, what an ass you must have thought me, not to know that this was a back way to Dr. Jekyll's! It was partly your own fault that I found it out even when I did."

"So you found it out, did you?" said Utterson. "But if that be so, we may step into the court and take a look at the windows. To tell you the truth, I am uneasy about poor Jekyll; and even outside, I feel as if the presence of a friend might do him good."

The court was very cool and a little damp, and full of premature twilight, although the sky, high up overhead, was still bright with sunset. The middle one of the three windows was halfway open; and sitting close beside it, taking the air with an infinite sadness of mien,[1] like some disconsolate[2] prisoner, Utterson saw Dr. Jekyll.

"What! Jekyll!" he cried. "I trust you are better."

"I am very low, Utterson," replied the doctor drearily; "very low. It will not last long, thank God."

"You stay too much indoors," said the lawyer. "You should be out, whipping up the circulation, like Mr. Enfield and me. (This is my cousin—Mr. Enfield—Dr. Jekyll.) Come now; get your hat and take a quick turn with us."

"You are very good," sighed the other. "I should like to very much; but no, no, no—it is quite impossible; I dare not. But indeed, Utterson, I am very glad to see you; this is really a great pleasure. I would ask you and Mr. Enfield up, but the place is really not fit."

"Why then," said the lawyer, good-naturedly, "the best thing we can do is to stay down here and speak with you from where we are."

"That is just what I was about to venture to propose," returned the doctor, with a smile. But the words were hardly uttered before the smile was struck out of his face and succeeded by an expression of such abject[3] terror and despair as froze the very blood of the two gentlemen below. They saw it but for a glimpse, for the window was instantly thrust down; but that glimpse had been sufficient, and they turned and left the court without a word. In silence, too, they traversed[4] the by-street; and it was not until they had come into a neighboring thoroughfare, where even upon a Sunday there were still some stirrings of life, that Mr. Utterson at last turned and looked at his companion. They were both pale, and there was an answering horror in their eyes.

"God forgive us! God forgive us!" said Mr. Utterson.

But Mr. Enfield only nodded his head very seriously, and walked on once more in silence.

[1] **mien:** manner
[2] **disconsolate:** hopelessly sad
[3] **abject:** of the most miserable kind; wretched
[4] **traversed:** traveled across

CHAPTER EIGHT

The Last Night

Mr. Utterson was sitting by his fireside one evening after dinner, when he was surprised to receive a visit from Poole.

"Bless me, Poole, what brings you here?" he cried; and then, taking a second look at him, "What ails you?" he added; "is the doctor ill?"

"Mr. Utterson," said the man, "there is something wrong."

"Take a seat, and here is a glass of wine for you," said the lawyer. "Now, take your time, and tell me plainly what you want."

"You know the doctor's ways, sir," replied Poole, "and how he shuts himself up. Well, he's shut up again in the cabinet; and I don't like it, sir—I wish I may die if I like it. Mr. Utterson, sir, I'm afraid."

"Now, my good man," said the lawyer, "be explicit. What are you afraid of?"

"I've been afraid for about a week," returned Poole, doggedly disregarding the question, "and I can bear it no more."

The man's appearance amply bore out his words. His manner was altered for the worse; and except for the moment when he had first announced his terror, he had not once looked the lawyer in the face. Even now, he sat with the glass of wine untasted on his knee and his eyes directed to a corner of the floor. "I can bear it no more," he repeated.

"Come," said the lawyer, "I see you have some good reason, Poole; I see there is something seriously amiss. Try to tell me what it is."

"I think there's been foul play," said Poole hoarsely.

"Foul play!" cried the lawyer, a good deal frightened, and rather inclined to be irritated in consequence. "What foul play? What does the man mean?"

"I daren't say, sir," was the answer, "but will you come along with me and see for yourself?"

Mr. Utterson's only answer was to rise and get his hat and greatcoat; but he observed with wonder the greatness of the relief that appeared upon the butler's face, and perhaps with no less, that the wine was still untasted when he set it down to follow.

It was a wild, cold, seasonable night of March, with a pale moon, lying on her back as though the wind had tilted her, and a flying wrack[1] of the most diaphanous[2] and lawny[3] texture. The wind made talking difficult and flecked the blood into the face. It seemed to have swept the streets unusually bare of passengers, besides, for Mr. Utterson thought he had never seen that part of London so deserted. He could have wished it otherwise; never in his life had he been conscious of so sharp a wish to see and touch his fellow-creatures; for, struggle as he might, there was borne in upon his mind a crushing anticipation of calamity. The square, when they got there, was all full of wind and dust, and the thin trees in the garden were lashing themselves along the railing. Poole, who had kept all the way a pace or two ahead, now pulled up in the middle of the pavement and, in spite of the biting weather, took off his hat and mopped his brow with a red pocket handkerchief. But for all the hurry of his coming, these were not the dews of exertion that he wiped away, but the moisture of some strangling anguish; for his face was white, and his voice, when he spoke, harsh and broken.

"Well, sir," he said, "here we are, and God grant there be nothing wrong."

"Amen, Poole," said the lawyer.

Thereupon the servant knocked in a very guarded manner; the door was opened on the chain; and a voice asked from within, "Is that you, Poole?"

"It's all right," said Poole. "Open the door."

The hall, when they entered it, was brightly lighted up; the fire was built high; and about the hearth the whole of the servants, men and women, stood huddled together like a flock of sheep. At the sight of Mr. Utterson, the housemaid broke into hysterical whimpering; and the cook, crying out, "Bless God! it's Mr. Utterson," ran forward as if to take him in her arms.

"What, what? Are you all here?" said the lawyer, peevishly. "Very irregular, very unseemly; your master would be far from pleased."

"They're all afraid," said Poole.

Blank silence followed, no one protesting; only the maid lifted up her voice, and now wept loudly.

"Hold your tongue!" Poole said to her, with a ferocity of accent that testified to his own jangled nerves; and indeed when the girl had so suddenly raised the note of her lamentation, they had all started and turned toward the inner door with faces of dreadful expectation. "And now," continued the butler, addressing the knife-boy, "reach me a candle, and we'll get this through hands at once." And then he begged Mr. Utterson to follow him, and led the way to the back gardens.

"Now, sir," said he, "you come as gently as you can. I want you to hear, and I don't want you to be heard. And see here, sir, if by any chance he was to ask you in, don't go."

Mr. Utterson's nerves, at this unlooked-for termination, gave a jerk that nearly threw him from his balance; but he re-collected his courage and followed the butler into the laboratory building and through the surgical theater, with its lumber of crates and bottles, to the foot of the stair. Here Poole motioned him to stand on one side and listen; while he himself, setting down the candle and making a great and obvious call on his resolution, mounted the steps and knocked with a somewhat uncertain hand on the red baize of the cabinet door.

"Mr. Utterson, sir, asking to see you," he called; and even as he did so, once more violently signed to the lawyer to give ear.

A voice answered from within: "Tell him I cannot see anyone," it said complainingly.

"Thank you, sir," said Poole, with a note of something like triumph in his voice; and taking up his candle, he led Mr. Utterson back across the yard and into the great kitchen, where the fire was out and the beetles were leaping on the floor.

"Sir," he said, looking Mr. Utterson in the eyes, "was that my master's voice?"

"It seems much changed," replied the lawyer, very pale but giving look for look.

"Changed? Well, yes, I think so," said the butler. "Have I been twenty years in this man's house, to be deceived about his voice? No, sir; master's made away with; he was made away with, eight days ago, when we heard him cry out upon the name of God; and *who's* in there instead of him, and *why* it stays there, is a thing that cries to Heaven, Mr. Utterson!"

"This is a very strange tale, Poole; this is rather a wild tale, my man," said Mr. Utterson, biting his finger. "Suppose it were as you suppose; supposing Dr. Jekyll to have been—well, murdered, what could induce the murderer to stay? That won't hold water; it doesn't commend itself to reason."

"Well, Mr. Utterson, you are a hard man to satisfy, but I'll do it yet," said Poole. "All this last week (you must know), him or it, or whatever it is that lives in that cabinet, has been crying night and day for some sort of medicine and cannot get it to his mind. It was sometimes his way—the master's, that is—to write his orders on a sheet of paper and throw it on the stair. We've had nothing else this week back; nothing but papers, and a closed door, and the very meals left there to be smuggled in when nobody was looking. Well, sir, every day—ay, and twice and thrice in the same day—there have been orders and complaints, and I have been sent flying to all the wholesale chemists in town. Every time I brought the stuff back, there would be another paper telling me to return it, because it was not pure, and another order to a different firm. This drug is wanted bitter bad, sir, whatever for."

"Have you any of these papers?" asked Mr. Utterson.

Poole felt in his pocket and handed out a crumpled note, which the lawyer, bending nearer to the candle, carefully examined. Its contents ran thus: "Dr. Jekyll presents his compliments to Messrs. Maw. He assures them that their last sample is impure and quite useless for his present purpose. In the year 18—, Dr. J. purchased a somewhat large quantity from Messrs. M. He now begs them to search with the most sedulous care, and should any of the same quality be left, to forward it to him at once. Expense is no consideration. The importance of this to Dr. J. can hardly be exaggerated." So far the letter had run composedly enough; but here, with a sudden splutter of the pen, the writer's emotion had broken loose. "For God's sake," he had added, "find me some of the old."

"This is a strange note," said Mr. Utterson; and then, sharply, "How do you come to have it open?"

"The man at Maw's was main angry, sir, and he threw it back to me like so much dirt," returned Poole.

"This is unquestionably the doctor's hand, do you know?" resumed the lawyer.

"I thought it looked like it," said the servant rather sulkily; and then, with another voice, "But what matters hand of write?" he said. "I've seen him!"

"Seen him?" repeated Mr. Utterson. "Well?"

"That's it!" said Poole. "It was this way: I came suddenly into the theater from the garden. It seems he had slipped out to look for this drug, or whatever it is; for the cabinet door was open, and there he was at the far end of the room, digging among the crates. He looked up when I came in, gave a kind of cry, and whipped upstairs into the cabinet. It was but for one minute that I saw him, but the hair stood upon my head like quills. Sir, if that was my master, why had he a mask upon his face? If it was my master, why did he cry out like a rat and run from me? I have served him long enough. And then . . ." The man paused, and passed his hand over his face.

"These are all very strange circumstances," said Mr. Utterson, "but I think I begin to see daylight. Your master, Poole, is plainly seized with one of those maladies that both torture and deform the sufferer; hence, for aught I know, the alteration of his voice; hence the mask and his avoidance of his friends; hence his eagerness to find this drug, by means of which the poor soul retains some hope of ultimate recovery—God grant that he be not deceived! There is my explanation. It is sad enough, Poole, ay, and appalling to consider; but it is plain and natural, hangs well together, and delivers us from all exorbitant alarms."

"Sir," said the butler, turning to a sort of mottled pallor, "that thing was not my master, and there's the truth. My master"—here he looked round him, and began to whisper—"is a tall, fine build of a man, and this was more of a dwarf." Utterson attempted to protest. "Oh, sir," cried Poole, "do you think I do not know my master after twenty years? Do you think I do not know where his head comes to in the cabinet door, where I saw him every morning of my life? No, sir, that thing in the mask was never Dr. Jekyll—God knows what it was, but it was never Dr. Jekyll; and it is the belief of my heart that there was murder done."

"Poole," replied the lawyer, "if you say that, it will become my duty to make certain. Much as I desire to spare your master's feelings, much as I am puzzled by this note, which seems to prove him to be still alive, I shall consider it my duty to break in that door."

"Ah, Mr. Utterson, that's talking!" cried the butler.

"And now comes the second question," resumed Utterson: "Who is going to do it?"

"Why, you and me, sir," was the undaunted reply.

"That is very well said," returned the lawyer; "and whatever comes of it, I shall make it my business to see you are no loser."

"There is an axe in the theater," continued Poole; "and you might take the kitchen poker for yourself."

The lawyer took that rude but weighty instrument into his hand and balanced it. "Do you know, Poole," he said, looking up, "that you and I are about to place ourselves in a position of some peril?"

"You may say so, sir, indeed," returned the butler.

"It is well, then, that we should be frank," said the other. "We both think more than we have said; let us make a clean breast. This masked figure that you saw, did you recognize it?"

"Well, sir, it went so quick, and the creature was so doubled up, that I could hardly swear to that," was the answer. "But if you mean, was it Mr. Hyde?—why, yes, I think it was! You see, it was much of the same bigness; and it had the same quick, light way with it; and then who else could have got in by the laboratory door? You have not forgot, sir, that at the time of the murder he had still the key with him? But that's not all. I don't know, Mr. Utterson, if ever you met this Mr. Hyde?"

"Yes," said the lawyer. "I once spoke with him."

"Then you must know, as well as the rest of us, that there was something queer about that gentleman—something that gave a man a turn—I don't know rightly how to say it, sir, beyond this: that you felt it in your marrow, kind of cold and thin."

"I own I felt something of what you describe," said Mr. Utterson.

"Quite so, sir," returned Poole. "Well, when that masked thing like a monkey jumped from among the chemicals and whipped into the cabinet, it went down my spine like ice. Oh, I know it's not evidence, Mr. Utterson; I'm book-learned enough for that; but a man has his feelings; and I give you my Bible word it was Mr. Hyde!"

"Ay, ay," said the lawyer. "My fears incline to the same point. Evil, I fear, founded—evil was sure to come of—that connection. Ay, truly, I believe you; I believe poor Harry is killed; and I believe his murderer (for what purpose, God alone can tell) is still lurking in his victim's room. Well, let our name be vengeance. Call Bradshaw."

The footman came at the summons, very white and nervous.

"Pull yourself together, Bradshaw," said the lawyer. "This suspense, I know, is telling upon all of you; but it is now our intention to make an end of it. Poole, here, and I are going to force our way into the cabinet. If all is well, my shoulders are broad enough to bear the blame. Meanwhile, lest anything should really be amiss, or any malefactor seek to escape by the back, you and the boy must go round the corner with a pair of good sticks and take your post at the laboratory door. We give you ten minutes to get to your stations."

As Bradshaw left, the lawyer looked at his watch. "And now,

Poole, let us get to ours," he said; and taking the poker under his arm, he led the way into the yard. The scud[4] had banked over the moon, and it was now quite dark. The wind, which only broke in puffs and draughts into that deep well of building, tossed the light of the candle to and fro about their steps, until they came into the shelter of the theater, where they sat down silently to wait. London hummed solemnly all around; but nearer at hand, the stillness was only broken by the sound of a footfall moving to and fro along the cabinet floor.

"So it will walk all day, sir," whispered Poole; "ay, and the better part of the night. Only when a new sample comes from the chemist, there's a bit of a break. Ah, it's an ill conscience that's such an enemy to rest! Ah, sir, there's blood foully shed in every step of it! But hark again, a little closer—put your heart in your ears, Mr. Utterson, and tell me, is that the doctor's foot?"

The steps fell lightly and oddly, with a certain swing, for all they went so slowly; it was different indeed from the heavy creaking tread of Henry Jekyll. Utterson sighed. "Is there never anything else?" he asked.

Poole nodded. "Once," he said. "Once I heard it weeping!"

"Weeping? how that?" said the lawyer, conscious of a sudden chill of horror.

"Weeping like a woman or a lost soul," said the butler. "I came away with that upon my heart, that I could have wept too."

But now the ten minutes drew to an end. Poole disinterred the axe from under a stack of packing straw; the candle was set upon the nearest table to light them to the attack; and then drew near with bated breath to where that patient foot was still going up and down, up and down in the quiet of the night.

"Jekyll," cried Utterson, with a loud voice, "I demand to see you." He paused a moment, but there came no reply. "I give you fair warning, our suspicions are aroused, and I must and shall see you," he resumed; "if not by fair means, then by foul—if not of your consent, then by brute force!"

"Utterson," said the voice, "for God's sake, have mercy!"

"Ah, that's not Jekyll's voice—it's Hyde's!" cried Utterson. "Down with the door, Poole!"

Poole swung the axe over his shoulder; the blow shook the building, and the red baize door leaped against the lock and hinges. A dismal[5] screech, as of mere animal terror, rang from the cabinet. Up went the axe again, and again the panels crashed and the frame bounded. Four times the blow fell, but the wood was tough and the fittings were of excellent workmanship; and it was not until the fifth, that the lock burst and the wreck of the door fell inwards on the carpet.

The besiegers,[6] appalled by their own riot and the stillness that had succeeded, stood back a little and peered in. There lay the cabinet before their eyes in the quiet lamplight, a good fire glowing and chattering on the hearth, the kettle singing its thin strain, a drawer or two open, papers neatly set forth on the business table, and nearer the fire, the things laid out for tea: the quietest room, you would have said, and, but for the glazed presses full of chemicals, the most commonplace that night in London.

Right in the midst there lay the body of a man sorely[7] contorted and still twitching. They drew near on tiptoe, turned it on his back, and beheld the face of Edward Hyde. He was dressed in clothes far too large for him, clothes of the doctor's bigness; the cords of his face still moved with a semblance of life, but life was quite gone; and by the crushed phial[8] in the hand and the strong smell of kernels[9] that hung upon the air, Utterson knew that he was looking on the body of a self-destroyer.

"We have come too late," he said sternly, "whether to save or punish. Hyde is gone to his account;[10] and it only remains for us to find the body of your master."

The far greater proportion of the building was occupied by the theater, which filled almost the whole ground story and was lighted from above, and by the cabinet, which formed an upper story at one end and looked upon the court. A corridor joined the theater to the door on the by-street, and with this, the cabinet communicated separately by a second flight of stairs. There were besides a few dark closets and a spacious cellar. All these they now thoroughly examined. Each closet needed but a glance, for all were empty; and all, by the dust that fell from their doors, had stood long unopened. The cellar, indeed, was filled with crazy lumber, mostly dating from the times of the surgeon who was Jekyll's predecessor; but even as they opened the door, they were advertised of the uselessness of further search by the fall of a perfect mat of cobwebs which had for years sealed up the entrance. Nowhere was there any trace of Henry Jekyll, dead or alive.

Poole stamped on the flags of the corridor. "He must be buried here," he said, hearkening to the sound.

"Or he may have fled," said Utterson, and he turned to examine the door in the by-street. It was locked; and lying near by on the flags, they found the key, already stained with rust.

"This does not look like use," observed the lawyer.

"Use!" echoed Poole. "Do you not see, sir, it is broken? much as if a man had stamped on it."

"Ah," continued Utterson, "and the fractures, too, are rusty." The two men looked at each other with a scare. "This is beyond me, Poole," said the lawyer. "Let us go back to the cabinet."

They mounted the stair in silence, and still, with an occasional awestruck glance at the dead body, proceeded more thoroughly to examine the contents of the cabinet. At one table, there were traces of chemical work, various measured heaps of some white salt being laid on glass saucers, as though for an experiment in which the unhappy man had been prevented.

"That is the same drug that I was always bringing him," said Poole; and even as he spoke, the kettle, with a startling noise, boiled over.

This brought them to the fireside, where the easy chair was drawn cozily up, and the tea things stood ready to the sitter's elbow, the very sugar in the cup. There were several books on a shelf; one lay beside the tea things open, and Utterson was amazed to find it a copy of a pious work, for which Jekyll had several times expressed a great esteem, annotated, in his own hand, with startling blasphemies.[11]

Next, in the course of their review of the chamber, the searchers came to the cheval glass, into whose depth they looked with an involuntary horror. But it was so turned as to show them nothing but the rosy glow playing on the roof, the fire sparkling in a hundred repetitions along the glazed front of the presses, and their own pale and fearful countenances stooping to look in.

"This glass has seen some strange things, sir," whispered Poole.

"And surely none stranger than itself," echoed the lawyer, in the same tone. "For what did Jekyll"—he caught himself up at the word with a start, and then conquering the weakness—"what could Jekyll want with it?" he said.

"You may say that!" said Poole.

Next they turned to the business table. On the desk among the neat array of papers, a large envelope was uppermost, and bore, in the doctor's hand, the name of Mr. Utterson. The lawyer unsealed it, and several enclosures fell to the floor. The first was a will, drawn in the same eccentric terms as the one which he had returned six months before, to serve as a testament in case of death and as a deed of gift in case of disappearance; but in place of the name of Edward Hyde, the lawyer, with indescribable amazement, read the name of Gabriel John Utterson. He looked at Poole, and then back at the papers, and last of all at the dead malefactor stretched upon the carpet.

"My head goes round," he said. "He has been all these days in possession; he had no cause to like me; he must have raged to see himself displaced; and he has not destroyed this document."

He caught the next paper; it was a brief note in the doctor's hand and dated at the top. "Oh, Poole!" the lawyer cried, "he was alive and here this day. He cannot have been disposed of in so short a space; he must be still alive, he must have fled! And then why fled? and how? And in that case can we venture to declare this suicide? Oh, we must be careful. I foresee that we may yet involve your master in some dire catastrophe."

"Why don't you read it, sir?" asked Poole.

"Because I fear," replied the lawyer solemnly. "God grant I have no cause for it!" And with that he brought the paper to his eyes and read as follows:

> My dear Utterson,
>
> When this shall fall into your hands, I shall have disappeared, under what circumstances I have not the penetration to foresee; but my instincts and all the circumstances of my nameless situation tell me that the end is sure and must be early. Go then, and first read the narrative which Lanyon warned me he was to place in your hands; and if you care to hear more, turn to the confession of
>
> Your unworthy and unhappy friend,
>
> HENRY JEKYLL.

"There was a third enclosure?" asked Utterson.

"Here sir," said Poole, and gave into his hands a considerable packet sealed in several places.

The lawyer put it in his pocket. "I would say nothing of this paper. If your master has fled or is dead, we may at least save his credit. It is now ten; I must go home and read these documents in quiet; but I shall be back before midnight, when we shall send for the police."

They went out, locking the door of the theater behind them; and Utterson, once more leaving the servants gathered about the fire in the hall, trudged back to his office to read the two narratives in which this mystery was now to be explained.

[1] **wrack:** thin clouds
[2] **diaphanous:** transparent
[3] **lawny:** having the quality of lawn (a thin cotton fabric)
[4] **scud:** wind-driven clouds
[5] **dismal:** causing dread
[6] **besiegers:** attackers
[7] **sorely:** extremely
[8] **phial:** vial
[9] **kernels:** granules of a drug
[10] **gone to his account:** dead
[11] **blasphemies:** words or deeds showing contempt for that which is sacred

CHAPTER NINE

Dr. Lanyon's Narrative

On the ninth of January, now four days ago, I received by the evening delivery a registered envelope, addressed in the hand of my colleague and old school companion, Henry Jekyll. I was a good deal surprised by this, for we were by no means in the habit of correspondence. I had seen the man, dined with him indeed, the night before; and I could imagine nothing in our intercourse that should justify the formality of registration. The contents increased my wonder, for this is how the letter ran:

10th December, 18—

Dear Lanyon,

You are one of my oldest friends; and although we may have differed at times on scientific questions, I cannot remember, at least on my side, any break in our affection. There was never a day when, if you had said to me, "Jekyll, my life, my honor, my reason, depend upon you," I would not have sacrificed my fortune or my left hand to help you. Lanyon, my life, my honor, my reason, are all at your mercy; if you fail me tonight, I am lost. You might suppose, after this preface, that I am going to ask you for something dishonorable to grant. Judge for yourself.

I want you to postpone all other engagements for tonight—ay, even if you were summoned to the bedside of an emperor; to take a cab, unless your carriage should be actually at the door; and, with this letter in your hand for consultation, to drive straight to my house. Poole, my butler, has his orders; you will find him waiting your arrival with a locksmith. The door of my cabinet is then to be forced; and you are to go in alone; to open the glazed press (letter E) on the left hand, breaking the lock if it be shut; and to draw out, *with all its contents as they stand,* the fourth drawer from the top or (which is the same thing) the third from the bottom. In my extreme distress of mind, I have a morbid[1] fear of misdirecting you; but even if I am in error, you may know the right drawer by its contents: some powders, a phial, and a paper book. This drawer I beg of you to carry back with you to Cavendish Square exactly as it stands.

That is the first part of the service: now for the second. You should be back, if you set out at once on the receipt of this, long before midnight; but I will leave you that amount of margin, not only in the fear of one of those obstacles that can neither be prevented nor foreseen, but because an hour when your servants are in bed is to be preferred for what will then remain to do. At midnight, then, I have to ask you to be alone in your consulting room, to admit with your own hand into the house a man who will present himself in my name, and to place in his hands the drawer that you will have brought with you from my cabinet. Then you will have played your part and earned my gratitude completely. Five minutes afterward, if you insist upon an explanation, you will have understood that these arrangements are of capital importance; and that by the neglect of one of them, fantastic as they must appear, you might have charged your conscience with my death or the shipwreck of my reason.

Confident as I am that you will not trifle with this appeal, my heart sinks and my hand trembles at the bare thought of such a possibility. Think of me at this hour, in a strange place, laboring under a blackness of distress that no fancy can exaggerate, and yet well aware that, if you will but punctually serve me, my troubles will roll away like a story that is told. Serve me, my dear Lanyon, and save

Your friend, H.J.

P.S.—I had already sealed this up when a fresh terror struck upon my soul. It is possible that the post office may fail me, and this letter not come into your hands until tomorrow morning. In that case, dear Lanyon, do my errand when it shall be most convenient for you in the course of the day; and once more expect my messenger at midnight. It may then already be too late; and if that night passes without event, you will know that you have seen the last of Henry Jekyll.

Upon the reading of this letter, I made sure[2] my colleague was insane; but till that was proved beyond the possibility of doubt, I felt bound to do as he requested. The less I understood of this farrago,[3] the less I was in a position to judge of its importance; and an appeal so worded could not be set aside without a grave responsibility. I rose accordingly from table, got into a hansom, and drove straight to Jekyll's house. The butler was awaiting my arrival; he had received by the same post as mine a registered letter of instruction, and had sent at once for a locksmith and a carpenter. The tradesmen came while we were yet speaking; and we moved in a body to old Dr. Denman's surgical theater, from which (as you are doubtless aware) Jekyll's private cabinet is most conveniently entered. The door was very strong, the lock excellent; the carpenter avowed he would have great trouble and have to do much damage if force were to be used; and the locksmith was near despair. But this last was a handy fellow, and after two hours' work the door stood open. The press marked E was unlocked; and I took out the drawer, had it filled up with straw and tied in a sheet, and returned with it to Cavendish Square.

Here I proceeded to examine its contents. The powders were neatly enough made up, but not with the nicety of the dispensing chemist; so that it was plain they were of Jekyll's private manufacture; and when I opened one of the wrappers, I found what seemed to me a simple crystalline salt of a white color. The phial, to which I next turned my attention, might have been about half full of a blood-red liquor,[4] which was highly pungent to the sense of smell, and seemed to me to contain phosphorus and some volatile ether. At the other ingredients I could make no guess. The book was an ordinary version book, and contained little but a series of dates. These covered a period of many years; but I observed that the entries ceased nearly a year ago, and quite abruptly. Here and there a brief remark was appended to a date, usually no more than a single word—"double" occurring perhaps six times in a total of several hundred entries; and once very early in the list, and followed by several marks of exclamation, "Total failure!!!" All this, though it whetted my curiosity, told me little that was definite. Here were a phial of some tincture,[5] a paper of some salt, and the record of a series of experiments that had led (like too many of Jekyll's investigations) to no end of practical usefulness. How could the presence of these articles in my house affect either the honor, the sanity, or the life of my flighty colleague? If his messenger could go to one place, why could he not go to another? And even granting some impediment,[6] why was this gentleman to be received by me in secret? The more I reflected, the more convinced I grew that I was dealing with a case of cerebral[7] disease; and though I dismissed my servants to bed, I loaded an old revolver, that I might be found in some posture of self-defense.

Twelve o'clock had scarce rung out over London ere the knocker sounded very gently on the door. I went myself at the summons, and found a small man crouching against the pillars of the portico.

"Are you come from Dr. Jekyll?" I asked.

He told me "yes" by a constrained gesture; and when I had bidden him enter, he did not obey me without a searching backward glance into the darkness of the square. There was a policeman not far off, advancing with his bull's-eye[8] open; and at the sight, I thought my visitor started and made greater haste.

These particulars struck me, I confess, disagreeably; and as I followed him into the bright light of the consulting room, I kept my hand ready on my weapon. Here, at last, I had a chance of clearly seeing him. I had never set eyes on him before, so much was certain. He was small, as I have said; I was struck besides with the shocking expression of his face, with his remarkable combination of great muscular activity and great apparent debility[9] of constitution, and—last but not least—with the odd, subjective disturbance caused by his neighborhood.[10] This bore some resemblance to incipient[11] rigor,[12] and was accompanied by a marked sinking of the pulse. At the time, I set it down to some idiosyncratic, personal distaste, and merely wondered at the acuteness of the symptoms; but I have since had reason to believe the cause to lie much deeper in the nature of man, and to turn on some nobler hinge than the principle of hatred.

This person (who had thus, from the first moment of his entrance, struck in me what I can only describe as a disgustful curiosity) was dressed in a fashion that would have made an ordinary person laughable; his clothes, that is to say, although they were of rich and sober fabric, were enormously too large for him in every measurement—the trousers hanging on his legs and rolled up to keep them from the ground, the waist of the coat below his haunches, and the collar sprawling wide upon his shoulders. Strange to relate, this ludicrous accoutrement[13] was far from moving me to laughter. Rather, as there was something abnormal and misbegotten in the very essence of the creature that now faced me—something seizing, surprising, and revolting—this fresh disparity seemed but to fit in with and to reinforce it; so that to my interest in the man's nature and character there was added a curiosity as to his origin, his life, his fortune and status in the world.

These observations, though they have taken so great a space to be set down in, were yet the work of a few seconds. My visitor was, indeed, on fire with somber excitement.

"Have you got it?" he cried. "Have you got it?" And so lively was his impatience that he even laid his hand upon my arm and sought to shake me.

I put him back, conscious at his touch of a certain icy pang along my blood. "Come, sir," said I. "You forget that I have not yet the pleasure of your acquaintance. Be seated, if you please." And I showed him an example and sat down myself in my customary seat, and with as fair an imitation of my ordinary manner to a patient as the lateness of the hour, the nature of my preoccupations, and the horror I had of my visitor would suffer me to muster.

"I beg your pardon, Dr. Lanyon," he replied, civilly enough. "What you say is very well founded, and my impatience has shown its heels to my politeness. I come here at the instance of your colleague, Dr. Henry Jekyll, on a piece of business of some moment; and I understood . . ." he paused, and put his hand to his throat, and I could see, in spite of his collected manner, that he was wrestling against the approaches of the hysteria—"I understand, a drawer . . ."

But here I took pity on my visitor's suspense, and some perhaps on my own growing curiosity.

"There it is, sir," said I, pointing to the drawer, where it lay on the floor behind a table, and still covered with the sheet.

He sprang to it, and then paused and laid his hand upon his heart. I could hear his teeth grate with the convulsive action of his jaws, and his face was so ghastly to see that I grew alarmed both for his life and reason.

"Compose yourself," said I.

He turned a dreadful smile to me, and, as if with the decision of despair, plucked away the sheet. At sight of the contents, he uttered one loud sob of such immense relief that I sat petrified. And the next moment, in a voice that was already fairly well under control, "Have you a graduated glass?"[14] he asked.

I rose from my place with something of an effort and gave him what he asked.

He thanked me with a smiling nod, measured out a few minims[15] of the red tincture, and added one of the powders. The mixture, which was at first of a reddish hue, began, in proportion as the crystals melted, to brighten in color, to effervesce[16] audibly, and to throw off small fumes of vapor. Suddenly, and at the same moment, the ebullition[17] ceased, and the compound changed to a dark purple, which faded again more slowly to a watery green. My visitor, who had watched these metamorphoses[18] with a keen eye, smiled, set down the glass upon the table, and then turned and looked upon me with an air of scrutiny.

"And now," said he, "to settle what remains: Will you be wise? will you be guided? will you suffer me to take this glass in my hand and to go forth from your house without further parley?[19]— or has the greed of curiosity too much command of you? Think before you answer, for it shall be done as you decide. As you decide, you shall be left as you were before, and neither richer nor wiser, unless the sense of service rendered to a man in mortal distress may be counted as a kind of riches of the soul. Or, if you shall so prefer to choose, a new province of knowledge and new avenues to fame and power shall be laid open to you, here, in this room, upon the instant; and your sight shall be blasted by a prodigy[20] to stagger the unbelief of Satan."

"Sir," said I, affecting a coolness that I was far from truly possessing, "you speak enigmas,[21] and you will perhaps not wonder that I hear you with no very strong impression of belief. But I have gone too far in the way of inexplicable service to pause before I see the end."

"It is well," replied my visitor. "Lanyon, you remember your vows: what follows is under the seal of our profession. And now, you who have so long been bound to the most narrow and material views, you who have denied the virtue of transcendental[22] medicine, you who have derided[23] your superiors—behold!"

He put the glass to his lips and drank at one gulp. A cry followed; he reeled, staggered, clutched at the table, and held on, staring with injected eyes, gasping with open mouth; and as I looked, there came, I thought, a change—he seemed to swell—his face became suddenly black, and the features seemed to melt and alter—and the next moment I had sprung to my feet and leaped back against the wall, my arm raised to shield me from that prodigy, my mind submerged in terror.

"O God!" I screamed, and "O God!" again and again; for there before my eyes—pale and shaken, and half-fainting, and groping before him with his hands, like a man restored from death—there stood Henry Jekyll!

What he told me in the next hour I cannot bring my mind to set on paper. I saw what I saw, I heard what I heard, and my soul sickened at it; and yet now, when that sight has faded from my eyes, I ask myself if I believe it, and I cannot answer. My life is shaken to its roots; sleep has left me; the deadliest terror sits by me at all hours of the day and night. I feel that my days are numbered and that I must die, and yet I shall die incredulous. As for the moral turpitude[24] that man unveiled to me, even with tears of penitence,[25] I cannot, even in memory, dwell on it without a start of horror. I will say but one thing, Utterson, and that (if you can bring your mind to credit it) will be more than enough. The creature who crept into my house that night was, on Jekyll's own confession, known by the name of Hyde and hunted for in every corner of the land as the murderer of Carew.

HASTIE LANYON

[1] **morbid:** psychologically unhealthy
[2] **made sure:** felt sure
[3] **farrago:** confusion
[4] **liquor:** liquid
[5] **tincture:** a solution of a medicinal substance
[6] **impediment:** something preventing one from doing something
[7] **cerebral:** related to the brain
[8] **bull's-eye:** lantern with a thick lens
[9] **debility:** feebleness
[10] **neighborhood:** nearness; proximity
[11] **incipient:** in the beginning stages of
[12] **rigor:** numbness; a death-like chill
[13] **ludicrous accoutrement:** ridiculous outfit
[14] **graduated glass:** glass used for measuring liquids
[15] **minims:** small amounts
[16] **effervesce:** to bubble
[17] **ebullition:** boiling; bubbling up
[18] **metamorphoses:** physical changes; transformations
[19] **parley:** discussion; dispute
[20] **prodigy:** extraordinary event
[21] **enigmas:** riddles; puzzles
[22] **transcendental:** extending beyond the limits of ordinary experience
[23] **derided:** ridiculed
[24] **moral turpitude:** corruptness; gross immorality
[25] **penitence:** the quality or state of being sorry for one's sins

A CLOSER LOOK

1. In the "Incident at the Window," how does Dr. Jekyll look and behave when Utterson first speaks to him? How does Jekyll look right before the window is so abruptly closed?

2. What prompts Poole to go to Mr. Utterson's house for help? What does Poole suspect has happened to Dr. Jekyll?

3. Why do Utterson and Poole decide to break down the door of Dr. Jekyll's cabinet? What do they find inside?

4. How has Dr. Jekyll's will been changed? Why is Utterson surprised to find that the revised document has not been destroyed?

5. Dr. Lanyon's narrative tells of the event that literally shocked him to death. What did Lanyon witness?

CHAPTER TEN

Henry Jekyll's Full Statement of the Case

I was born in the year 18— to a large fortune, endowed besides with excellent parts, inclined by nature to industry, fond of the respect of the wise and good among my fellow men, and thus, as might have been supposed, with every guarantee of an honorable and distinguished future. And indeed, the worst of my faults was a certain impatient gaiety of disposition, such as has made the happiness of many, but such as I found it hard to reconcile with my imperious[1] desire to carry my head high and wear a more than commonly grave countenance before the public. Hence it came about that I concealed my pleasures; and that when I reached years of reflection and began to look round me, and take stock of my progress and position in the world, I stood already committed to a profound duplicity of life. Many a man would have even blazoned[2] such irregularities as I was guilty of; but from the high views that I had set before me, I regarded and hid them with an almost morbid sense of shame. It was thus rather the exacting[3] nature of my aspirations, than any particular degradation in my faults, that made me what I was, and, with even a deeper trench than in the majority of men, severed in me those provinces of good and ill which divide and compound man's dual nature. In this case, I was driven to reflect deeply and inveterately[4] on that hard law of life which lies at the root of religion, and is one of the most plentiful springs of distress. Though so profound a double-dealer, I was in no sense a hypocrite; both sides of me were in dead earnest. I was no more myself when I laid aside restraint and plunged in shame than when I labored in the eye of day, at the furtherance of knowledge or the relief of sorrow and suffering. And it chanced that the direction of my scientific studies, which led wholly toward the mystic and the transcendental, reacted and shed a strong light on this consciousness of the perennial war among my members. With every day, and from both sides of my intelligence, the moral and the intellectual, I thus drew steadily nearer to that truth, by whose partial discovery I have been doomed to such a dreadful shipwreck: that man is not truly one, but truly two. I say two, because the state of my own knowledge does not pass beyond that point. Others will follow, others will outstrip me on the same lines; and I hazard the guess that man will be ultimately known for a mere polity of multifarious, incongruous and independent denizens.[5] I, for my part, from the nature of my life, advanced infallibly in one direction, and in one direction only. It was on the moral side, and in my own person, that I learned to recognize the thorough and primitive duality of man; I saw that, of the two natures that contended in the field of my consciousness, even if I could rightly be said to be either, it was only because I was radically both; and from an early date, even before the course of my scientific discoveries had begun to suggest the most naked possibility of such a miracle, I had learned to dwell with pleasure, as a beloved daydream, on the thought of the separation of these elements. If each, I told myself, could but be housed in separate identities, life would be relieved of all that was unbearable; the unjust might go his way, delivered from the aspirations and remorse of his more upright twin; and the just could walk steadfastly and securely on his upward path, doing the good things in which he found his pleasure, and no longer exposed to disgrace and penitence by the hands of this extraneous evil. It was the curse of mankind that these incongruous faggots[6] were thus bound together—that in the agonized womb of consciousness, these polar twins should be continuously struggling. How, then, were they dissociated?

I was so far in my reflections when, as I have said, a sidelight began to shine upon the subject from the laboratory table. I began to perceive, more deeply than it has ever yet been stated, the trembling immateriality, the mistlike transience,[7] of this seemingly so solid body in which we walk attired. Certain agents I found to have the power to shake and to pluck back that fleshly vestment, even as a wind might toss the curtains of a pavilion. For two good reasons, I will not enter deeply into this scientific branch of my confession. First, because I have been made to learn that the doom and burden of our life is bound forever on man's shoulders; and when the attempt is made to cast it off, it but returns upon us with more unfamiliar and more awful pressure. Second, because, as my narrative will make, alas! too evident, my discoveries were incomplete. Enough, then, that I not only recognized my natural body from the mere aura and effulgence[8] of certain of the powers that made up my spirit, but managed to compound a drug by which these powers should be dethroned from their supremacy, and a second form and countenance substituted, none the less natural to me because they were the expression, and bore the stamp of lower elements in my soul.

I hesitated long before I put this theory to the test of practice. I knew well that I risked death; for any drug that so potently controlled and shook the very fortress of identity might, by the least scruple of an overdose, or at the least inopportunity in the moment of exhibition, utterly blot out that immaterial tabernacle[9] which I looked to it to change. But the temptation of a discovery so singular and profound at last overcame the suggestions of alarm. I had long since prepared my tincture; I purchased at once, from a firm of wholesale chemists, a large quantity of a particular salt, which I knew, from my experiments, to be the last ingredient required; and, late one accursed night, I compounded the elements, watched them boil and smoke together in the glass, and when the ebullition had subsided, with a strong glow of courage, drank off the potion.

The most racking pangs succeeded: a grinding in the bones, deadly nausea, and a horror of the spirit that cannot be exceeded at the hour of birth or death. Then these agonies began swiftly to subside, and I came to myself as if out of a great sickness. There was something strange in my sensations, something indescribably new, and, from its very novelty, incredibly sweet. I felt younger, lighter, happier in body; within I was conscious of a heady recklessness, a current of disordered sensual images running like a mill race in my fancy, a solution[10] of the bonds of obligation, an unknown but not an innocent freedom of the soul. I knew myself, at the first breath of this new life, to be more wicked, tenfold more wicked—sold a slave to my original evil; and the thought, in that moment, braced and delighted me like wine. I stretched out my hands, exulting in the freshness of these sensations; and in the act, I was suddenly aware that I had lost in stature.

There was no mirror, at that date, in my room; that which stands beside me as I write was brought there later on, and for the very purpose of those transformations. The night, however, was far gone into the morning—the morning, black as it was, was nearly ripe for the conception of the day; the inmates of my house were locked in the most rigorous hours of slumber; and I determined, flushed as I was with hope and triumph, to venture in my new shape as far as to my bedroom. I crossed the yard, wherein the constellations looked down upon me, I could have thought, with wonder—the first creature of that sort that their unsleeping vigilance had yet disclosed to them. I stole through the corridors, a stranger in my own house; and coming to my room, I saw for the first time the appearance of Edward Hyde.

I must here speak by theory alone, saying not that which I know, but that which I suppose to be most probable. The evil side of my nature, to which I had now transferred the stamping efficacy, was less robust and less developed than the good which I had just deposed. Again, in the course of my life, which had been after all nine tenths a life of effort, virtue, and control, it had been much less exercised and much less exhausted.[11] And hence, as I think, it came about that Edward Hyde was so much smaller, slighter, and younger than Henry Jekyll. Even as good shone upon the countenance of the one, evil was written broadly and plainly on the face of the other. Evil besides (which I must still believe to be the lethal side of man) had left on that body an imprint of deformity and decay. And yet when I looked upon that ugly idol in the glass, I was conscious of no repugnance—rather of a leap of welcome. This, too, was myself. It seemed natural and human. In my eyes it bore a livelier image of the spirit, it seemed more express and single, than the imperfect and divided countenance I had been hitherto accustomed to call mine. And in so far I was doubtless right. I have observed that when I wore the semblance of Edward Hyde, none could come near to me at first without a visible misgiving of the flesh. This, as I take it, was because all human beings, as we meet them, are commingled out of good and evil: and Edward Hyde, alone, in the ranks of mankind, was pure evil.

I lingered but a moment at the mirror: the second and conclusive experiment had yet to be attempted. It yet remained to be seen if I had lost my identity beyond redemption and must flee before daylight from a house that was no longer mine; and hurrying back to my cabinet, I once more prepared and drank the cup, once more suffered the pangs of dissolution, and came to myself once more with the character, the stature, and the face of Henry Jekyll.

That night I had come to the fatal crossroads. Had I approached my discovery in a more noble spirit, had I risked the experiment while under the empire of generous or pious aspirations, all must have been otherwise, and from these agonies of death and birth I had come forth an angel instead of a fiend. The drug had no discriminating action; it was neither diabolical nor divine; it but shook the doors of the prisonhouse of my disposition, and like the captives of Philippi, that which stood within ran forth. At that time my virtue slumbered; my evil, kept awake by ambition, was alert and swift to seize the occasion; and the thing that was projected was Edward Hyde. Hence, although I had now two characters as well as two appearances: one was wholly evil; and the other was still the old Henry Jekyll, that incongruous compound of whose reformation and improvement I had already learned to despair. The movement was thus wholly toward the worse.

Even at that time I had not yet conquered my aversion to the dryness of a life of study. I would still be merrily disposed at times; and as my pleasures were (to say the least) undignified, and I was not only well known and highly considered, but growing toward the elderly man, this incoherency of my life was daily growing more unwelcome. It was on this side that my new power tempted me until I fell in slavery. I had but to drink the cup, to doff at once the body of the noted professor, and to assume, like a thick cloak, that of Edward Hyde. I smiled at the notion; it seemed to me at the time to be humorous, and I made my preparations with the most studious care. I took and furnished that house in Soho, to which Hyde was tracked by the police; and engaged as housekeeper a creature whom I well knew to be silent and unscrupulous. On the other side, I announced to my servants that a Mr. Hyde (whom I described) was to have full liberty and power about my house in the square; and, to parry[12] mishaps, I even called and made myself a familiar object, in my second character. I next drew up that will to which you so much objected; so that if anything befell me in the person of Dr. Jekyll, I could enter on that of Edward Hyde without pecuniary[13] loss. And thus fortified, as I supposed, on every side, I began to profit by the strange immunities of my position.

Men have before hired bravos to transact their crimes, while their own person and reputation sat under shelter. I was the first that ever did so for his pleasures. I was the first that could thus plod in the public eye with a load of genial respectability, and in a moment, like a schoolboy, strip off these lendings and spring headlong into the sea of liberty. But for me, in my impenetrable mantle, the safety was complete. Think of it: I did not even exist! Let me but escape into my laboratory door; give me but a second or two to mix and swallow the draught that I had always standing ready; and, whatever he had done, Edward Hyde would pass away like the stain of breath upon a mirror, and there in his stead, quietly at home trimming the midnight lamp in his study, a man who could afford to laugh at suspicion, would be Henry Jekyll.

The pleasures which I made haste to seek in my disguise were, as I have said, undignified; I would scarce use a harder term. But in the hands of Edward Hyde, they soon began to turn toward the monstrous. When I would come back from these excursions, I was often plunged into a kind of wonder at my vicarious depravity. This familiar that I called out of my own soul, and sent forth alone to do his good pleasure, was a being inherently malign and villainous. His every act and thought centered on self, drinking pleasure with bestial avidity[14] from any degree of torture to another, relentless like a man of stone. Henry Jekyll stood at times aghast before the acts of Edward Hyde; but the situation was apart from ordinary laws, and insidiously[15] relaxed the grasp of conscience. It was Hyde, after all, and Hyde alone, that was guilty. Jekyll was no worse; he woke again to his good qualities seemingly unimpaired; he would even make haste, where it was possible, to undo the evil done by Hyde. And thus his conscience slumbered.

Into the details of the infamy at which I thus connived (for even now I can scarce grant that I committed it) I have no design of entering; I mean but to point out the warnings and the successive steps with which my chastisement approached. I met with one accident which, as it brought on no consequence, I shall no more than mention. An act of cruelty to a child aroused against me the anger of a passer-by, whom I recognized the other day in the person of your kinsman. The doctor and the child's family joined him; there were moments when I feared for my life; and at last, in order to pacify their too just resentment, Edward Hyde had to bring them to the door and pay them in a check drawn in the name of Henry Jekyll. But this danger was easily eliminated from the future by opening an account at another bank in the name of Edward Hyde himself; and when, by sloping my own hand backward, I had supplied my double with a signature, I thought I sat beyond the reach of fate.

Some two months before the murder of Sir Danvers, I had been out for one of my adventures, had returned at a late hour, and woke the next day in bed with somewhat odd sensations. It was in vain I looked about me, in vain I saw the decent furniture and tall proportions of my room in the square, in vain that I recognized the pattern of the bed curtains and the design of the mahogany frame; something still kept insisting that I was not where I was, that I had not awakened where I seemed to be, but in the little room in Soho where I was accustomed to sleep in the body of Edward Hyde. I smiled to myself and, in my psychological way, began lazily to inquire into the elements of this illusion, occasionally, even as I did so, dropping back into a comfortable morning doze. I was still so engaged when, in one of my more wakeful moments, my eye fell upon my hand. Now the hand of Henry Jekyll (as you have often remarked) was professional in shape and size; it was large, firm, white, and comely. But the hand which I now saw, clearly enough, in the yellow light of a mid-London morning, lying half shut on the bedclothes, was lean, corded, knuckly, of a dusky pallor, and thickly shaded with a swart[16] growth of hair. It was the hand of Edward Hyde.

I must have stared upon it for near half a minute, sunk as I was in the mere stupidity of wonder, before terror woke up in my breast as sudden and startling as the crash of cymbals; and bounding from my bed, I rushed to the mirror. At the sight that met my eyes, my blood was changed into something exquisitely thin and icy. Yes, I had gone to bed Henry Jekyll, I had awakened Edward Hyde. How was this to be explained? I asked myself; and then, with another bound of terror, how was it to be remedied? It was well on in the morning; the servants were up; all my drugs were in the cabinet, a long journey—down two pairs of stairs, through the back passage, across the open court, and through the anatomical theater—from where I was then standing horror-struck. It might indeed be possible to cover my face; but of what use was that, when I was unable to conceal the alteration in my stature? And then, with an overpowering sweetness of relief, it came back upon my mind that the servants were already used to the coming and going of my second self. I had soon dressed, as well as I was able, in clothes of my own size: had soon passed through the house, where Bradshaw stared and drew back at seeing Mr. Hyde at such an hour and in such a strange array; and ten minutes later, Dr. Jekyll had returned to his own shape, and was sitting down, with a darkened brow, to make a feint of breakfasting.

Small indeed was my appetite. This inexplicable incident, this reversal of my previous experience, seemed, like the Babylonian finger on the wall,[17] to be spelling out the letters of my judgment; and I began to reflect more seriously than ever before on the issues and possibilities of my double existence. That part of me which I had the power of projecting had lately been much exercised and nourished; it had seemed to me of late as though the body of Edward Hyde had grown in stature, as though (when I wore that form) I were conscious of a more generous tide of blood; and I began to spy a danger that, if this were much prolonged, the balance of my nature might be permanently overthrown, the power of voluntary change be forfeited, and the character of Edward Hyde become irrevocably mine. The power of the drug had not been always equally displayed. Once, very early in my career, it had totally failed me; since then I had been obliged on more than one occasion to double, and once, with infinite risk of death, to treble the amount; and these rare uncertainties had cast hitherto the sole shadow on my contentment. Now, however, and in the light of that morning's accident, I was led to remark that whereas, in the beginning, the difficulty had been to throw off the body of Jekyll, it had of late gradually but decidedly transferred itself to the other side. All things therefore seemed to point to this: that I was slowly losing hold of my original and better self, and becoming slowly incorporated with my second and worse.

Between these two, I now felt I had to choose. My two natures had memory in common, but all other faculties were most unequally shared between them. Jekyll (who was composite), now with the most sensitive apprehensions, now with a greedy gusto, projected and shared in the pleasures and adventures of Hyde; but Hyde was indifferent to Jekyll, or but remembered him as the mountain bandit remembers the cavern in which he conceals himself from pursuit. Jekyll had more than a father's interest; Hyde had more than a son's indifference. To cast in my lot with Jekyll was to die to those appetites which I had long secretly indulged and had of late begun to pamper. To cast it in with Hyde was to die to a thousand interests and aspirations, and to become, at a blow and forever, despised and friendless. The bargain might appear unequal, but there was still another consideration in the scales; for while Jekyll would suffer smartingly in the fires of abstinence, Hyde would be not even conscious of all that he had lost. Strange as my circumstances were, the terms of this debate are as old and commonplace as man; much the same inducements and alarms cast the die for any tempted and trembling sinner; and it fell out with me, as it falls with so vast a majority of my fellows, that I chose the better part, and was found wanting in the strength to keep it.

Yes, I preferred the elderly and discontented doctor, surrounded by friends and cherishing honest hopes; and bade a resolute farewell to the liberty, the comparative youth, the light step, leaping pulses, and secret pleasures that I had enjoyed in the disguise of Hyde. I made this choice perhaps with some unconscious reservation, for I neither gave up the house in Soho, nor destroyed the clothes of Edward Hyde, which still lay ready in my cabinet. For two months, however, I was true to my determination; for two months I led a life of such severity as I had never before attained to, and enjoyed the compensations of an approving conscience. But time began at last to obliterate[18] the freshness of my alarm; the praises of conscience began to grow into a thing of course; I began to be tortured with throes[19] and longings, as of Hyde struggling after freedom; and at last, in an hour of moral weakness, I once again compounded and swallowed the transforming draught.

I do not suppose that when a drunkard reasons with himself upon his vice, he is once out of five hundred times affected by the dangers that he runs through his brutish physical insensibility; neither had I, long as I had considered my position, made enough allowance for the complete moral insensibility and insensate[20] readiness to evil which were the leading characters of Edward Hyde. Yet it was by these that I was punished. My devil had been long caged; he came out roaring. I was conscious, even when I took the draught, of a more unbridled, a more furious propensity to ill. It must have been this, I suppose, that stirred in my soul that tempest of impatience with which I listened to the civilities of my unhappy victim; I declare at least, before God, no man morally sane could have been guilty of that crime upon so pitiful a provocation, and that I struck in no more reasonable spirit than that in which a sick child may break a plaything. But I had voluntarily stripped myself of all those balancing instincts by which even the worst of us continues to walk with some degree of steadiness among temptations; and in my case, to be tempted, however slightly, was to fall.

Instantly the spirit of hell awoke in me and raged. With a transport of glee, I mauled the unresisting body, tasting delight from every blow; and it was not till weariness had begun to succeed that I was suddenly, in the top fit of my delirium, struck through the heart by a cold thrill of terror. A mist dispersed; I saw my life to be forfeit; and fled from the scene of these excesses, at once glorying and trembling, my lust of evil gratified and stimulated, my love of life screwed to the topmost peg.[21] I ran to the house in Soho, and (to make assurance doubly sure) destroyed my papers; thence I set out through the lamplit streets, in the same divided ecstasy of mind, gloating on my crime, light-headedly devising others in the future, and yet still hastening and still hearkening in my wake for the steps of the avenger. Hyde had a song upon his lips as he compounded the draught, and as he drank it pledged the dead man. The pangs of transformation had not done tearing him, before Henry Jekyll, with streaming tears of gratitude and remorse, had fallen upon his knees and lifted his clasped hands to God. The veil of self-indulgence was rent from head to foot. I saw my life as a whole: I followed it up from the days of childhood, when I had walked with my father's hand, and through the self-denying toils of my professional life, to arrive again and again, with the same sense of unreality, at the horrors of the evening. I could have screamed aloud; I sought with tears and prayers to smother down the crowd of hideous images and sounds with which my memory swarmed against me; and still, between the petitions, the ugly face of my iniquity stared into my soul. As the acuteness of this remorse began to die away, it was succeeded by a sense of joy. The problem of my conduct was solved. Hyde was thenceforth impossible; whether I would or not, I was now confined to the better part of my existence; and, oh, how I rejoiced to think it! with what willing humility I embraced anew the restrictions of natural life! with what sincere renunciation I locked the door by which I had so often gone and come, and ground the key under my heel!

The next day came the news that the murder had been overlooked,[22] that the guilt of Hyde was patent to the world, and that the victim was a man high in public estimation. It was not only a crime, it had been a tragic folly. I think I was glad to know it; I think I was glad to have my better impulses thus buttressed and guarded by the terrors of the scaffold.[23] Jekyll was now my city of refuge; let but Hyde peep out an instant, and the hands of all men would be raised to take and slay him.

I resolved in my future conduct to redeem the past, and I can say with honesty that my resolve was fruitful of some good. You know yourself how earnestly in the last months of last year I labored to relieve suffering; you know that much was done for others, and that the days passed quietly, almost happily for myself. Nor can I truly say that I wearied of this beneficent and innocent life; I think instead that I daily enjoyed it more completely. But I was still cursed with my duality of purpose; and as the first edge of my penitence wore off, the lower side of me, so long indulged, so recently chained down, began to growl for license. Not that I dreamed of resuscitating Hyde; the bare idea of that would startle me to frenzy: no, it was in my own person that I was once more tempted to trifle with my conscience, and it was as an ordinary secret sinner that I at last fell before the assaults of temptation.

There comes an end to all things; the most capacious measure[24] is filled at last; and this brief condescension to my evil finally destroyed the balance of my soul. And yet I was not alarmed; the fall seemed natural, like a return to the old days before I had made my discovery. It was a fine, clear January day, wet under foot where the frost had melted, but cloudless overhead; and the Regent's Park was full of winter chirrupings and sweet with spring odors. I sat in the sun on a bench; the animal within me licking the chops of memory; the spiritual side a little drowsed, promising subsequent penitence, but not yet moved to begin. After all, I reflected I was like my neighbors; and then I smiled, comparing myself with other men, comparing my active good will with the lazy cruelty of their neglect. And at the very moment of that vainglorious[25] thought, a qualm came over me, a horrid nausea, and the most deadly shuddering. These passed away, and left me faint; and then as in its turn the faintness subsided, I began to be aware of a change in the temper of my thoughts—a greater boldness, a contempt of danger, a solution of the bonds of obligation. I looked down: my clothes hung formlessly on my shrunken limbs; the hand that lay on my knee was corded and hairy. I was once more Edward Hyde. A moment before I had been safe of all men's respect, wealthy, beloved—the cloth laying for me in the dining room at home; and now I was the common quarry[26] of mankind, hunted, houseless, a known murderer, thrall[27] to the gallows.

My reason wavered, but it did not fail me utterly. I have more than once observed that, in my second character, my faculties seemed sharpened to a point and my spirits more tensely elastic; thus it came about that, where Jekyll perhaps might have succumbed, Hyde rose to the importance of the moment. My drugs were in one of the presses of my cabinet: how was I to reach them? That was the problem that (crushing my temples in my hands) I set myself to solve. The laboratory door I had closed. If I sought to enter by the house, my own servants would consign me to the gallows. I saw I must employ another hand, and thought of Lanyon. How was he to be reached? how persuaded? Supposing that I escaped capture in the streets, how was I to make my way into his presence? and how should I, an unknown and displeasing visitor, prevail on the famous physician to rifle the study of his colleague,

Dr. Jekyll? Then I remembered that, of my original character, one part remained to me: I could write my own hand; and once I had conceived that kindling spark, the way that I must follow became lighted up from end to end.

Thereupon, I arranged my clothes as best I could and, summoning a passing hansom, drove to an hotel in Portland Street, the name of which I chanced to remember. At my appearance (which was indeed comical enough, however tragic a fate these garments covered), the driver could not conceal his mirth. I gnashed my teeth upon him with a gust of devilish fury; and the smile withered from his face—happily for him—yet more happily for myself, for in another instant I had certainly dragged him from his perch. At the inn, as I entered, I looked about me with so black a countenance as made the attendants tremble; not a look did they exchange in my presence, but obsequiously took my orders, led me to a private room, and brought me wherewithal to write. Hyde in danger of his life was a creature new to me: shaken with inordinate anger, strung to the pitch of murder, lusting to inflict pain. Yet the creature was astute: mastered his fury with a great effort of the will, composed his two important letters—one to Lanyon and one to Poole—and, that he might receive actual evidence of their being posted, sent them out with directions that they should be registered.

Thenceforward, he sat all day over the fire in the private room, gnawing his nails; there he dined, sitting alone with his fears, the waiter visibly quailing before his eye; and thence, when the night was fully come, he set forth in the corner of a closed cab and was driven to and fro about the streets of the city. "He," I say; I cannot say "I." That child of hell had nothing human; nothing lived in him but fear and hatred. And when at last, thinking the driver had begun to grow suspicious, he discharged the cab and ventured on foot, attired in his misfitting clothes, an object marked out for observation, into the midst of the nocturnal passengers, these two base passions raged within him like a tempest. He walked fast, haunted by his fears, chattering to himself, skulking through the less frequented thoroughfares, counting the minutes that still divided him from midnight. Once a woman spoke to him, offering, I think, a box of lights. He smote[28] her in the face, and she fled.

When I came to myself at Lanyon's, the horror of my old friend perhaps affected me somewhat: I do not know; it was at least but a drop in the sea to the abhorrence with which I looked back upon these hours. A change had come over me. It was no longer the fear of the gallows; it was the horror of being Hyde that racked me. I received Lanyon's condemnation partly in a dream; it was partly in a dream that I came home to my own house and got into bed. I slept after the prostration of the day, with a stringent and profound slumber which not even the nightmares that wrung me could avail to break. I awoke in the morning shaken, weakened, but refreshed. I still hated and feared the thought of the brute that slept within me, and I had not of course forgotten the appalling dangers of the day before; but I was once more at home, in my own house and close to my drugs, and gratitude for my escape shone so strong in my soul that it almost rivaled the brightness of hope.

I was stepping leisurely across the court after breakfast, drinking the chill of the air with pleasure, when I was seized again with those indescribable sensations that heralded the change: and I had but the time to gain the shelter of my cabinet before I was once again raging and freezing with the passions of Hyde. It took on this occasion a double dose to recall me to myself; and, alas! six hours after, as I sat looking sadly in the fire, the pangs returned, and the drug had to be readministered. In short, from that day forth it seemed only by a great effort as of gymnastics, and only under the immediate stimulation of the drug, that I was able to wear the countenance of Jekyll. At all hours of the day and night I would be taken with the premonitory[29] shudder; above all, if I slept, or even dozed for a moment in my chair, it was always as Hyde that I awakened. Under the strain of this continually impending doom and by the sleeplessness to which I now condemned myself, ay, even beyond what I had thought possible to man, I became, in my own person, a creature eaten up and emptied by fever, languidly weak both in mind and body, and solely occupied by one thought: the horror of my other self. But when I slept, or when the virtue of the medicine wore off, I would leap almost without transition (for the pangs of transformation grew daily less marked) into the possession of a fancy brimming with images of terror, a soul boiling with causeless hatreds, and a body that seemed not strong enough to contain the raging energies of life. The powers of Hyde seemed to have grown with the sickliness of Jekyll. And certainly the hate that now divided them was equal on each side. With Jekyll, it was a thing of vital instinct. He had now seen the full deformity of that creature that shared with him some of the phenomena of consciousness and was co-heir with him to death; and beyond these links of community, which in themselves made the most poignant part of his distress, he thought of Hyde, for all his energy of life, as of something not only hellish but inorganic. This was the shocking thing, that the slime of the pit seemed to utter cries and voices; that the amorphous dust gesticulated and sinned; that what was dead and had no shape should usurp the offices of life. And this again, that that insurgent horror was knit to him closer than a wife, closer than an eye; lay caged in his flesh, where he heard it mutter and felt it struggle to be born; and at every hour of weakness, and in the confidence of slumber, prevailed against him and deposed him out of life. The hatred of Hyde for Jekyll was of a different order. His terror of the gallows drove him continually to commit temporary suicide and return to his subordinate station of a part instead of a person; but he loathed the necessity, he loathed the despondency into which Jekyll was now fallen, and he resented the dislike with which he was himself regarded. Hence the apelike tricks that he would play me, scrawling in my own hand blasphemies on the pages of my books, burning the letters and destroying the portrait of my father; and indeed, had it not been for his fear of death, he would long ago have ruined himself in order to involve me in the ruin. But his love of life is wonderful; I go further: I, who sicken and freeze at the mere thought of him, when I recall the abjection and passion of this attachment, and when I know how he fears my power to cut him off by suicide, I find it in my heart to pity him.

It is useless, and the time awfully fails me, to prolong this description. No one has ever suffered such torments, let that suffice; and yet even to these, habit brought—no, not alleviation—but a certain callousness of soul, a certain acquiescence of despair; and my punishment might have gone on for years but for the last calamity which has now fallen, and which has finally severed me from my own face and nature. My provision of the salt, which had never been renewed since the date of the first experiment, began to run low. I sent out for a fresh supply and mixed the draught; the ebullition followed, and the first change of color—not the second. I drank it, and it was without efficiency.[30] You will learn from Poole how I have had London ransacked: it was in vain; and I am now persuaded that my first supply was impure, and that it was that unknown impurity which lent efficacy to the draught.

About a week has passed, and I am now finishing this statement under the influence of the last of the old powders. This, then, is the last time, short of a miracle, that Henry Jekyll can think his own thoughts or see his own face (now how sadly altered!) in the glass. Nor must I delay too long to bring my writing to an end; for if my narrative has hitherto escaped destruction, it has been by a combination of great prudence and great good luck. Should the throes of change take me in the act of writing it, Hyde will tear it in pieces; but if some time shall have elapsed after I have laid it by, his wonderful selfishness and circumscription to the moment will probably save it once again from the action of his apelike spite. And indeed the doom that is closing on us both has already changed and crushed him. Half an hour from now, when I shall again and forever reindue[31] that hated personality, I know how I shall sit shuddering and weeping in my chair, or continue, with the most strained and fearstruck ecstasy of listening, to pace up and down this room (my last earthly refuge) and give ear to every sound of menace. Will Hyde die upon the scaffold? or will he find the courage to release himself at the last moment? God knows; I am careless. This is my true hour of death, and what is to follow concerns another than myself. Here, then, as I lay down the pen and proceed to seal up my confession, I bring the life of that unhappy Henry Jekyll to an end.

[1] **imperious:** haughty; arrogant
[2] **blazoned:** to make known far and wide
[3] **exacting:** demanding
[4] **inveterately:** habitually
[5] **polity of multifarious, incongruous and independent denizens:** society of varied, ill-matched and independent inhabitants
[6] **faggots:** bundles of sticks bound together
[7] **transience:** temporariness
[8] **effulgence** radiance; brightness
[9] **tabernacle:** the human body as the temporary dwelling place of the soul
[10] **solution:** dissolving
[11] **exhausted:** used up
[12] **parry:** avoid
[13] **pecuniary:** financial
[14] **avidity:** eagerness
[15] **insidiously:** working harmfully in a subtle way
[16] **swart:** dark
[17] **Babylonian finger on the wall:** doom. This expression refers to the Biblical story of King Belshazzar of Babylon, who hosted a feast at which wine was drunk from vessels stolen from a temple. During the feast, fingers from a man's hand came and wrote on the wall a message that spelled Belshazzar's doom.
[18] **obliterate:** erase; do away with
[19] **throes:** violent pangs
[20] **insensate:** unthinking

[21] **screwed to the topmost peg:** at the highest possible level
[22] **overlooked:** witnessed
[23] **scaffold:** platform on which a criminal is hanged
[24] **most capacious measure:** container that has a great capacity
[25] **vainglorious:** boastful
[26] **quarry:** prey
[27] **thrall:** slave
[28] **smote:** struck; hit
[29] **premonitory:** forewarning
[30] **efficiency:** effectiveness
[31] **reindue:** put on again

A CLOSER LOOK

1. What basic conflict existed within Henry Jekyll?

2. What did Jekyll want to achieve through his scientific experiments? Why did Jekyll want to achieve this? Were his motivations noble? Explain your answer.

3. What was Hyde the embodiment (physical representation) of?

4. Why was Hyde so much smaller, slighter and younger than Jekyll?

5. The confession states that Jekyll's conscience slumbered. Why didn't Jekyll feel any guilt for Hyde's misdeeds, at first?

6. What did Jekyll begin to fear when he woke up one morning as Hyde, without having taken the drug? How was the body of Hyde changing?

7. Why couldn't Jekyll renew his supply of the salt? Explain what Jekyll meant by the statement, "this is my true hour of death."

8. Why did Hyde commit suicide?